The Spioenkop Campaign

The Battles to Relieve Ladysmith 17-27 January 1900

Robert Davidson

Helion & Company

Helion & Company Limited
Unit 8 Amherst Business Centre
Budbrooke Road
Warwick
CV34 5WE
England
Tel. 01926 499 619
Email: info@helion.co.uk
Website: www.helion.co.uk
Twitter: @helionbooks
Visit our blog at blog.helion.co.uk

Published by Helion & Company 2023
Designed and typeset by Mary Woolley (www.battlefield-design.co.uk)
Cover designed by Paul Hewitt, Battlefield Design (www.battlefield-design.co.uk)

Text © Robert Davidson 2023
Images © from author's collection unless otherwise stated.
Maps drawn by Robert Davidson © 2023

Cover: Foreground: Burghers Sias de Kock (Left) and Nicolaas Prinsloo (Right) of the
Middelburg Commando. Background: Royal Field Artillery 15-pdr ammunition wagon
crossing the pontoon bridge at Trichardt's Drift. (Courtesy of Tinus le Roux and Neville
Constantine)

ISBN 978-1-804513-31-6

British Library Cataloguing-in-Publication Data.
A catalogue record for this book is available from the British Library.

For details of other military history titles published by Helion & Company Limited contact the
above address or visit our website: http://www.helion.co.uk.

We always welcome receiving book proposals from prospective authors.

Contents

List of Illustrations and Maps

Cover: Foreground: Burghers Sias de Kock (Left) and Nicolaas Prinsloo (Right) of the Middelburg Commando. Background: Royal Field Artillery 15-pdr ammunition wagon crossing the pontoon bridge at Trichardt's Drift. Courtesy of Tinus le Roux and Neville Constantine.

Acknowledgements

I first slept out on the battlefields of the Upper Tugela well over half a century before I began work on this book. The subject fascinated me then, and it still does. I am grateful for the unflagging support from my wife, Mary Rutherford, and from our children Joe, Alice, Rose and William. I am indebted to Christopher Brice and the team at Helion, the indexer Richard van Rensburg, the staff at the War Museum of the Boer Republics in Bloemfontein, Cape Archives, National Army Museum, Liddell Hart Archives, Imperial War Museum and Wellcome Trust, and to many who have enthusiastically helped me, including: Berenice Baynham, Ron Bester, David Biggins, Simon Blackburn, Cheryl Blackburn, Tony Braithwaite, Neville Constantine, Barry Coventry, Neil Drummond, Ron Gold, Alan Green, MC Heunis, Vicky Heunis, Brent Janse van Rensburg, Meurig Jones, Jon Kaplan, Etna Labuschagne, Janine and Ruben Lee, Henk Loots, Elmarie Malherbe, Pam McFadden, Duggie MacMaster, Dewald Nel, Fransjohan Pretorius, Robin Phillips, Nicholas Riall, Melanie Rossouw, Tinus le Roux, Tony Scott, George Shaw, Arnold van Dyk, and Trish Woodman.

Introduction

Spioenkop, like Majuba and Isandhlwana, is famous for the heroism of doomed men.[1] It also owes much of its fame to the camera. The Kodak box camera became popular after 1896, and during the South African War, many British officers carried cameras and kept photograph albums. Officers' albums all have much in common: small box camera images of soldiers disembarking, on board ship, or relaxing; distant soldiers or artillery in the field; scenes in camp or hospital; and perhaps a friend with a pet monkey. However, to enhance his album, almost every officer included photographs of the dead on Spioenkop. These propaganda photographs were taken after the battle by the Boer photographers, Lund and van Hoepen, and they were sold, for over a shilling each, at numerous shops and kiosks. The picture of dead soldiers in the Lancashire Fusiliers' trench is the most famous image of the war. In the long history of the British Empire, photographs like these had never been seen before. They show details of men's faces, bodies lying on the veldt, clothes in disarray, wounds obvious. The bodies were moved after rigor mortis, so their limbs are frozen in mid-air. They were an instant antidote to Richard Caton Woodville's popular images of Empire; these were the real thing. They were eagerly published by newspapers and magazines, from Newfoundland to New Zealand, and were soon accompanied by letters from the ordinary soldiers at the front giving lurid accounts of the horrors on Spioenkop. Today, in Lancashire but also elsewhere, 19 football stadiums have a raised bank or stand for spectators called 'Spion Kop' or 'The Kop'. Yet at the time, both sides referred to the whole campaign of 17 to 27 January 1900 as Spioenkop, or Spion Kop in its anglicised form. The night attack on Spioenkop summit was carried out by less than one tenth of the British force on the Upper Tugela, and only about 300 Boers counter-attacked. An eyewitness account by Captain Grant of the Devons sums it up:

> I refer to the battle of Spion Kop, which did not at all, as many seem to suppose, begin and end with the catastrophe upon the kop itself. The actual fighting, the 'rush and hold on' which distinguishes a battle from an engagement, began on Saturday, January 20, and ended when our troops dragged their exhausted limbs back over the Tugela pontoon again in the dawn of Saturday, January 27. Between these two dates the fighting was uninterrupted and dogged, and it is of these seven days of strain, with

---

1   The name "Spioenkop" means "lookout hill' in Dutch and Afrikaans. When the Voortrekkers reached the area in 1837, it was the name they gave to this lofty vantage point. "Spion Kop" is the phonetic equivalent in English. The word "spion" does mean "spy", but "kop" has no meaning in English. Thus the spelling "Spioenkop" is preferable and will be used throughout, unless quoting from sources who spelled it "Spion Kop".

the thousands charging, firing, dying along the crest of the mountains, that one who was present will think when he hears the battle of Spion Kop mentioned in after-days.[2]

This was the first war in which British soldiers faced modern rifle and artillery fire, and British losses were large compared to the preceding campaigns in Sudan and Benin. Many survivors suffered what would become known as 'shell shock', or Post-Traumatic Stress Disorder; some took their own lives in later years. Until the First World War, the 'fame' and horror of Spioenkop was unsurpassed, and many people from all walks of life confabulated or exaggerated their presence at Spioenkop. From 1919 onwards, Boer veterans could apply for a campaign medal, the *Anglo–Boere Oorlogmedalje*, and a majority of those who had fought in Natal managed to mention Spioenkop on their application form. Winston Churchill is famous for being at Spioenkop, and he twice climbed Spioenkop Spur to deliver messages; but he was never actually on the summit. He acknowledged he had only crawled a short way onto the plateau: '…the fire was much too hot for mere sight-seeing.'[3] Mohandas (Mahatma) Gandhi exaggerated his role, claiming: '…the action at Spion Kop found us working within the firing line.'[4] Yet Gandhi and his stretcher-bearers were several kilometres away. So was John Black Atkins, writing for the *Manchester Guardian*, who coined the phrase 'acre of massacre'.[5]

Spioenkop remains famous because it is easy to visit and it is a haunting experience. The summit is only the size of Trafalgar Square, and has many monuments and graves. Visitors can park their cars on the summit, and follow, to the minute and to the metre, the events of 24 January 1900. The battlefields of Tabanyama, which is where the larger Spioenkop campaign was fought, are sprawling, hardly accessible, and almost never visited. Tabanyama is an area of rolling veldt, grazed by cattle and antelope, lacking monuments, landmarks or roads. Few natural features are named, and the names of hills are confused. As a consequence, the actions around Tabanyama are poorly understood, and have been glossed over by historians. The whole campaign has had a vagueness about it. Events like the ambush at Acton Homes were thought to have happened in altogether the wrong place. Other events, like the heroism of Slegtkamp, Hindon and de Roos, had no known location. This book is an attempt at a more detailed account of what happened on the Upper Tugela.

Much of the effort of historians has been spent deciding whom to blame for Spioenkop. The more I have studied the battlefield, the less I have found myself able to assign blame to senior officers. Where possible, I quote eyewitnesses, as I have found that the opinions of those who wrote later are often lacking in value. For consistency, I have kept the 1900 spelling for the Tugela River and Tabanyama, rather than their modern isiZulu names, Thukela and iNtabamnyama. I freely use Afrikaans/Dutch words like burgher, donga, laager, schanz, spruit, veldt and of course Spioenkop. To assist future battlefield wanderers, I have tried to locate many sites by GPS.

Robert Davidson 2023

2   Linesman (Captain Maurice H. Grant), *Words by an Eyewitness – the Struggle in Natal* (London: Blackwood, 1901), p.38.
3   Winston S. Churchill, *My Early Life*, (London: Thornton Butterworth, 1930), p.309.
4   Mohandas K. Gandhi, *The Story of My Experiments with Truth*, Vol. 1, (Ahmedabad: Navajivan Press, 1927), p.500.
5   John Black Atkins, *The Relief of Ladysmith*, 2nd Edition (London: Methuen, 1900), p.237.

1

Preparations for War

> '...the war had two causes. The first and principal cause was the wealth of the goldfields of the Republic; the second, revenge for Majuba Hill.' Paul Kruger[1]

The Inevitable War

The Boers realised that their victory at Majuba in 1881 had humiliated Britain and that, sooner or later, they would need to fight again. The Jameson Raid in January 1896 demonstrated that the time had come to prepare. The Transvaal (the *Zuid Afrikaansche Republiek* or ZAR) was by then wealthy from the gold mines, and for the next 3 years, over one-third of the Transvaal's annual revenues were allocated to defence.[2] They purchased 49 modern field guns from France and Germany, and twenty-two 37mm Vickers-Maxim pom-poms from England.[3] In 1897 the Transvaal signed an alliance with the Orange Free State (*Oranje Vrijstaat* or OVS), who also re-armed, though with less enthusiasm and less purchasing power. This would be a war of riflemen, and central to Boer firepower was the Boer Mauser rifle. For their 60,000 burghers, the republics bought over 95,000 rifles, including 38,000 Mauser rifles, 7,000 Mauser carbines, and 50 million Mauser cartridges.[4] The magic of Boer riflemen lay not in their rifles, but in their ability to ride and fight independently, use cover, judge distance, and take snap-shots when a target was glimpsed. The Boer Mauser is, undeniably, an excellent rifle. It is sighted up to 2,000 metres; a person with good vision can put most shots into a postcard at 100 metres. It has an internal 5-shot magazine, rapidly loaded by stripper clips. Each burgher with a Mauser could comfortably shoot 15 aimed shots per minute, and could keep this up as long as he had ammunition. Smokeless ammunition made the Boers invisible, and burghers with older Martini Henrys, which produced a cloud of smoke, were banished from shooting near other burghers.[5] Mauser bullets were fully jacketed in mild steel, and resisted distortion on impact. The 7mm

---

1   Paul Kruger, *The Memoirs of Paul Kruger*, (New York: Century, 1902), p.120.
2   Martin Meredith, *Afrikaner Odyssey* (Johannesburg: Jonathan Ball, 2017), p.59.
3   Darrell D. Hall, *The Hall Handbook of the Anglo-Boer War 1899–1902*, (Pietermaritzburg: University of Natal Press, 1999), p.6.
4   Hall, *Handbook*, p.2.
5   Fransjohan Pretorius, *Life on Commando During the Anglo-Boer War 1899–1902*, (Cape Town: Human & Rousseau, 1999), p.147.

calibre bullets weighed only 11.2g and flew at 670 metres per second, with a 'flat' trajectory. Bullets that missed their target continued for very long distances, turning the battlefield into a swept zone of bullets. The British infantryman experienced: '...many hours lying on your belly in the scorching sun, while the air is vocal above you with the singing of bullets from an invisible foe... the bird-like notes are in the air above, and bitter little sounds against stones, and tiny little fountains of dust spurt from the ground around.'[6]

The British .303-inch Lee-Metfords and Lee-Enfields were also excellent rifles; they were almost as accurate as the Mauser, and also used smokeless ammunition. The problem with British soldiers' shooting was their musketry training. They still fired volleys on command, except at shorter ranges. They had not been trained in snap-shooting or judgement of distances. Accuracy was so little valued in the British Army that thousands of Lee-Enfield Mk I rifles were issued with defective sights which gave a point of impact 50cm to the right at 500m, an error which was only discovered in December 1899.[7]

The Humane Mauser Bullet

With new rifles and new bullets came new injuries. British military doctors were intrigued by Mauser bullet wounds, and reported their findings in multiple publications. At short ranges, less than 200m, the 'hydraulic shock' of the high-velocity jacketed bullet caused a large wound, just as if a heavy lead bullet or an expanding hunting bullet had been used. Frederick Treves, a famous London surgeon who was a volunteer in Natal and correspondent for the *British Medical Journal*, noted: 'At 500 yards or less [a Mauser bullet] will smash a femur or humerus to fragments.'[8] However, Mauser bullets striking at long distances, typically beyond 1,000 m, produced wounds that were altogether different. Largely depleted of energy, the bullets caused very small entrance and exit wounds, which healed quickly in the dry South African climate. Treves, again, observed: 'The [Mauser] bullet at long range acts more like a fine-pointed instrument, going through bone without splintering it, and dividing nerve and arteries with remarkable neatness.'[9]

This gave rise to the concept of 'humane' bullets. The correspondent for the *Illustrated London News* was particularly impressed:

> Death from a Mauser bullet is less painful than the drawing of a tooth... As a rule a sudden exclamation, "I'm hit!" "My God!" "Damn it!"... They look as if staggering from the blow of a fist rather than that from a tiny pencil of lead – then a sudden paleness, perhaps a grasping of the hands occasionally as if to hold on to something, when the bottom seems to be falling out of all things stable, but generally no sign of aught else than the dulling of death – dulling to sleep – a drunken sleep – drunken death it often seems – very commonplace as a rule. A smile as often as, or oftener than, any sign of pain, but generally no sign of either... just as dropping off dully to sleep,

6   George Lynch, *Impressions of a War Correspondent* (London: George Newnes, 1903), pp.49 & 75.
7   Owen Coetzer, *The Road to Infamy* (London: Arms & Armour, 1996), p.24.
8   Frederick Treves, 'The War in South Africa' in *British Medical Journal*, 1900, p.220.
9   Treves, British Medical Journal, 1900, p.534.

most probably with no thought of you or home, without anxiety or regret. Merciful Mauser!... Merciful Mauser be thanked! [10]

Captain Jourdain described a Sergeant in the Dublin Fusiliers with a lucky escape from a long range Mauser bullet:

> The bullet penetrated his buff belt in front, then his drill jacket and his trousers and his shorts, entered his body going only skin deep, and then travelled under the skin almost completely round his body and was extracted from under the skin on his left side... He was at duty a few days afterwards.[11]

Long range bullets could still be lethal: Colonel Dick-Cunyngham in Ladysmith was struck in the back by a stray bullet fired 3,000 metres away during the battle of Platrand. He died the following day.

The ratio of killed to wounded was low: 1 killed to 3.5 wounded amongst officers, and 1 killed to 3.9 wounded amongst other ranks. Less than one in ten wounded men would go on to later die of their wounds.[12] Long-range bullets might often pass through the limbs, chest, or even the head, without serious consequences. Very few limbs needed emergency amputation. Only one in seven penetrating wounds of the chest were fatal.[13] Surgeon Lieutenant Ernest Blake Knox described two soldiers who survived being shot in the chest at Tabanyama:

> Shot through the chest, just half an inch from his heart... I dressed him, gave him a little brandy, and wrote out a surgical tally, [a page from the surgeon's note-book] which I fastened to a button on his tunic, and sent him on to Major Moir's Hospital [at Fairview Farm]. He afterwards recovered... One young fellow had been struck by a long – range Mauser bullet in the chest, directly over the heart. He had been temporarily stunned by the force of the blow, but on recovering consciousness inquisitively felt the wound with his fingers while I cut up his shirt with my scissors. Before I could prevent him, he had reached the bullet and pulled it out. Luckily, it was a spent bullet, and had not penetrated far, for the wound was but half an inch deep.[14]

Head wounds at close range were invariably fatal, but at long ranges, more than half the men shot in the head survived.[15] Lord Dundonald described a man in his Mounted Brigade wounded '...by a rifle bullet which passed through his head behind the eyes, going in at one temple and out at the other. It seemed almost a faithful fatal wound but what was my astonishment to see him back at duty in a month and he did not even complain of a headache!'[16] A nurse in the

---

10   Lynch, *Impressions of a War Correspondent*, pp.1, 2, 11.
11   Henry F. N. Jourdain, *Ranging Memories* (Oxford: John Johnson, University Press, 1934), p.92.
12   William F. Stevenson, Surgeon-General, editor, *Report on the Surgical Cases Noted in the South African War, 1899–1902*, (London: Printed for H.M. Stationery Office by Harrison and Sons, 1905), p.277.
13   Stevenson, *Report*, pp.196, 157
14   Ernest Blake Knox, *Buller's Campaign with the Natal Field Force of 1900* (London: R. B. Johnson, 1902), p.42.
15   Stevenson, *Report*, p.42.
16   Douglas M. B. H. C. Dundonald, 12th Earl of, *My Army Life* (London: E. Arnold, 1926), p.112.

Russian ambulance described the good recovery of a Boer youth who had an entrance wound in the nape of his neck, with the bullet exiting beneath the inner corner of his eye.[17]

Even the Bishop of Natal was fascinated:

> The wounds in some cases are very remarkable. There was one man hit in the side of the head, and the bullet is supposed to be there still, in his brain, as one would think, yet he seems happy. There was another who was hit just above the hip, and the bullet was found just under the skin above the breast-bone on the other side. He has the bullet, and he shows you the dark mark where the bullet was lodged in him.[18]

Abdominal or pelvic wounds were dreaded, for once surgery became necessary, they carried a 70 percent risk of death.[19] As Treves wrote: '… operations were done 'practically in the open air, that is, under the shelter of a widely-opened square tent. The light, therefore, is good. A great trouble is from flies; they cover the surgeon's hands, and with all care cannot be kept from alighting on exposed intestine, etc.'[20]

Men on both sides believed their chances of survival from an abdominal wound improved if one fought on an empty stomach, so they often declined to eat before going into action.

There were reports of happy outcomes, like two soldiers recovering from abdominal wounds who developed urinary retention, which eased when they passed Mauser bullets in their urine.[21]

Lieutenant Charlton of the Lancashire Fusiliers confided: 'A flesh wound would be gratifying, but heaven forbid that he should ever be hit in the genitals!'[22]

Spinal injuries were usually hopeless; paralysis led to a lingering death from pressure sores or urinary infection.[23]

The Boer Forces

Each man had to join his Commando, but he was unpaid, and not obliged to fight unless he volunteered to do so:

> There were hundreds of men in the Natal laagers who never engaged in one battle and never fired a shot in the first six months of the war. Again, there were hundreds of men who took part in almost every one of the battles, whether their commando was engaged or not, but they joined the fighting voluntarily and not because they were compelled to do so.[24]

17   Sophia Izedinova, *A Few Months with the Boers* (Johannesburg: Perskor, 1977), p.50.
18   Arthur H. Baynes, *My Diocese During the War* (London: Bell, 1900), p.135.
19   Stevenson, *Report*, p.120.
20   Treves, *British Medical Journal*, 1900, p.600.
21   George H. Makins, *Surgical Experiences in South Africa, 1899–1900, Being Mainly a Clinical Study of the Nature and Effects of Injuries Produced by Bullets of Small Calibre* London: Smith, Elder, & Co., 1901, p.110. Stevenson, *Report*, p.96.
22   Lionel E.O .Charlton, Charlton (London: Faber & Faber, 1931), p.103.
23   Stevenson, *Report*, p.65
24   Howard C. Hillegas, *The Boers in War; the story of the British-Boer war of 1899–1900* (New York, Appleton, 1900), p.87.

The head of the Transvaal forces, *Commandant*-General Piet Joubert, was assisted by five Assistant *Commandant*-Generals, equivalent to Lieutenant-Generals in the British Army. Below them were *Vecht*-Generals, fighting generals, equivalent to Major-Generals or Brigadiers, followed by *Commandants*, equivalent to Colonels, each of whom commanded the Commando of a district. The Commandos varied greatly in size. Each district was divided into wards (*wyke*), each *wyk* being commanded by a *Veldkornet*, equivalent to a Major. The burghers of each *wyk* were subdivided into squads of about 25 men under a Corporal, equivalent to a Lieutenant. Burghers elect their officers, and could vote to demote them. Boer battle plans were decided at a *Krijgsraad*, or council of war, which carried the highest military authority. Every officer voted at the *Krijgsraad*, and experienced officers could be out-voted by juniors.

Fig 1: *Krijgsraad* before Colenso. Before battle, Boer officers would discuss the plan of attack and vote on the plan. Once approved, the plan was then communicated to the burghers, who participated voluntarily. (Courtesy of the Lee Family)

Once a decision had been reached, the officers explained the action to their burghers, and asked for volunteers. No officer could compel a man to do any duty, and no power on earth could compel him to move out of his tent if he did not desire to go. [25] Boers moved on horseback, but fought on foot. They left their horses tethered under cover, looked after by grooms (*agterryers*) or by burghers who were shy of the fighting line. [26] Once in defensive positions, as around Ladysmith,

25   Hillegas, *The Boers in War*, pp.86–88.
26   Roland W. Schikkerling, *Commando Courageous* (Johannesburg: Keartland, 1964), p.209.

Colenso, and Tabanyama, Boer mobility was reduced, and it felt to them like an unnatural phase of the war. During battle, withdrawal was not seen as particularly dishonourable; there was always another hill to fight on. Roland Schikkerling of the Pretoria Commando was on the Upper Tugela:

> As a rule [the Boer] waits for the attack, but will often unexpectedly become offensive. He will never brook an enemy behind or around him, and never grows sentimental over a position. With him retreat is no less a stratagem than assault... The English at first disdained cover and fought in solid formation, advancing openly to the attack. They seemed indifferent to their ground and in the first days gave little heed to field-craft. The Boer – and here he showed his greatest skill – studied its contours and took every advantage of its irregularities, folds and depressions... The resource and individuality of the Boer unit gave the line a brain at every point which stood in the stead of an Officer, who, in a confused fight, could at best only give orders to the few immediately around him...[27]

Boer riflemen acted independently, but to a common end. They had no military training; only some useful practical experience and a few inborn fighting qualities:

> The old veterans from whom we expected miracles... were sadly disappointing and unreasonably cautious. The best work was done by the young men, principally by townsmen, and men of breeding and education... In war, more than in any other occupation, it is the quality and virtue of the individual, not bravery alone, that counts. Unhappily, there is with us a great lack of discipline. The men, though always ready and willing to fight, are not very obedient to their officers, often arguing with them as to the manner of conducting operations. This condition of things might have ended more disastrously had it not been for the individualism and patriotism of the men, and for volunteers who were always ready for any hazard.[28]

27   Schikkerling, *Commando Courageous*, p.208.
28   Schikkerling, *Commando Courageous*, p.210.

2

The South African War Before the Spioenkop Campaign

As the events of January 24 [Spion Kop] overshadow the week, the important
affair… which so nearly terminated in a tactical success – has never received
full credit – its story being engulfed, as it were, in the annals of the Majuba-like
proceedings at Spion Kop.'—Lieutenant Ernest Blake Knox.[1]

The Opening Phase of the War in Natal

On 16 September 1899, while the final negotiations to avert war were still in progress, General
Sir George White V.C. was sent out to Natal to command an army of 14,000 men. At that
time, British regiments consisted of two battalions, each about 1,000 strong, of which one
was usually in Britain and available to go to South Africa. The other battalion was usually in
India. By November, a further 48,000 men sailed for South Africa, commanded by General
Sir Redvers Buller V.C.

General White intended to hold his army in readiness at Ladysmith, but before he could
do so, 4,000 men under Major General William Penn Symons had already moved off towards
the Transvaal border. White tried to withdraw them, but the Boers attacked on 20 October at
Dundee (Talana). The British infantry made a bayonet charge up Talana Hill, and technically
they won the battle. However, they suffered 253 casualties, including Penn Symons himself
who was mortally wounded, shot in the abdomen. Embarrassingly, the cavalry had been cut off
and 150 mounted men were captured. While the British column trudged back to Ladysmith,
White's force won the battle of Elandslaagte near Ladysmith on 21 October, but White was
then defeated on 30 October at Nicholson's Nek. He drew his men into Ladysmith, and on
2 November 1899 the siege began.

Ladysmith sits in terrain shaped like a saucer – Sir Archibald Hunter described it as being the
'bottom of a teacup.'[2] The British held the inner circle of low hills while the Boers held the outer
circumference of taller hills, on which they placed artillery to bombard the town.[3] Trapped in

---

1   Blake Knox, *Buller's Campaign*, pp.30–31.
2   Coetzer, *The Road to Infamy*, p.58.
3   John Y. F .Blake, *A West Pointer with the Boers* (Boston: Angel Guardian Press, 1903), p.122.

Fig 2: General Buller on board the *Dunottar Castle*. General Sir Redvers Henry Buller (1839–1908) embarked for South Africa on 14 October 1899 and reached Cape Town on 31 October. This photograph shows him taking a stroll on the deck with two of his staff. (Arnold van Dyk collection)

Ladysmith were 13,436 troops, 5,400 white residents, and 2,400 loyal Africans and Indians.[4] Overnight, the besieged towns, Kimberley and Mafeking and especially Ladysmith, all became famous, and throughout the Empire people closely followed their fortunes. Lieutenant Charlton of the Lancashire Fusiliers, awaiting the order to go to South Africa, wrote: 'The invulnerability of British troops was an article of faith in every soldier's creed, and to hear of reverses at this early stage was to reach the bottom of belief.'[5]

The inhabitants of Ladysmith soon began to get ill from enteric fever (typhoid). Typhoid is a bacterial infection transmitted by faecally-contaminated water and food, and by flies feeding on human excrement. George Steevens, the *Daily Mail* correspondent and celebrated author of *'With Kitchener to Khartoum'* was in Ladysmith. Not long before he contracted typhoid, from which he died, Steevens wrote:

> We wait and wonder, first expectant, presently apathetic, and feel ourselves grow old. Furthermore, we are in prison. We know now what Dartmoor feels like. The practised vagabond tires in a fortnight of a European capital; of Ladysmith he sickens in three hours… I know how a fly in a beer-bottle feels. I know how it tastes, too.[6]

One in seven of those with typhoid died; the survivors gradually recovered over several weeks, with some later relapsing.[7] Professor Almoth Wright, chief bacteriologist at the Army Medical School, had developed a sterilised culture of *Salmonella Typhi* to use as a vaccine, which would

4   Blake Knox, *Buller's Campaign*, p. XV.
5   Charlton, *Charlton*, p.82.
6   George W. Steevens, *From Capetown to Ladysmith; an unfinished record of the South African War* (New York: Dodd, Mead & Co., 1900), p.139.
7   De Villiers, *Healers, Helpers and Hospitals*, Vol. 2, p.111.

be shown to halve the mortality of typhoid. Immunisation was offered on the troop ships, but side effects were so severe that many declined. Captain Jourdain of the Connaught Rangers recalled:

> Of the seventeen who underwent this rather drastic mode of making a hole in one's arm and putting in about a tablespoon or more of serum, I was the only one who was on his legs at 9.30 p.m. that night and the only one except one who had breakfast the next morning. One youth fainted even before the overdose of liquid was put inside him.[8]

General White, writing to his wife on 9 December 1899, foresaw the coming typhoid epidemic:

> Ladysmith is a nasty place, & I fear there will be a terrible plague of enteric if we are kept here much longer. Already there are 80 cases, & the numbers are increasing rapidly. We had more enteric fever here last year than in any other station of the British Army, & I dread the result of siege conditions this year far more than the shells & bullets of the enemy.[9]

George Lynch, correspondent for the *Illustrated London News* in Ladysmith was one of those who fell ill with typhoid. He went out to Intombi Hospital Camp on the 6:00 a.m. train, with its load of wounded and sick:

> It was a sad journey out; men could not help cursing their bad luck and wondering what would be before them as a result of the journey, wondering if they should ever rejoin their regiments or if their next journey would not be back to the cemetery they were now passing on their right, growing every day more ominously populous.[10]

General Neville Lyttelton, outside Ladysmith, had no inkling of this, writing to his wife: 'It is a marvellously healthy country with no malaria or fever, and nobody, however wet, seems to catch cold or get rheumatism.'[11]

When Buller disembarked at Cape Town on 31 October, the news of White's defeat at Nicholson's Nek awaited him, and he decided to make Ladysmith his priority: '...the deliverance of South Natal must be my first object, combined if possible with the rescue of Sir George White's force for active operations.'[12] Buller delegated the relief of Kimberley and the invasion of the OVS to Lord Methuen, while he sailed for Durban. It was a popular decision, as Lieutenant Blake Knox wrote: 'Ladysmith must be relieved from within Natal... by this decision [General

8   Jourdain, *Ranging Memories*, p.84.
9   Henry M. Durand, *The life of Field-Marshal Sir George White, V.C.*, (London: Blackwood & Sons, 1915), Vol. II, p.136.
10 Lynch, *Impressions of a War Correspondent*, p.17.
11 Neville Lyttelton, *Letter* to his wife of 1 February 1900, Liddell Hart Archives GB0099 KCLMA Lyttelton.
12 Durand, *The life of Field-Marshal Sir George White*, p.114.

Buller] saved the Empire from great disaster.'[13] Buller himself recognised that: 'The fall of Ladysmith would have a terrible effect, especially in India.'[14]

Part of the Boer force, under Louis Botha, wished to avoid being involved in the siege, bypassed Ladysmith and invaded southern Natal. They were defeated at Willow Grange, near Estcourt, on 23 November 1899. Two days later, Buller landed in Durban, taking command of an army to relieve Ladysmith: the Natal Field Force. The Boers fell back to the natural line of defence of the Tugela River, dynamiting the railway bridges at Frere on 26 November, and at Colenso on 28 November.

The British Army in Natal

The British soldier arriving in South Africa in 1899 was well-equipped for modern warfare. He marched with a load of only 20kg, comprising: a Lee-Metford or Lee-Enfield magazine rifle with a bayonet; in buff leather pouches, 150 Mk II cordite .303 cartridges; a haversack containing a tinned emergency ration and usually his own supply of rusks, tea, coffee, chocolate, sugar, salt, pepper and rice. He had a change of flannel shirt, socks and underpants; a towel and night cap, a blanket and a tin canteen, knife, spoon and fork. He wore a grey flannel shirt, woollen socks, and a khaki cotton drill tunic and breeches; puttees and lace-up boots. As a lingering superstition against diarrhoeal diseases, most men wore next to their skin a colourful flannel 'cholera' belt.[15] In the sun, no soldier should remove his foreign service helmet, which was made of cork and well-ventilated. The helmet was thought, correctly, to prevent heatstroke and, erroneously, to prevent malaria and other tropical fevers. However, the helmet brims came down so low at the front and back that it was almost impossible to aim a rifle while lying down, unless one reversed the helmet or removed it altogether. The climate in South Africa was not as harsh as in Sudan, so quilted spinal pads to guard against heat stroke were not worn, and khaki neck flaps, initially worn by some units, were soon discarded. Richard Harding Davis, correspondent for *The Times*, was impressed by khaki kit:

> Some of these hills are green, but the greater part are a yellow or dark red, against which at two hundred yards a man in khaki is indistinguishable from the rocks around him. Indeed, the khaki is the English soldier's sole protection. It saves him in spite of himself, for he apparently cannot learn to advance under cover, and a sky-line is the one place where he selects to stand erect and stretch his weary limbs. I have come to within a hundred yards of a hill before I saw that scattered among its red and yellow boulders was the better part of a regiment as closely packed together as the crowd on the bleaching boards at a base-ball match.**[16]**

13   Blake Knox, *Buller's Campaign*, p. XVII.
14   Commission into the War in South Africa; Report of His Majesty's Commissioners Appointed to Inquire into the Military Preparations and Other Matters Connected with the War in South Africa (London: H.M.S.O 1903), Vol. II, p.164.
15   Jourdain, *Ranging Memories*, p.93.
16   Richard Harding Davis, *Notes of a War Correspondent* (New York: C. Scribner's Sons, 1911), p.142.

The British Army quickly adopted new inventions. They carried to the Upper Tugela sufficient pontoons to make several prefabricated bridges, a field telegraph linking the generals to London, an observation balloon with compressed cylinders of hydrogen, plus zinc and hydrochloric acid to make more gas.

Fig 3: Pontoons were transported by rail to Frere and by ox-wagon to the Upper Tugela to allow the Royal Engineers to build bridges across the Tugela very quickly. The prefabricated chesses are in the foreground. (Arnold van Dyk collection)

Their field hospitals were equipped with chloroform anaesthesia and carbolic sterilising sprays, and the stationary hospitals had X-ray apparatus to locate bullets and shrapnel, and help set bone fragments. A cinematographer with a Mutograph cine camera was on hand to record the events for the public at home.

The Natal Landscape

Natal has a very varied landscape, rising from the warm Indian Ocean with subtropical beaches, through coastal bush, to the snow-capped Drakensberg Mountains. The Upper Tugela valley is a series of flat-topped hills (*koppies*), covered in long grass, which is bright green in the rainy summer from October to April, and bleaches to a pale khaki in the dry winter. The soil is iron-rich and red, with plentiful Mountain Aloes and occasional Acacia thorn trees. It is fertile grassland, well-suited for antelope or cattle, and in 1900 it was largely devoid of trees. Arriving in Natal, *The Times* Correspondent was amazed by the hills:

> They are illegitimate children of no line, abandoned broadcast over the country, with no family likeness and no home. They stand alone, or shoulder to shoulder, or at right angles, or at a tangent, or join hands across a valley. They never appear the same; some run to a sharp point, some stretch out, forming a table-land, others are gigantic anthills, others perfect and accurately modelled ramparts. In a ride of half a mile, every hill completely loses its original aspect and character. They hide each other, or disguise each other. Each can be enfiladed by the other, and not one gives up the secret of its strategic value until its crest has been carried by the bayonet... To add to this confusion, the river Tugela … doubles on its tracks, it sinks out of sight between them, and in the open plain rises to the dignity of water-falls. It runs uphill, and remains motionless on an incline, and on the level ground twists and turns so frequently that when one says he has crossed the Tugela, he means he has crossed it once at a drift, once at the wrecked railroad bridge, and once over a pontoon. And then he is not sure that he is not still on the same side from which he started.[17]

The Battle of Colenso

To relieve Ladysmith from the south, Buller had only three possible routes. The direct route was through Colenso up the railway, and the indirect routes meant either crossing the Upper Tugela to the west, or the Lower Tugela to the east. Buller considered the direct route to be too strongly defended. The eastern route passed through rough, hot country, and would have involved much bush fighting. In the 9th Frontier War 20 years earlier, Buller had learned not to send British troops to fight in thick bush before they had been thoroughly trained and acclimatised.[18] The western route seemed promising, for at higher altitude the terrain was grassy, more open, and cooler. Buller initially planned to cross the Tugela at Potgieter's Drift, 25km upstream of Colenso, but after the defeats in the Cape at Stormberg and Magersfontein, Buller revised his plans. He saw a long march away from the railway as hazardous: 'I might share the fate of Sir George White, and be cut off from Natal.'[19] Being 'cut off' was one of two persistent fears of all the British commanders – the other was the fear of being attacked at night. There had been several recent disasters where British units were cut off: Talana, Stormberg and Nicholson's Nek. Indeed, being cut off was the sure way to lose a battle. So, on 15 December 1899, Buller attacked directly up the railway line at Colenso. It was a resounding defeat, adding a third humiliation to what came to be known as 'Black Week'. But, by a strange trick of memory, Buller later gave sworn testimony that no battle had taken place:

---

17   Davis, *Notes of a War Correspondent*, p.141.
18   Charles H. Melville, *Life of General the Right Hon. Sir Redvers Buller* London: Edward Arnold, 1923, p.83.
19   Durand, *The Life of Field-Marshal Sir George White*, p.130.

I hope I have practically made it clear that I never attacked on the 15th [December 1899] at all. I have been accused of having done so, and it has been said that every military man condemned the execution of that attack. But I made no attack. I stopped at the very earliest moment in the morning every General from moving, and no attack was made on Colenso at all on the 15th of December. I have tried to make that clear here... My left Brigade moved too soon, contrary to my orders, I did not succeed in stopping it, but withdrew it at once. But no other troops, except some artillery that got into the wrong place, moved forward at all for any purpose of any attack.[20]

The battle of Colenso undoubtedly did happen, and it was Buller's first experience of long range Mauser fire. To the west of the railway, General Arthur Fitzroy Hart led his Irish Brigade across an open plain into a loop of the Tugela River, where they were shot at by Boers concealed in trenches 1,000 to 2,000 metres away. Within a few minutes, 216 of 900 men of the leading battalion, the Dublin Fusiliers, were dead or wounded. East of the railway, Colonel Long unlimbered the 66th and 14th Batteries of field artillery too far ahead of their infantry supports, and within 1,100 metres of entrenched Boers. Soon 16 gunners were dead, 89 wounded and 52 captured.[21] Captain Walter Congreve tried to retrieve a field gun; his horse was shot in three places and, wounded, he crawled into a donga (dry stream bed) 500 metres back. Next, Lieutenant Freddy Roberts, the only son of Field Marshal Lord Roberts, galloped up to retrieve a gun and fell wounded. Congreve carried Freddy back to the donga, getting shot through his leg, elbow, shoulder and toe. Freddy Roberts was hit in three places. Roberts lay for seven hours in the donga, attended to by Major Babtie, RAMC, who rode out to him in a hail of bullets, and whose horse was killed under him. All at a rifle range of over 1km.

Once he reached the field hospital at Chieveley, Freddy was examined by the civil surgeon Frederick Treves and Major Hamilton, RAMC: 'From a surgical point of view the case was hopeless, and had been hopeless from the first... In addition to a penetrating wound of the abdomen, his forearm was shattered by a Mauser and his knee wounded by a shell. He was pulseless.'[22]

Freddy Roberts died at midnight, and was buried at 4:00 p.m. on 16 December, in what is now Chieveley Military Cemetery. Many came to pay their last respects, including Generals Clery and Hildyard, and Lord Dundonald; but not Buller. The pall-bearers, who would become famous, were Colonels Buchanan-Riddell and Wortley, Major Bewicke-Copley and Prince Christian Victor. The Bishop of Natal conducted the funeral service. The firing party went through their movements, but they did not fire, as this might be misunderstood by the Boers who were within artillery range.[23]

The British public were not at all prepared for casualties. Throughout Imperial history, the British Army had enjoyed considerable technological advantages. At the battle of Omdurman, just 15 months earlier, Kitchener's troops had faced 50,000 Mahdists armed with what Churchill

20 Commission into the War in South Africa, Vol. II, p.201.
21 Darrell D. Hall, *Halt! Action Front!* (South Africa, Covos-Day, 1999), p.10.
22 Treves, *British Medical Journal*, 1900, pp.27 and 200.
23 Baynes, *My Diocese during the War,* pp.119—121.

called 'trashy rifles.' Kitchener's force killed 9,700 Mahdists, losing only 47 of their own men.[24] Hillaire Belloc captured the mood of 1898 in a witty rhyme: 'Whatever happens, we have got the Maxim gun, and they have not.'[25] But the Boer Mauser was anything but a 'trashy rifle', and Boers were not fanatical tribesmen. The casualty figures at Colenso were the reverse of Omdurman: 1,139 British compared to 38 Boer casualties.[26]

During the battle of Colenso Buller was struck in the ribs by a spent bullet. It did not penetrate, but left him shaken, and he dismounted 'limply and wearily from his horse like an old, old man.'[27] Buller telegraphed the Secretary of State for War despondently: 'I do not think either a Boer or a gun was seen by us all day, yet the fire brought to bear was very heavy. Our infantry were quite willing to fight, but were absolutely exhausted by the intense heat...my men have not seen a dead Boer, and that dispirits them.'[28][29] Buller now wanted to be 'rid of the incubus of Ladysmith,'[30] and the next day he sent a heliogram to White in Ladysmith, which became notorious as Buller's 'surrender telegram':

> I tried Colenso yesterday, but failed; the enemy is too strong for my force, except with siege operations, and those will take one full month to prepare. Can you last so long? If not, how many days can you give me in which to take up defensive positions? After which I suggest your firing away as much ammunition as you can, and making best terms you can. I can remain here if you have alternative suggestion, but, unaided, I cannot break in.[31]

White received the message while in bed with 'fever', which was a euphemism for typhoid. He could not believe Buller had sent it, and muttered: 'The Boers have got hold of the cypher.'[32] White replied:

> Make every effort to get reinforcements as early as possible, including India, and enlist every man in both Colonies who will serve and can ride... The loss of 12,000 men here would be a heavy blow to England. We must not think of it... Enteric fever is increasing alarmingly here. There are now 180 cases, all within last month.[33]

24   Winston S. Churchill, *The River War. An Historical Account of the Reconquest of the Soudan* (London: Longmans, 1902), p.308.
25   Hillaire Belloc, *The Modern Traveller* London: Edward Arnold, 1898, p.41.
26   Coetzer, *The Road to Infamy*, p.81.
27   John Black Atkins, *The Relief of Ladysmith*, p.174.
28   Commission into the War in South Africa, Vol. II, p.175.
29   Durand, *The life of Field-Marshal Sir George White*, p.141.
30   Commission into the War in South Africa, Vol. II, p.206.
31   Commission into the War in South Africa, Vol. II, p.161.
32   Durand, *The life of Field-Marshal Sir George White*, p.138.
33   Commission into the War in South Africa, Vol. II, p.161.

3

General Sir Charles Warren Arrives in South Africa

'The fact of the matter is that there were two Bullers.' General Sir Charles
Warren.[1]

The British government reacted swiftly to the 'surrender telegram'. Buller was dismissed as Commander-in-Chief, and Field Marshal Frederick Sleigh Roberts, still grieving for his son, was appointed to replace him. Roberts understood the challenges:

> Modern weapons make war almost impossible and offensives unthinkable... Two new factors have made their appearance: first, the terrible force of firing; and second, the significant weakening of the impulse in the soldier to go forward... during the frightful moments of the advance he thinks only about how to best take cover, and afterwards how to get out safely from that hell.[2]

Roberts sailed from Southampton on 23 December 1899 and would assume command as soon as he disembarked in Cape Town on 10 January. Until then, Buller was still Commander-in-Chief. On 17 December, Buller's spirits lifted: reinforcements, in the form of Lieutenant General Sir Charles Warren's 5th Division, had reached South Africa. They had been intended for the Cape and OVS, but while Buller was still Commander-in-Chief he could divert Warren to Natal, which he did.

Buller heliographed Ladysmith: 'Fifth Division just arriving at the Cape. Have telegraphed for it to come on at once. It will make me strong enough to try Potgieter's. How long can you hang on?'[3]

In a desperate attempt to capture Ladysmith before Warren reached Natal, on 6 January 1900 the Boers attacked Platrand (Wagon Hill and Caesar's Camp). The attack was unenthusiastically delivered and poorly coordinated, and the defenders were victorious. Ladysmith received a heliogram on 8 January: 'From Her Majesty the Queen to General Sir George White. Warmly

---

1   Coetzer, *The Road to Infamy*, p.117.
2   Pavel A. Stakhovich, 'The Despatches of Colonel Stakhovich, of the General Staff Despatched to the Theatre of Military Operations in South Africa', in *Scientia Militaria, South African Journal of Military Studies*, Vol.5, No.3, 1975, p.13.
3   Durand, *The life of Field-Marshal Sir George White*, p.146.

Fig 4: General Sir Charles Warren and his Staff in South Africa. Warren (1840–1927) commanded 5th
Division in Natal. (Arnold van Dyk collection)

congratulate you and all under your command for your brilliant success. Greatly admire conduct of the Devonshire Regiment.'[4]

While waiting for Warren's arrival, Buller's force stayed near their camps on the railway at Chieveley, 10km south of Colenso, and Frere, 10km further south. Conditions in Ladysmith worsened, and on 10 January 1900, White heliographed Buller: 'My sick list now amounts to 2,000, including 615 cases of typhoid.'[5] 'Black Week', the hat-trick of defeats at Stormberg, Magersfontein, and Colenso, was followed by 'a long pause, sombre and bewildering to the nation beyond anything in the annals of English history, with three defeated British armies pulling themselves together and compiling terrible casualty lists out of range of the positions from which they had been rolled back.'[6] Despite the shadow that lay over England, jollity permeated the camps.[7] From Chieveley the gunners of HMS *Terrible* daily shelled the Boer trenches at Colenso, and on 19 December Lieutenant England's 4.7 inch naval gun, at a range of 7km, destroyed the Colenso wagon bridge, the only remaining bridge across the Tugela. It was: 'a very lucky and good shot, at which, needless to say, Sir F. Clery was very pleased.'[8]

4   Commission into the War in South Africa, Vol. II, p.163.
5   Commission into the War in South Africa, Vol. II, pp.163, 178.
6   Linesman, *Words by an Eyewitness*, p.27.
7   Linesman, *Words by an Eyewitness*, p.29.
8   Charles R. N. Burne *With the Naval Brigade in Natal, 1899–1900* (London: Arnold, 1902), p.20.

Fig 5: General Francis Clery watching the naval guns shelling the Colenso road bridge. On
19 December 1899 the naval gunners destroyed the last remaining bridge over the Tugela, to limit Boer
mobility. Clery (1838–1926) is on the right, marked 'X'. The 4.7-inch gun of HMS *Terrible*, centre, was
commanded by Lieutenant England. (Arnold van Dyk collection)

While the destruction of the bridge restricted the mobility of the Boers, it also meant that,
thereafter, any crossing of the Tugela by the British would have to be by pontoon bridge. The
10km of open veldt between British and Boer lines was patrolled by mounted men, and the
British armoured train regularly probed north from Estcourt. British heliographers exchanged
jokes with Boer signallers, asking whether they would prefer Cecil Rhodes or Winston Churchill
as President, and advising the Boers: 'not to dig those trenches too deep or they would get
through to England.'[9]

Warren's 5th Division, re-routed to Natal, arrived at Frere on 9 January. General Sir
Charles Warren was a 59-year old who, like Buller, had served in South Africa more than
20 years previously. Warren was familiar with the northern Cape, Orange Free State, and
Bechuanaland; thus, the War Office had intended he should return to that region and join the
advance on Kimberley and Bloemfontein. Warren did not protest when Buller re-directed him
to Natal. In 1876, Warren had mapped the boundary between the Orange Free State and the
Cape Colony. He discovered, to nobody's surprise, that the highly lucrative diamond fields of
Kimberley belonged to the Cape, not to the OVS nor to the Griqua tribe. Colonel Warren then
went on to command the Diamond Fields Horse in 1878 during the 9th Frontier War in the
Eastern Cape, where he was wounded and mentioned in despatches. In 1879, he was appointed

9   Baynes, *My Diocese During the Wa*r, p.142.

Administrator of Griqualand West, near Kimberley. Around that time, he met Colonel Buller, a young, bearded officer in command of the Frontier Light Horse, who would win a V.C. in the Zulu War of 1879.[10] But, as Winston Churchill observed:

> I am doubtful whether the fact that a man has gained the Victoria Cross for bravery as a young officer fits him to command an army twenty or thirty years later. I have noticed more than one serious misfortune which arose from such assumptions. Age, easy living, heaviness of body, many years of promotion and success in time of peace, dissipate the vital forces indispensable to intense action.[11]

Warren's force comprised about 8,000 men in two Brigades, the 11th and the 4th, and each Brigade had 4 Battalions (Appendix I). The 11th, or Lancashire, Brigade was under Major General Edward Robert Prevost Woodgate and consisted of the 2nd Lancashire Fusiliers, 2nd King's Royal Lancasters, 1st South Lancashires, and 1st York and Lancasters. Woodgate, aged 54, had served in the Royal Lancasters since 1865, including in the Zulu War.

The 4th Brigade, under Major General Sir Neville Lyttelton, comprised the 3rd Battalion King's Royal Rifle Corps, 2nd Scottish Rifles, 1st Durham Light Infantry, and 1st Rifle Brigade. Lyttelton, aged 54, had commanded the 2nd Infantry Brigade at Omdurman.

Major General Talbot Coke's 10th Infantry Brigade, though not part of 5th Division, also reached Frere on 9 January.

Coke's force comprised the 2nd Middlesex, 2nd Dorsets, 2nd Somerset Light Infantry, the Imperial Light Infantry (Appendix I).

Soon after his arrival, Warren unwisely ventured some advice to Buller. He suggested the next

Fig 6: Major-General John Talbot Coke (1841–1912) joined the Army in 1859 and was to command Right Attack in the Spioenkop campaign. He was partially in command at Spioenkop.

10   Coetzer, *The Road to Infamy*, pp.111–112.
11   Churchill, *My Early Life*, pp.300–301.

attempt to relieve Ladysmith should be from Hlangwane Hill, to which Buller snapped: 'What do you know about it?'[12] Events would prove Warren correct – Hlangwane would be the key to the relief of Ladysmith, 6 weeks later. Warren saw the problem as one of mobility: 'The great difficulty with the British commanders was that they could not realise the tremendous mobility of the Boers; they kept thinking that Infantry moving 10 miles a day could outflank Boers moving 10 miles in two hours.'[13] In addition, Warren was concerned by Buller's state of mind:

> When I arrived at Durban on the 25th December 1899, [Major-General Neville] Lyttelton begged me to come at once and buck up Buller, otherwise the army would go smash. Up to that point Buller was a counsel of despair: he could not see his way to relieve Ladysmith. My business was to tell him that it could be done and that I could do it.
>
> The fact of the matter is that there were two Bullers... The first General Buller was my old friend, but the second General Buller was full of uncertainty and suspicion. At first, I did not know how to meet this second General Buller, but by the 28th January I recognised that he was merely a phantom that required to be resisted, and when that was done, the real old General Buller took his place.[14]

Major General Neville Lyttelton's 4th Brigade, Major General Hildyard's 2nd Brigade, and Major General Hart's 5th, or Irish, Brigade had all been in Natal since November, and all had fought at Colenso. Warren's men of the 11th Brigade had never been in South Africa, and Warren needed them to practice in field conditions:

> ...meeting the Boers with their good weapons of precision and their powers of shooting and taking cover was a new experience to which our troops must get accustomed, while the advent of smokeless powder added to the intricacy of the operations... The troops I was taking into action were quite unfitted for immediately fighting the Boer... They had not seen him yet, dead or alive ... It was my mission to introduce Mr Thomas Atkins to Mr Boer, face to face...[15]

Warren's men picked up tips from the veterans of Willow Grange and Colenso. They stained their buff leather straps brown using Condy's Fluid (potassium permanganate), which was on hand as a disinfectant for water and as an antiseptic for sores. White horses got the same treatment. To avoid being picked off by Boers, officers discarded their swords and revolvers and carried rifles, also donning the buff leather straps of a private soldier.[16] Private Charles O'Mahony of the West Yorks, a seasoned campaigner, approved:

12   Christiaan J. Barnard, 'General Botha in the Spioenkop Campaign January 1900' in *Military History Journal, South African Military History Society*, Vol. 2 No1, June 1971.
13   Coetzer, *The Road to Infamy*, p.414.
14   Coetzer, *Road to Infamy*, p.117.
15   Coetzer, *Road to Infamy*, p.130.
16   Charlton, *Charlton*, p.100.

For some time now the officers had adopted the dress of the rank and file; that is to say they wore a belt with two pouches, brace straps and carried a rifle, marched in the ranks, fired, etc., acting exactly like one of the rank and file, but in command as usual giving the words to advance, halt, etc. ... Our officers never lost dignity by doing so and became more popular on the contrary, which counts for a good deal more than dignity on active service.[17]

The Boer Command in Natal

There were fewer than 16,000 Boers in Natal, and their numbers dwindled as burghers drifted off home on leave. Around Ladysmith, the commandos were idle under two veterans: Free Staters under 71-year-old General Marthinus Prinsloo and Transvaalers under 68-year-old *Commandant*-General Petrus 'Piet' Joubert. On 22 November, a shell had exploded near Joubert, who fell from his horse, and complications set in. Eventually Joubert was hospitalised at Volksrust; he partly recovered, but died on 27 March 1900, probably from peritonitis.[18] With Joubert incapacitated, General Lucas Meyer, the 'Lion of Vryheid', aged 53, assumed command in Natal. Meyer had fought the British in 1881, and had been wounded in the neck at Ingogo. Meyer's Assistant *Veldkornet* was Louis Botha. Botha had grown up barefoot, tending sheep, and received little formal education and no military training. He served as *Volksraad* member for Vryheid alongside Meyer. Botha became known as a calm, kind and tactful man, and a good orator, but at 36 years of age he was too young to be made a general.[19] Meyer fell ill on 30 October. His doctors prescribed complete rest, and Meyer returned to Pretoria. Louis Botha was temporarily promoted to *Vechtgeneraal*, commanding the Utrecht, Vryheid and Wakkerstroom Commandos. This force, 6,000 strong, manned the Colenso trenches, so Botha found himself in command at the battle of Colenso.[20] A burgher on the Tugela described Botha's tactics, which had led to the resounding victory:

Our tactics here and everywhere along the fighting line are – keep in your trenches; we get ourselves entrenched and wait for the enemy. The English make their attack in the open, thinking that they fight the Soudanese... As we are all mounted, we do our movements quickly. The hardest things we have to endure are the terrible heat, which keeps us in our shirt sleeves all day, and the Siberian cold of the nights, the heavy downpours of rain and the dust storms.[21]

17   Charles J. O'Mahony, writing as 'Jack the Sniper,' *A Peep over the Barleycorn. In the firing line with the P.W.O., 2nd West Yorkshire Regiment, through The Relief of Ladysmith,* (Dublin: J.T. Drought, 1911), p.181.
18   J. C.de Villiers, *Healers, Helpers and Hospitals* (Pretoria: Protea Book House, 2008), Vol.2, p.163.
19   Frederik Rompel, *Heroes of the Boer War* (London, Review of Reviews, 1903), p.115.
20   Leopold S. Amery ed., *The War in South Africa 1899–1902* (London: Sampson Low, Marston & Co, 1905) Vol. III, p.206.
21   Anon, *Glasgow Herald*, Letter, Wednesday 10th January 1900

Botha showed his men exactly where to dig their trenches, and how to conceal them. He slept among his men and carried a rifle in battle, with no signs of rank to distinguish him. If he received a gift, such as biltong or dry sausage, he would invariably share it with his men. At first, he went unrecognised and was sometimes asked by burghers: 'Where can I find General Botha?' His energy became legendary. After Colenso, and even more so after Spioenkop, Botha became a celebrity. Boers passing him would nudge each other, with obvious pleasure, saying: "'That's him." – "Who?" - "Man, our general, Lewies Botha, don't you know him?"' Botha's secretary knew him as: 'A good leader, and a best friend. An example of a gentleman.'[22] During the Natal campaign, even after days of fighting, if he was roused from sleep, he was ready for action. But, by the end of December 1899, his hands-on approach had exhausted him. He was short of sleep, and since his victory at Colenso he had been under daily shellfire. When Meyer returned to Colenso at the beginning of January 1900 after two months' medical leave, Botha hoped that he, too, might be allowed a period of leave, but this was not granted.[23]

Like the British camps at Chieveley and Frere, and like the town of Ladysmith, the Boer trenches at Colenso had become increasingly unpleasant. Burgher Cornelis Plokhooy complained in a letter:

> After a few rainy nights, our beds resemble mud puddles rather than places of rest. Everything is miry and when we get up we can find no firm footing; our feet sink into the squelchy mud... After such a night the burghers always felt queasy, so that in the mornings they would sit in the sun until they recovered... When it rained, the burghers snuggled into their blankets, whereupon the mosquitoes attacked four or five at a time in places where they could not be driven away... It toughened us for all life's vicissitudes. No eventuality will strike us as too hard, for many of the things that may yet befall us can hardly be worse than a night of thunder and pouring rain, spent with brown and other tormentors on a pile of dry grass in mud that slithers away from underneath one at every movement and with a few bandoliers, each holding 300 cartridges, for a pillow.[24]

It was the rainy season, and burgher Hilhorst of the Swaziland Police complained: 'The ground is soaked, bedding drenched, raincoats mouldering from the water, clothing and shoes in much the same state, tents and other shelter miles away... Everything you touched was damp and soggy: rifles, cartridges, salt, coffee, bread. And how was one supposed to light a fire?'[25] The Boers endured regular shelling from naval guns at Chieveley. One of the Boksburg Commando wrote: 'The shelling would start early in the morning on one flank, then work their way steadily to and fro. Some days the British fired no more than 10 shells at the trenches, but on other days several hundreds.'[26]

22   Christof G. S. Sandberg, *De Zesdaagsche Slag aan de Boven Tugela* (Amsterdam: De Gids, 1901), p.87.
23   Barnard, *General Botha in the Spioenkop Campaign.*
24   Pretorius, *Life on Commando During the Anglo-Boer War*, p.131.
25   Pretorius, *Life on Commando During the Anglo-Boer War*, p.132.
26   Pretorius, *Life on Commando During the Anglo-Boer War*, p.133.

Meanwhile, Chieveley and Frere were becoming distinctly unsanitary, and dysentery broke out.[27] The days were hot, with swarms of flies attracted by plentiful unburied horses and occasional unburied soldiers on the Colenso battlefield, and by the daily accumulation of the excreta of tens of thousands of men, horses, slaughter-cattle and oxen. Men were starting to come down with typhoid, just as they were in Ladysmith. Private Harry Phipps of the 1st Borders wrote in his diary at Frere: 'I am getting thoroughly bloodthirsty & at present would sooner have another go at the enemy than have a good dinner, which is saying a lot.'[28] Private Walter Abbott of the Dorsets wrote that he had always thought that Chieveley was a big place 'but when we got there I found only one house. That was the station.'[29] Frere boasted a little hotel and a water supply in the form of the Blaaukrans Spruit. The Bishop of Natal was enchanted with Frere camp which 'spreads everywhere, converting these silent hills and plains into a busy town.'[30] To Treves, Frere was 'simply a speck – a corrugated iron oasis – on the vast undulating plains of the veldt. These plains roll away to the horizon, and are broken only by kopjes and dongas and the everlasting ant-hills… everyone is glad to leave Frere – dreary, sweltering Frere.'[31]

27   Jourdain, *Ranging Memories*, p.95.
28   Harry Phipps, *Diary, 1st Battalion Border Regiment*, National Army Museum 1983-02-15, entry 3 January 1900.
29   Walter Abbott, Private, Dorsetshire Regiment, *Diary*, National Army Museum 1992-08–335, entry 27 January 1900.
30   Baynes, *My Diocese During the War*, p.139.
31   Treves, *The Tale of a Field Hospital*, pp.3 &10.

4

The March from Frere and Chieveley

'…against such slow opponents as Buller and Warren we were pretty safe.'
Veldkornet Jan Kemp.[1]

Buller Revisits His Plan

After his defeat at Colenso on 15 December 1899, Buller looked again at his original plan to break through the Boers' Tugela line upstream of Colenso. There were at least 15 drifts (fords) on this stretch of river. The Upper Tugela had been reconnoitred, and no Boers had been seen on the north bank of the river, nor on the Brakfontein heights, which commanded Potgieter's Drift from the north. Across Potgieter's Drift and through Brakfontein ran a good wagon road to Ladysmith, only 27km away. As a second option, 8km further upstream there was a second wagon road, which crossed the Tugela at Trichardt's Drift. The march upstream of the bulk of the army in Natal would require heavy transport, good roads, and a secure line of communication with the railway to prevent the force being cut off. The movement west would be slow and in full view of the Boers, but Buller still hoped to retain some element of initiative, if not surprise. The slowness of the march meant it could not be considered a turning movement, but rather as a march to the flank in preparation for frontal attacks. Buller's troops would march from Chieveley and Frere and meet at Pretorius' Farm, about 10km from the railway.

The route of Warren's 5th Division from Frere roughly followed the current R74 road, while Clery's 2nd Division from Chieveley had 5km further to march. The combined column would then proceed to Springfield (today called Winterton) about 20km further. From Springfield, it was about 12–15km to the drifts on the Tugela. Buller later blamed his decision on poor advice: 'The line of advance by Potgieter's Drift was recommended to me by those whom I was bound to trust, as being easier; but it was not, and if I had then known the line of advance by Potgieter's Drift as well as I did after I had been fighting there, I should never have gone there.'[2] Local guides were lacking. The countryside belonged to a handful of loyal farmers like the Coventry brothers John, Harry, George, and Charles, who had gone into Ladysmith for safety, and were now besieged. There were no maps of the country, so Buller ordered one to be compiled in

1   Jan C. G. Kemp, *Vir Vryheid en Vir Reg*, (Pretoria: Nasionale Pers, 1941), p.275.
2   Commission into the War in South Africa, Vol. II, p.198.

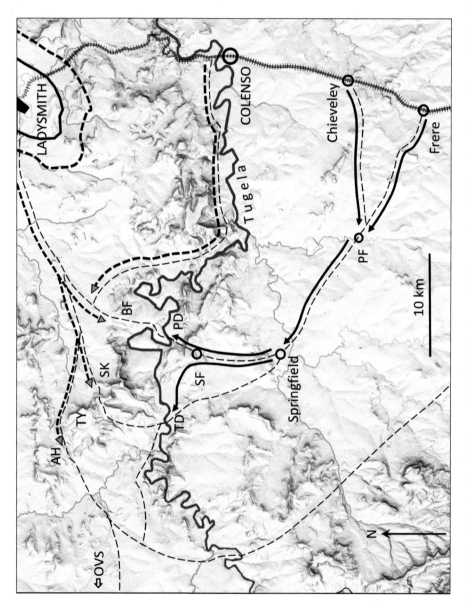

Map 1: March to the Upper Tugela, 10 to 17 January 1900. British columns (solid arrows) march from the railway at Frere and Chieveley, converge at Pretorius' Farm (PF) and proceed to Springfield and then Spearman's Farm (SF). Lyttelton's force then crosses the Tugela at Potgieter's Drift (PD) and Warren's force at Trichardt's Drift (TD). The Boers send reinforcements (dotted arrows) from Colenso and Ladysmith, to the OVS road at Acton Homes (AH), Tabanyama (TY), Spioenkop (SK) and Brakfontein (BF). Dashed lines indicate wagon roads.

Pietermaritzburg from property boundaries. Reproduced as a blueprint, it became known as the 'Blue Map'. It indicated the wagon roads and drifts on the Tugela, but the hills and valleys were crudely drawn artist's impressions. Buildings were not shown, and there was no grid to provide coordinates. Some features were wrongly located, making the map worse than useless when trying to trek cross-country. To cross the Tugela, temporary bridges would be built by the Pontoon Section of the Royal Engineers. They had brought from England flat-bottomed pontoons, which reached Frere by ship and by railway, to be transported across the veldt on ox-wagons. Contrary to British expectations, crossing the Tugela would prove easier than moving across the veldt. Marching away from the railway, the army would be short of water, as Buller admitted after Colenso: 'I find that my infantry cannot fight further than 10 miles from camp, and even then only if water is to be had, and it is scarce here…'[3]

For some time, there had been rumours in the British camps that there would be a march upstream, and the rumours became credible on 7 January when the hospitals in Pietermaritzburg cleared out their wounded in the expectation of new arrivals. The following day the field hospitals at Frere were also emptied, and 700 civilian stretcher-bearers of the Natal Volunteer Ambulance Corps (NVAC) turned up. The NVAC had just been organised by Colonel Gallwey, the Principal Medical Officer of Natal, and were instantly known as the 'Body Snatchers'. The NVAC were needed in large numbers because 12 men were allocated to each stretcher, so they could carry the wounded in shifts for many miles.[4] Their presence at the front could only mean one thing: a campaign was about to begin.[5,6]

Wet Weather

The storms on 6 January, which helped save Ladysmith during the battle of Platrand, were followed by downpours on 8 and 9 January, so the 2nd Division at Chieveley and the 5th Division at Frere had to postpone their departures. The ship's carpenter of HMS *Terrible* spent an idle day making two dummy 4.7-inch guns to take the place of the guns going west, but the Boers heliographed the British signal station: 'Do you take us to be such fools as not to know a dummy from a real gun?'[7][8]

Wednesday morning, 10 January, was dry and bright, and both divisions set off.

The only combat that day was a small skirmish. At first light, the Boers on the heights north of Colenso saw the columns forming up, and 35 scouts of Edwards' *Verkenner Korps* (Edwards' Reconnaissance Corps) rode out to spy. British mounted patrols fired at them, and a burgher named Harry Campbell was shot in the abdomen. He rode 750 metres, then dropped from his saddle. His comrades purloined poles and blankets from a Zulu hut, and fashioned a stretcher. They carried Campbell back to their lines, keeping the British away by sniping. Campbell was

3   Commission into the War in South Africa, Vol. II, p.161.
4   Treves, *British Medical Journal* 1900, p.219.
5   Inniskilling Fusiliers Regimental Historical Records Committee, *The Royal Inniskilling Fusiliers* London: Constable, 1928, p.410.
6   Winston S. Churchill, *London to Ladysmith via Pretoria* (London: Longmans, 1900), p.248.
7   Bennet Burleigh, *The Natal Campaign* (London: Chapman & Hall, 1900), p.278.
8   Thomas T. Jeans, *Naval Brigades in The South African War 1899–1900* (London: Sampson Low, Marston & Co 1901), p.253.

Fig 7: The 1st Battalion, York and Lancasters, leaves Frere. The battalion, about 1,000 men, are just leaving camp, and stand at attention for the picture. The stationmaster's house and Frere Hotel are in the background. An ox-wagon is in the foreground, and behind the infantry column are ox-wagons, horse-drawn ambulance wagons and infantry. (Arnold van Dyk collection)

in agony, and repeatedly asked them to put him down. After 2 hours, they reached a Boer ambulance. Campbell survived, which was attributed to his having fought on an empty stomach.[9] Buller's columns which trekked west comprised 23,000 infantry, 2,000 mounted men, forty-two 15-pdr field guns, six 5-inch howitzers, and, from HMS *Terrible*, eight naval 12-pdrs and two naval 4.7-inch guns. There was a long column of commissariat, field hospitals and equipment, bearer companies, and the Royal Engineers with their balloon, pontoon, telegraph, and various other sections.[10] The men were in good spirits: Bennet Burleigh, with the *Daily Telegraph*, wrote 'General Hart's Brigade were in raptures at not being left behind to lose the chance of participating in the big scrimmage. Dublins, Inniskillings, and Connaught "boys" were gay and chirpy, going singing to war.'[11] Ahead of the marching men and wagons rode Lord Dundonald's mounted brigade, with Major Coghill's 64th Battery of 15-pdrs, under secret orders to rush ahead to secure Springfield.[12]

9   Dirk Mostert, *Slegtkamp van Spioenkop: Oorlogsherinneringe van Kapt Slegtkamp* (Pretoria: Nasionale Pers, 1935), pp.31–32.
10   Blake Knox, *Buller's Campaign*, p.4
11   Burleigh, *The Natal Campaign*, p.280.
12   John F. Maurice *History of The War in South Africa, 1899–1902* (London: Hurst and Blackett, 1907), Vol. II, p.342.

Fig 8: Douglas Cochrane, 12th Earl of Dundonald (1852–1935). With the rank of Colonel, Lord Dundonald commanded the Mounted Brigade in the Natal Field Force. (*Black and White Budget*)

Scouts in two local units, the Natal Carbineers and Imperial Light Horse, rode well in advance to screen the column against surprises.[13] The columns stretched out for 24km and comprised 324 ox-wagons, which were the traditional heavy transports of South Africa. Each wagon, drawn by 8 or 16 trek oxen, made two trips.[14] At best, the shambling oxen could cover 20km a day,[15] but Buller's column managed a speed of only 1 mile an hour.[16] The *Manchester Guardian* correspondent described the scene as being like a rope being drawn slowly across the country as far as you could see. 'It seemed endless, this rope made of all the strands that hold an army together...'[17]

The rains had saturated the ground, and once the army left the railway, they found *spruits* were muddy torrents, the drifts quagmires, and the wagons got continually stuck. Teams of oxen were doubled and even trebled, and the soldiers repeatedly dug wagons and artillery out of the mud. The *Daily Telegraph* reported: 'The tracks, by profound flattery called roads, were utterly blocked. Hundreds upon hundreds of waggons were jammed together in mile-long lanes; the baggage-guards and other bodies of troops had to while away the time, and bivouac as best they could upon the open veldt.'[18] The leading wagon bogged down at the first crossing, Blaauwkrans Spruit, within sight of Frere camp. Even 80 oxen were unable to move it an inch, and mules and horses dropped dead from exhaustion. A traction engine was requisitioned from Frere, and a steel hawser was passed from the engine and made fast to the disselboom: 'Then steam was turned on, and with snort and whirr the steamer walked away with the wagon, conveying it some

13   George Crowe, *The Commission of H.M.S. "Terrible" 1898–1902* (London: George Newnes, 1903), p.135.
14   Coetzee, *Road to Infamy*, p.121.
15   Louis Creswicke, *South Africa and the Transvaal War* (Edinburgh: TC & EC Jack, 1900), Vol. III, p.93.
16   Maurice *History of The War in South Africa,1899–1902* (London: Hurst and Blackett, 1907), Vol. II, p.341.
17   Atkins, *The Relief of Ladysmith*, p.206.
18   Burleigh, *The Natal Campaign*, p.282.

distance to a high and dry part of the roadway...'[19] Soon enough, the traction engine was on its side, marooned. One of the sailors of HMS *Terrible* asked the engine driver: '...if he wanted a sky-pilot [chaplain] to read the burial service over it?' 'There's plenty of life in the beggar yet!' came the reply.[20] Private O'Mahony of the West Yorkshires observed: 'Traction engines ... would have as much chance of getting round the left flank to Spion Kop in the rainy season as they would have of flying the Channel.'[21] The rearguard departed Chieveley only at 5.30 p.m., by which time the men had been drenched by an evening thunderstorm, as is customary in Natal in the summer.[22][23] A Private in the Middlesex found it a trying day – by 10:00 p.m. he had only marched about 5km, 'moving on only a few yards, halting and so on all day, and the wagons sticking in the mud.' To add to their discomfort, about midnight while crossing a ridge they had to lie down in the mud to avoid the Boers' searchlight.[24] Private O'Mahony blamed the roads:

> Except in the vicinity of the towns there are no made or prepared roads in South Africa. The way of travel is simply a path beaten down by animals and wagons. You can easily imagine what quagmires these would become in wet weather; and, bad as they were, matters got much worse when... you cast off across-country... Our progress was so slow that we hadn't negotiated four miles in six hours.[25]

Veldkornet Kemp of the Krugersdorp Commando was reassured by the British lack of mobility: '...against such slow opponents as Buller and Warren we were pretty safe.'[26]

Barton Remains on the Railway

Eventually the camps at Frere and Chieveley were almost deserted: 'There is something almost uncanny in the way in which a populous city suddenly reverts to bare and solitary veldt.'[27] Almost deserted, but not quite: Major General Barton with 6th Brigade remained behind to guard Chieveley, Frere, and the lines of communication to Pietermaritzburg. Without them, Buller could be cut off entirely. Barton kept the 2nd Royal Scots Fusiliers, 2nd Royal Irish Fusiliers, 1st Royal Welch Fusiliers, two naval 12-pdr guns under Lieutenant Richards, and the only two surviving 15-pdr field guns of Colonel Long's 66th Battery. Frere Camp was protected by the Rifle Reserve Battalion.[28] Mounted patrols were carried out by the 14th Hussars, South African Light Horse (SALH) and Bethune's Mounted Infantry. Outposts guarded the railway to Pietermaritzburg, with two naval 12-pdrs at Frere, two at Mooi River and two more at Estcourt.

19   Burleigh, *The Natal Campaign*, p.286.
20   Crowe, *The Commission of H.M.S. "Terrible"*, p.137.
21   O'Mahony, *A Peep over the Barleycorn*, p.132.
22   Inniskillings, *The Royal Inniskilling Fusiliers*, p.412.
23   Blake Knox, *Buller's Campaign*, p.5.
24   Walter John Putland, *Personal Diary of Lance Corporal Walter Putland 2785 2nd Middlesex Regiment*, National Army Museum, 8107-18.
25   O'Mahony, *A Peep over the Barleycorn*, p.135.
26   Jan C. G. Kemp, *Vir Vryheid en Vir Reg* (Pretoria: Nasionale Pers, 1941), p.275.
27   Baynes, *My Diocese During the War*, p.145.
28   Blake Knox, *Buller's Campaign*, p. XIX.

Warren and Clery's columns reached Pretorius' Farm (approx. GPS -28.82968, 29.66291) at noon on 10 January. The farm was 'a tin-roofed house, a few sheds, a dozen trees, and an artificial pond filled to the brim by the recent rains.'[29] At the farm, they had the Kaal Spruit to cross: '...the worst drift in the Colony...',[30] and the naval gunners stuffed the muzzles of their guns with straw to keep the water out.[31] 'Tramp-tramp-tramp, hour after hour, through a pitiless rain, went battalion after battalion, brigade after brigade; the early dawn breaking before the division had crossed the spruit – many of whom were destined never to recross.'[32]

The first night on the open veldt was miserable; even General Lyttelton and the Bishop of Natal had to sleep out in the open, though they borrowed a tarpaulin and stretchers from an ambulance wagon.[33] The Dorsets lost Private McKenzie from disease at Pretorius' Farm. Typhoid, notoriously difficult to diagnose, was blamed: 'Interic fever... A lot of men fell sick with interic & dysentery & had to be sent back.'[34] The next day, 11 January, the Natal summer heat made itself felt. 'The army, indeed, had a general terra-cotta appearance from their dust-like covering... a few men began to fall out of the ranks and rest on the roadside. Some were footsore, others were exhausted from the heat, and a few even showed signs of sunstroke.'[35] General Lyttelton and the Bishop of Natal ate lunch under a groundsheet propped up by rifles, drinking soda water made on the spot with 'Sparklets'. 'Then we lay down under our little awning and tried to sleep. A strange sight – close to the road – under this improvised tent, a General and a Bishop full length upon the ground. Such extremities does war reduce one to.'[36] Some units remained at Pretorius' Farm to guard the transport columns, while the Mounted Brigade pressed on and reached Springfield at daybreak on 11 January. They found the Boers had, unexpectedly, not dynamited the iron bridge across the Little Tugela. This was probably out of consideration for the local farmers, who were mainly Afrikaners.[37] Dundonald left 300 mounted men and 2 field guns at Springfield to protect the bridge, and pushed north to occupy, at 6:00 a.m., Spearman's Hill (a ridge also known as Mount Alice and Naval Gun Hill).

Capturing Potgieter's Ferry

Spearman's Hill overlooks Potgieter's Drift. From its summit, Dundonald could see no Boers, but on the north bank was a ferry used for taking wagons across the Tugela.

Major Charles Childe's G Squadron, South African Light Horse, volunteered to bring the ferry to the south bank. Lieutenant Carlisle, Sergeant Turner, Corporals Cox and Barkley, and Troopers Howell, Godden, and Collingwood stripped off and crept down to the river. They swam across to the cutting where the boat was moored, and worked it back by its hauling-line and block, covered by the SALH on the southern bank. They had reached mid-stream when

29   Churchill, *London to Ladysmith via Pretoria*, p.254.
30   Jeans, *Naval Brigades in The South African War*, p.253.
31   Burne, *With the Naval Brigade in Natal*, p.28.
32   Crowe, *The Commission of H.M.S. "Terrible"*, p.139.
33   Baynes, *My Diocese During the War*, p.148.
34   Abbott, *Diary*.
35   Blake Knox, *Buller's Campaign*, p.9.
36   Baynes, *My Diocese During the War*, p.151.
37   Baynes, *My Diocese During the War*, p.150.

Fig 9: Ferry at Potgieter's Drift. Men of Bethune's Mounted Infantry haul the ferry across at Potgieter's Drift. The ferry was captured by G Squadron, SALH on 11 January 1900. It could transport wagons, artillery, or 50 or more men. (National Army Museum)

some Boers opened fire. Corporal Cox hacked through the hawser linking it to the north side, and the SALH hauled the boat across under a scattering of Mauser bullets. Nobody was hit.[38]

By the time Warren's 5th Division reached Springfield at dawn on January 12, 'The soldiers' uniforms looked 'so bedraggled that a ragpicker might hesitate about appropriating them.'[39] Buller and his staff left Frere at 3:00 a.m. on 12 January, and when they reached Spearman's Hollow, the sheltered area behind Spearman's Hill, they requisitioned Marthinus Pretorius' farmhouse as Buller's headquarters. Buller addressed the troops at Springfield (Appendix II (a)), then spent hours on Spearman's Hill studying the terrain through his telescope. The panorama was breathtaking, as it is today. Buller looked down on the winding Tugela in the valley, and onto the high hills north of the river, beyond which a hazy plain stretched to Ladysmith, with Lombard's Kop and Umbulwana in the distance. To the west rose the great escarpment of the Drakensberg. The Bishop of Natal counted about 120 Boers passing from east to west on the hills north of the Tugela:

38   Burleigh, *The Natal Campaign*, p.284.
39   Burleigh, *The Natal Campaign*, p.282.

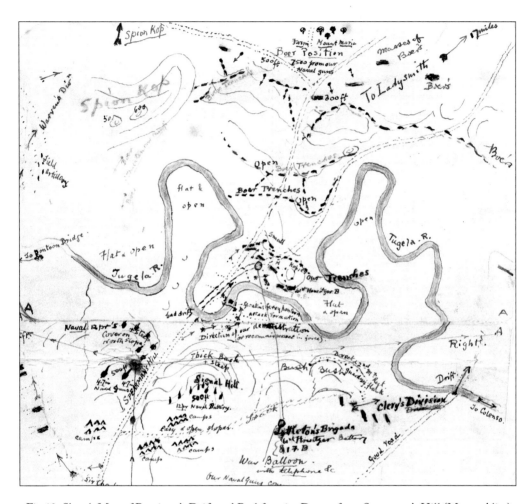

Fig 10: Sketch Map of Potgieter's Drift and Brakfontein. Drawn from Spearman's Hill (Mount Alice) by Lieutenant Colonel Frederic Harvey, RAMC, on 19 January 1900, it shows the British positions across Potgieter's Drift on the Maconochie Koppies, including the 61st (howitzer) Battery and the observation balloon. North are shown several lines of Boer trenches comprising the Brakfontein position. The drawing is based on the Blue Map, so the eastern Twin Peak is wrongly labelled as Spion Kop. (National Army Museum)

Then, looking along the lower hills and kopjes which skirt the meandering river on the north, one could make out long lines of intrenchments, and could see the Boers at work in them with pick and shovel. At Colenso we could see nothing, but here with a good glass one can see line after line of earth-works and watch the Boers shovelling out the earth, and making rifle-pits and gun emplacements, and see them riding to and fro and standing and sitting on hill-tops watching us. It is a unique position thus to be able to look across the valleys and see your enemy and all his works.[40]

Burleigh could see Boers arriving from Ladysmith and working:

in their shirt-sleeves, digging trenches, piling up stone walls, and constructing small semi-circular forts. Every favourable bit of ground they could be seen inspecting, while hundreds toiled in every direction. Their object was unmistakable – to draw line after line of trenches, and to erect forts which would command every inch of ground from the river-front up to and beyond the crested ridges four miles north.[41]

The naval contingent took possession of the eastern summit of Spearman's Hill and started making gun positions. Naval Surgeon Thomas Jeans was with them: 'Through our telescopes we could plainly see the enemy digging for dear life on the sides of these hills, extending their trenches and building schanzes and gun emplacements.'[42]

Communication

Spearman's Hill has a direct line of sight to Ladysmith and Frere. Dundonald's heliographer soon flashed a signal to Captain Walker, the chief signaller Ladysmith, and to Frere.[43] From then on, the besieged garrison received regular updates from the Upper Tugela.[44] White in Ladysmith despaired that, weakened by typhoid, hunger, and the losses at Platrand, his garrison was no longer able to assist Buller by offensive action:

I only wish I could help, but my force is terribly reduced, principally by loss of officers in action... I have therefore to play what to me is the painful part of sitting quietly in Ladysmith awaiting the success of Buller's force. If he is repulsed again we shall be in a bad way. I dread to think of what the effect on our Cause will be if Ladysmith is reduced by famine or taken by assault.[45]

When night came, Spearman's Hill and Ladysmith communicated by searchlight. The Boer searchlight interfered, sending rude messages such as: 'What is Mr. Buller going to do, now

---

40   Baynes, *My Diocese During the War*, pp.154—155.
41   Burleigh, *The Natal Campaign*, p.290.
42   Jeans, *Naval Brigades in the South African War*, p.255.
43   Blake Knox, *Buller's Campaign*, p.11.
44   Durand, *The life of Field-Marshal Sir George White*, p.173.
45   Durand, *The life of Field-Marshal Sir George White*, p.168.

Mr Roberts is coming out?'[46] North of the Tugela, the Boers moved in parallel with Buller's westward movement. They laid telegraph cables connecting their laagers with Colenso and Pretoria.[47] Phillip 'Flip' Pienaar, a Boer telegraphist, unspooled more than 25km of rubber-insulated copper wire:

> A wooden "saddle" holding one roll of wire was strapped on the back of one of the natives; …the native marched forward, the wire unrolling as he went, and the other boys placing stones upon it here and there in order to prevent its being dragged about by cattle… In this manner… every commando was always fully informed as to the situation of all the others, and the enemy's every movement immediately known to the entire forces, enabling reinforcements to be sent anywhere at any time.[48]

South of the Tugela, the Royal Engineers also unspooled their drum of telegraph wire, from Frere to Spearman's Camp.[49] During the day, telegraph machines buzzed their messages; at night, on both sides of the Tugela, the telegraphists slept by their apparatus. From 17 January Pienaar was kept so busy at the Spioenkop telegraph office that for a week he had no time for a decent wash.

The Boer Response

Before 8 January, there were fewer than 1,000 Boers along the Tugela from Vaalkrans to beyond Acton Homes. They comprised Free Staters under General Andries Cronjé and Transvaalers under Generals Tobias Smuts and Ben Viljoen.[50] On 8 January, the rumours of an impending British march westwards reached the Boer command. General Schalk Burger with the Carolina and Leydenburg Commandos moved westwards from Ladysmith, establishing their laager behind the eastern of the *Drielingkoppe* (Twin Peaks), where their scouts could watch the Upper Tugela but from where they could easily return to Ladysmith if needed.[51]

Botha, at Colenso, summoned volunteers, and during the night of 10 January the first groups rode to the Upper Tugela. From 11 January Botha worked non-stop. Each day before sunrise he rode from his tent at Colenso to the Upper Tugela, a journey of 3½ hours. His priority was the construction of trenches on the Brakfontein ridge, opposite Potgieter's Drift, where he expected the British to attack. After sunset, Botha rode back to Colenso to organise reinforcements, ammunition, and supplies, and to dictate reports to *Commandant*-General Joubert and President Kruger. Botha still hoped to go home on leave before the impending attack, and so he kept his headquarters at Colenso. He confided to President Kruger that he was unwell, and asked for a few days' leave, suggesting Schalk Burger or Daniel Erasmus be put in command on the Upper Tugela. President Kruger replied that he considered it essential Botha should

---

46   Jourdain, *Ranging memories*, p.98.
47   Alan R. I. Hiley and John A. Hassell, *The Mobile Boer; being the record of the observations of two burgher officers* (New York: Grafton press, 1902), p.113.
48   Philip Pienaar, *With Steyn and De Wet* (London: Methuen, 1902), p.34.
49   Baynes, *My Diocese during the War*, p.164.
50   Barnard, *General Botha in the Spioenkop Campaign*.
51   Amery, *The War in South Africa*, Vol. III, p.207.

Fig 11: General Schalk Burger (1852–1918) was in command of the sector between Brakfontein and Spioenkop, and withdrew when the Kings Royal Rifles captured Twin Peaks. More suited to politics than military leadership, he became acting State President when Kruger left for Europe. (Free State Archives)

command the new front. Here, Kruger said, every man would have to fight to the limit. He respectfully asked Botha not to request leave until the battle had been fought: 'I regard your presence in the difficult circumstances on your front as indispensable. God will help and sustain you in your onerous task.' Botha accepted this, and on 14 January he informed Pretoria that 650 men had been sent from Ladysmith to the Upper Tugela, and that evening another 200 would follow.[52]

While the British watched the Boers from Spearman's Hill, the Boers watched the British from Spioenkop. It is the highest hill on the north bank of the Upper Tugela and faces Spearman's Hill across the valley. Spioenkop means 'lookout hill' in Afrikaans, and was the hill from which the Voortrekkers had looked out on Natal in 1837. From its summit, the Boers now saw the Tugela winding and cutting its way through the plain; to the south-east the main road passed through the river at Potgieter's Drift, leading towards Ladysmith. To the south-west at Trichardt's Drift was another road which crossed the river and then split; one branch went due north across the heights, and the other branch went west to join the road from the OVS to Ladysmith via Acton Homes Farm. It was obvious to Reverend John 'Danie' Kestell, chaplain to the Boers, that: '...if General Buller intended fording the Tugela from Springfield, at either Potgieter's or Trichardt's Drift to go to Ladysmith, he would have to bring his troops along one or both of these roads.'[53] The Boers found entrenching hard going. At the beginning, their tools were so scarce, that the commandos had to borrow from each other, and work alternately. The Boer trenches were far from the railway and difficult for wagons to reach. Christof 'Sandjie' Sandberg, Botha's secretary, wrote: 'As a result, Boer food was not

52   Barnard, *General Botha in the Spioenkop Campaign*.
53   Kestell, *Through Shot and Flame*, p.56.

plentiful – it was mainly hard rusks, which needed soaking in water; there was no coffee, and the burghers subsisted on meat from recently slaughtered animals, cooked on a grill or ramrod.'[54]

Final Preparations at Spearman's Camp

On 13 January, the naval gunners prepared their guns for action. Captain Percy Scott had had them removed from HMS *Terrible* at Simonstown and installed on carriages, drawn by oxen. Two 4.7-inch naval guns under Captain Jones and Lieutenant Hunt were on top of Spearman's Hill (approx. GPS -28.70768, 29.56191), a pretty spot covered with long grass and shaded by cassia, mimosa, and euphorbia trees. On a plateau lower down the hill were eight 12-pdr guns, 6 under Lieutenant Ogilvy and Lieutenant James, and 2 under Lieutenant Burne (approx. GPS -28.68901, 29.54179).[55] The naval guns fired shells filled with Lyddite, a newly invented high explosive made from picric acid and gun cotton. The 12-pdrs could fire shells up to 7,300 metres and the 4.7-inch guns up to 9,100 metres.[56] The air was bracing and the atmosphere so clear that the naval gunners often fell into the error of underestimating distances.[57][58]

Civil surgeon Frederick Treves was allocated to Major Kirkpatrick's No.4 Stationary Field Hospital, which was dismantled before dawn on 13 January and packed onto wagons. Their pace was very slow; the surgeons rode alongside, the sergeants and the orderlies walked, and the nurses rode in ambulance carts. With them were 100 Indians attached to the hospital for camp work. Treves called them:

> a dismal crowd as they stalked along, with their thin, bare legs and their picturesque tatters of clothing, with all their earthly possessions in bundles on their heads, and with apparently a vow of funereal silence in their hearts... The heat was intense, and the march monotonous: ever the same shadeless veldt, the same unending brown road, relieved by nothing but an occasional dead horse or mule; the same creeping, creaking, wallowing wagons, the everlasting cloud of dust, and over all the blazing sun that neither hat nor helmet could provide shelter from.[59]

No.4 Stationary Hospital was initially erected at Springfield but on 18 January it moved in 16 ox-wagons to what is today Spearman's Military Cemetery (GPS -28.72226, 29.54326). The hospital had 60 tents, 10 marquees and 12 surgeons, including Majors Kirkpatrick and Mallins, Lieutenant Simson, and Treves.[60]

By 15 January, the troops had all assembled. Warren's camp at Springfield was clearly visible to the Boers on Spioenkop, while Lyttelton's camp at Spearman's Hollow, though closer to the

54   Sandberg, *De Zesdaagsche Slag aan de Boven Tugela*, p.89.
55   Charles Holmes Wilson, *The Relief of Ladysmith. The Artillery in Natal* (London: William Clowes & Sons, 1901), p.55.
56   Hall, *Halt! Action Front!* pp.24—25.
57   Jeans, *Naval Brigades in the South African* War, p.255
58   Burleigh, *The Natal Campaign*, p.293.
59   Treves, *Tale of a Field Hospital*, pp.50–51.
60   Treves, *British Medical Journal* 1900, pp.219, 470.

Tugela, was out of sight. Sixteen days' supply for the whole army, comprising 600,000 rations, had been accumulated. The Army was ready for the second attempt to relieve Ladysmith.[61,62]

The Strength of Brakfontein

The longer General Buller spent on Spearman's Hill studying Potgieter's Drift and Brakfontein, the less confident he became of a breakthrough. Everything ahead of him, from Doornkop in the east to the southern slopes of Twin Peaks, was well fortified. Trench after trench was being built, and extensive deep defences were completed and concealed. Straddling the Ladysmith road was an immense trench, extending from a donga on the one side to a donga on the other, about 200 metres in length.[63] Buller heliographed Ladysmith: 'I find the enemy's position covering Potgieter's Drift so strong that I shall have to turn it, and I expect it will be four or five days from now before I shall be able to advance towards Ladysmith.' White replied bravely 'I can wait. Wish you best of luck.'[64] He concealed the extent to which typhoid was stalking his garrison. By 16 January, 2,400 of White's men were in hospital, and many others were weak, including White himself who had recurrent fever.[65]

Buller looked at other options besides Potgieter's Drift, and conferred with Warren. His question to Warren was: if Lyttelton's Brigade were to cross at Potgieter's Drift, and made feint attacks to pin down as many Boers as possible, could Warren cross at Trichardt's Drift, 8km upstream, with a larger force? Warren reconnoitred Trichardt's Drift on the morning of 15 January and reported that it was indeed feasible. He suggested the crossing should be followed up by the capture of Spioenkop, but Buller preferred the idea of a turning movement west of Spioenkop around the hills, which were locally known as Tabanyama. In isiZulu 'iNtabamnyama' means 'black hill'. On the 'Blue Map', it is shown as 'Rangeworthy' and a few squiggles.[66]

Crossing at Potgieter's Drift

Lord Roberts summarised Buller's strategy as being to cross the Tugela at Trichardt's Drift, and then: 'by following the road past 'Fair View' and 'Acton Homes', to gain the open plain north of Spion Kop, the Boer position in front of Potgieter's Drift being too strong to be taken by direct attack.'[67] To distract the Boers, Lyttelton's force would need to cross earlier than Warren's, so at 2.30 p.m. on 16 January, they left Spearman's Camp, a storm soaking them as they marched towards the river. The men knew the Boers asked God's blessing before going into action, so the Bishop of Natal also said prayers with the men.[68] They reached Potgieter's Drift late in the

61   Blake Knox, *Buller's Campaign*, p.13.
62   Inniskillings, *The Royal Inniskilling Fusiliers*, p.413
63   Baynes, *My Diocese during the War*, p.161.
64   Commission into the War in South Africa, Vol. II, p.163.
65   Durand, *The life of Field-Marshal Sir George White*, p.172.
66   Amery, *The War in South Africa*, Vol. III, p.214.
67   H. M. Govt, *The Spion Kop Despatches* London: H.M.S.O., 1902, p.3.
68   Baynes, *My Diocese During the War*, p.181.

afternoon. The Tugela was about 80 metres wide, and as they waded across they held on to each other, making a snake-like line.

They made it across unopposed and advanced in open, or skirmishing, order over the boulder-strewn country, settling themselves onto some low kopjes.[69] The first officer across was Captain Frederick Talbot of the Rifle Brigade, who wondered: 'We crossed without opposition – can't think why – they could have made it very hot for us while crossing & also coming across the open here... Then we were told to occupy three rocky hills & bivouac for the night.'[70]

The reason why they were unopposed soon became apparent. The Boers were in their trenches on hills 4,000 metres away in a semi-circle around them, and the British were safe as long as they were out of Mauser range. Lyttelton's orders were for his force to stay there while Warren crossed upstream, then advance with him: '...meanwhile to 'make demonstrations' & keep the enemy busy to prevent them going against Warren. So we sally forth and draw their fire, keeping well out of range, and as soon as they have lined their trenches, go back to breakfast.'[71]

The Scottish Rifles struggled across the Tugela as night fell; Corporal Carr was swept away, but rescued by Corporal Cousins, who was later awarded the Humane Society's Bronze Medal. The ferry was then brought back into service. It could take 50 or more men at a time, and by the early hours of 17 January, Lyttelton's force was across. It comprised the 2nd Scottish Rifles, 3rd King's Royal Rifles, 1st Rifle Brigade, 2 squadrons of Bethune's Mounted Infantry and 61st Battery (howitzers).[72] The next day, the 64th Battery of field artillery joined them. Two squadrons of Bethune's Mounted Infantry (BMI) patrolled the lines of communication with Frere. The soldiers occupied the low hills, which are covered in red soil and boulders, with little vegetation. They were initially called the Red Koppies (*Rooikoppies*) or One Tree Hill, but soon they became known as the Maconochie Koppies. Cooking fires were not allowed, and the ground became littered with empty tins of stew and vegetables from the Maconochie Company of Aberdeen. British lines on the Upper Tugela can today still be identified by large quantities of tins and disposable tin openers. The diet would prove monotonous, as Treves recorded: 'Tinned provisions are, no doubt, excellent and nourishing, but oh, the weariness of them! And oh, the squalor of the single tin mug, which never loses the taste of what it last had in it!'[73]

17 January 1900

The sun rose at 4:30 a.m. on 17 January. Dense mist hung over the hills, and at 5:00 a.m., the naval guns began to shell the Boer trenches on Brakfontein.[74] The observation balloon under Captain Phillips was filled with hydrogen and trundled forward on its cart to report the fall of shot for the gunners. After 5 hours' bombardment, the signal came that Warren's force had

69   Creswicke, *South Africa and the Transvaal War*, Vol. III, p.305.
70   Frederick G. Talbot, Captain, Rifle Brigade, Letter of 28 January 1900, Liddell Hart archive, GB0099 KCLMA Lyttelton.
71   Talbot, Letter.
72   Dundonald, *My Army Life*, p.120. Baynes, *My Diocese During the War*, p.183.
73   Treves, *Tale of a Field Hospital*, p.51.
74   Christiaan J. Barnard, *Generaal Louis Botha op die Natalse Front 1899–1900* (Cape Town: Balkema, 1970), p.85.

Fig 12: Spioenkop from the Ladysmith side. Looking south from the Fairview-Rosalie road, this shows a group of visitors returning from Spioenkop. Note the lack of trees and thorn bushes. All the territory shown was in Boer hands in January 1900. The skyline shows: TPE = the eastern Twin Peak. At its base was General Schalk Burger and the Carolina and Lydenburg Commando laagers, and an OVS Krupp. TPW = western Twin Peak. S = saddle, where a Boer pom-pom was sited just below the skyline during the battle. AK = Aloe Knoll. SK Summit = the dome-shaped summit of Spioenkop. CH = Conical Hill, held by the Boksburg Commando during the battle. General Louis Botha's headquarters were just north of this. GH = Green Hill, held by Utrecht Commando during the battle. (Arnold van Dyk collection)

begun crossing at Trichardt's Drift, and the 4.7s swung their barrels round to shell Spioenkop and Twin Peaks, to keep the Boers' heads down.

The 5-inch howitzers of 61st Battery, which had crossed to the Maconochie Koppies at midnight, also opened fire. Howitzers were heavy guns, with a range of 4,400 metres. They fired at a high angle, their 50-pound percussion shells containing 4.5kg of Lyddite. Unlike the 15-pdr field guns, howitzers could fire at targets that were out of sight – called indirect fire. They could also fire magnesium star shells, to light up the battlefield at night. The howitzers concentrated on Brakfontein, while Lieutenant Charles Burne of HMS *Terrible* counted their shells: 'six at a time, all bursting within fifty yards of one another and right on the Boer works on the skyline, where our Naval 4.7's were also working away at a greater distance off.'[75] Still no reply came from the Boer riflemen or their artillery. The naval gunners kept up the bombardment all day, and that night, as on the following nights, they slept in their clothes by their guns.[76]

75   Burne *With the Naval Brigade in Natal,* p.30.
76   Baynes, *My Diocese During the War,* p.185.

Warren at Trichardt's Drift

Warren's orders were to break through the Boer lines, march until arriving at Dewdrop – that is, north of the Brakfontein heights – and attack the enemy in the rear. Buller would simultaneously mount a frontal assault on Brakfontein. The march from Frere had shown how vulnerable a slowly moving column would be, especially if not on a proper road. For his column of ox-wagons and artillery, Warren needed to capture one of two wagon roads, both of which were overlooked by high ground that was in Boer hands. The more direct road, 17km to the rendezvous with Buller, went from Trichardt's Drift, past Fairview Farm (today called Rangeworthy Farm), and past Rosalie Farm (today called Roseleigh Farm). The Fairview-Rosalie road is overlooked for much of its route by Spioenkop. The alternative was a low-lying track, not shown on the Blue Map, which ran west from Trichardt's Drift, across Venter's Spruit drift, and joined the road from the Orange Free State to Ladysmith. This was also called the Acton Homes road. This route would entail a 16km longer march, overlooked by Tabanyama for most of its route.

Warren commanded 529 officers, 14,853 NCOs and men, plus 7th, 19th, 28th, 63rd, 73rd and 78th Batteries of 15-pdr field guns. He had 14 .303-inch machine guns and 4,856 horses. Warren's force would be in effect a huge, slow, 'flying column', detached from its base and carrying only three and a half days' provisions. All tents, camp equipment and stores would be left behind at Springfield. Nonetheless, there were still 600 vehicles, including 322 ox-wagons, and moving by ox-wagon from Frere had been hard enough, even without facing the Boers. It would take 13 hours for Warren's column to crawl past a given point, provided they encountered no opposition.[77] But first, before one of the two roads could be chosen, they had to cross the Tugela. Warren paraded his force for a night march at Springfield at 5:45 p.m. on 16 January. Lieutenant Laurie Wedd, 2nd Queen's, wrote that, to deceive the Boers: 'The camp was left standing and men were left behind to simulate a brigade, blow bugle calls, light the tents at night and light cooking fires.'[78] At about 7:00 p.m., Warren's division moved out. Smoking was forbidden and no talking was allowed.[79] They reached the koppies above Trichardt's Drift about 1:00 a.m.; the artillery horses were tied to the limber and carriage wheels, and the men lay down to sleep. Private O'Mahony of the West Yorks saw Spioenkop looming up across the Tugela valley, and heard the Boers singing hymns in the dead of night: 'the words in Dutch and the tune floating weirdly across the valley, caused a momentary commotion in our bivouac, everyone imagining it was the preliminary to attack.'[80] The *Illustrated London News* correspondent had seen a commando at prayers like these:

> The chant rose and fell with a swinging solemnity. There was little of pleading or supplication in its tones; they were calling on the God of Battles; the God of the Old Testament... sometimes there was a strain of almost stern demand about it that gave it more the ring of a war-song than a prayer... these men were calling on an unseen Power whose actual existence was as real to their minds as that of their Mauser rifles

77 Coetzer, *The Road to Infamy*, p.128.
78 Laurie D. Wedd, Lieutenant 2nd Queen's Royal West Surrey Regiment, Letter, National Army Museum 1999-06-94.
79 Blake Knox, *Buller's Campaign*, pp.15–17.
80 O'Mahony, *Peep over the Barleycorn*, p.135.

Fig 13: Boer Prayer Meeting Just Before Spioenkop. Stereoscope view by B. W. Kilburn. The minister is thought to be Reverend John Daniel ('Danie') Kestell, (1854 - 1941) who was at Tabanyama from 22 January. He described the Spioenkop campaign in *Through Shot and Flame*.

stacked around the tent-pole…the hymns they were singing were old Dutch ones. "We keep this up every night in camp… just the same as at home."[81]

In the dark, the British infantry lay in lines. In Woodgate's Brigade, the South Lancashires lay in front, then the Lancashire Fusiliers, and behind them the York and Lancaster. They waited for dawn, wet and cold, without greatcoats or blankets.[82] Around 3:00 a.m., they were startled by an extraordinary wailing sound which increased in volume until it reached a crescendo. Lieutenant George Hyde Harrison of the Border Regiment described the alarm: 'It was most weird and produced a feeling of scared apprehension. Then followed a horde of excited men running into us from the front. Alarmed, everyone sprang to his feet wondering what on earth was coming next…' The officers dashed down the lines shouting, 'Fix Bayonets!' 'This had a very steadying effect upon the men and consequently very few of them joined in what had almost become a general stampede, with mules dashing about in all directions. Gradually the tumult subsided – an officer's charger had got frightened and galloped through the ammunition mules

81   Lynch, *Impressions of a War Correspondent*, pp.63–65.
82   Alec H. C. Kearsey, *War Record of the York & Lancaster Regiment 1900–1902* London: George Bell & Sons, 1903, p.12.

tethered in rear. These, in their turn, dashed through the ranks of sleeping men. Half an hour later, order having been restored, the bivouac relapsed into tranquillity and sleep.'[83] Once the sun was up, a pall of mist and cloud blanketed Spioenkop and Tabanyama, as often happens on summer mornings.[84] No Boers could be seen across the Tugela, so Lieutenant Bridges and three scouts of the Imperial Light Horse waded their horses across, while the pontoon wagons moved slowly down towards the river. Suddenly, four Boers at Wright's Farm, just across the Tugela (GPS approx. -28.68132, 29.47896), fired at the pontoon train, and a soldier of the Devons was killed at a range of almost 2,000 metres,[85] his name is not recorded on the casualty rolls. In response, 28th Battery unlimbered and fired its first shot of the campaign at Wright's Farm.[86] Private Neligan of the South Lancashires described his first experience of artillery: '…although they were our own guns firing, the bursting of the shells, as they threw up the sand and earth, was horribly alarming, and made one shudder at the very thought of being in close proximity to them when they exploded.'[87] The incident of Wright's Farm was, as Private O'Mahony recognised:

> a splendid illustration of what can be done by a few men using modern rifles and smokeless powder. Imagine four men defending a farm-house surrounded by a wood, and a company of infantry unsupported by artillery advancing against them over an open space of 1,700 yards… It's no wonder Buller moved cautiously after crossing the Tugela at Trichardt's Drift. The greatest soldier, the greatest critic, the greatest fool would behave similarly when coming into contact with a hidden foe using smokeless powder; each would move cautiously.[88]

Once the four Boers had galloped away from Wright's Farm, the infantry advanced in long lines down towards Trichardt's Drift. The white canvas hoods on the ambulance wagons were thought to be too conspicuous and were removed. Lieutenant Blake Knox had his first view of the Tugela:

> …winding erratically like a huge tortuous snake in its dying agonies through the valley below. Little dots in long extended lines were advancing on Trichardt s Farm near the riverside – these were the infantry; other dots in closer formation, moving more rapidly and appearing larger and darker, were flitting through the scrub – these were the Irregular Cavalry. A few scattered rifle-shots now fell on our ears, then a rattle of musketry.[89]

83 George Hyde Harrison, Border Regiment, unpublished memoir, Cumbria's Museum of Military Life: Ch. 5, pp.92–93.
84 Amery, *The War in South Africa*, Vol. III, p.219.
85 Blake Knox, *Buller's Campaign*, p.18.
86 Anon, *28th Battery Digest of Service 1900*, Royal Artillery Institution Archives.
87 T. Neligan, *From Preston To Ladysmith With The 1st Bn. South Lancashire Regt.*, Preston: 1900, p.22.
88 O'Mahony, *A Peep Over the Barleycorn*, p.187.
89 Blake Knox, *Buller's Campaign*, p.18.

Crossing at Trichardt's Drift

The Tugela at Trichardt's Drift was about 55 metres wide, confined by steep banks, and flowed swiftly following the rains. The Tugela River's name in isiZulu is Thukela, meaning 'startling', indicating its power. At 7:00 a.m., four companies of the 2nd West Yorkshires rowed across in the engineers' pontoons, and took up positions on the opposite bank, to protect Major Irvine's Bridging Battalion against Boer sniping. At 7:30 a.m., 63rd Battery of 15-pdrs opened fire over their heads from the south bank, shelling possible Boer hiding places on the slopes to the north.[90] By 11:00 a.m. the engineers had completed the bridge, with 12 pontoons tethered about 4 metres apart, bows pointing upstream. Across the pontoons they placed beams, and over the beams, planks, or chesses.[91]

Fig 14: Ammunition Column Crossing the Tugela. Looking south over the pontoon bridge. The Tugela is flowing from the right. Taken on 17 January 1900, the bridge has just been completed and the engineers' tools can be seen on the far bank. Ammunition wagons have halted on the bridge, while more wait on the south to cross. (Wellcome collection)

90   Anon, *63rd Battery Digest of Service 1900*, Royal Artillery Institution Archives.
91   O'Mahony, *A Peep over the Barleycorn*, p.136.

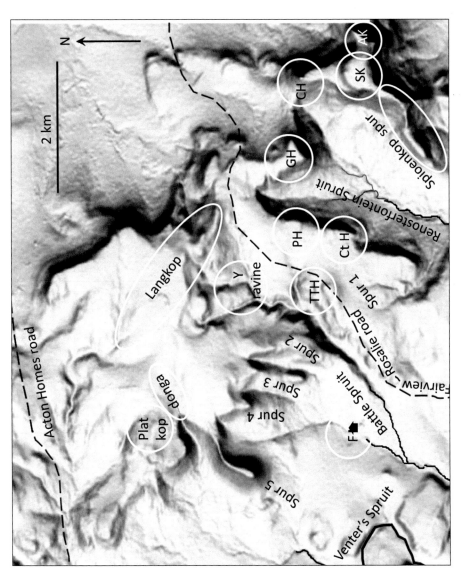

Map 2: Names of Features on Tabanyama and Spioenkop. AK = Aloe Knoll; CH = Conical Hill or 'the northern extension of Spion Kop'; CtH = Connaught Hill; F = Fairview Farm or Rangeworthy Farm or Coventry's Farm; GH = Green Hill or Groenkop; Langkop = not named by the British; PH = Picquet Hill or 'a small koppie northeast of Three Tree Hill' or South Lancashire Hill; Platkop = 'the hill north of Bastion Hill'; Spur 5 = Bastion Hill or Conical Hill or Sugarloaf Hill or Childe's Hill; Spur 3–4 = Sugarloaf Hill; Spur 4 = Hart's Hill or 'the amphitheatre'; Spur 2 or '20th Hill'; TTH = Three Tree Hill or Gun Hill; Y ravine = origin of Battle Spruit or 'the long ravine'.

Woodgate's 11th, or Lancashire, Brigade crossed first, followed at 1:30 p.m. by Hart's 5th, or Irish, Brigade. Those who had helped build the bridge fell in with their battalions as they marched past.[92] By late afternoon, the koppies north of the drift were occupied by Woodgate's and Hart's Brigades, Woodgate's men being higher up. The brigades was split, half on the ridge where the current Three Tree Hill lodge stands (approx. GPS -28.66179, 29.48708), and half on a koppie across the Renosterfontein Spruit (approx. GPS -28.66930, 29.50030). Private Phipps of the 1st Borders was in Hart's Brigade. Though his battalion was not Irish, it replaced the Royal Irish Rifles, who had been sent to join Methuen. Phipps found the terrain: '…the most hilly country it has been my fortune to be in…' adding that he felt '…thoroughly tired out, also very hungry, having had only two hard biscuits the whole of the day.'[93] The Boers were nowhere

Fig 15: Building the Trestle Bridge at Trichardt's Drift. Taken on 17 January 1900, the 17th Royal Engineers Company have completed a trestle bridge from the south bank to the island, the final pontoon is being brought into position, while the gradient above the bridge is improved. Trek oxen graze on the south bank. The river is flowing from the right, the pontoon bridge is out of sight to the left.

92   Amery, *The War in South Africa*, Vol. III, p.221. Harrison, 'Unpublished Memoir,' p.94. Anon., *Connaught Rangers Regimental Records*, p.16
93   Phipps, *Diary, 1st Border Regiment*.

to be seen. In the mist, they had withdrawn northwards, to Three Tree Hill, Picquet Hill, and the saddle (*wapadnek*) where the wagon road passes between Langkop and Green Hill.

A few harmless long range shots were exchanged. It was found that oxen crossing the pontoon bridge were alarmed by the swaying of the bridge and the booming of their hooves on the planks, so the engineers began a second bridge, about 600 metres upstream, where a sandbank formed an island in mid-stream. This bridge consisted of three trestles between the south bank and the island, and five pontoons between the island and the north bank. The pontoon bridge was mainly used for men, mules and carts, and the trestle bridge for cattle and ox-wagons.[94]

The Mounted Brigade Crosses

At noon, while the trestle bridge was still being built, the Mounted Brigade commanded by Colonel Douglas Cochrane, 12th Earl of Dundonald, waded across on horseback 350 metres downstream at Wagon Drift. Dundonald was lauded in the British press for his boldness, but was nicknamed 'Dundoodle' by his men. He was described by Stevenson, one of his troopers, as a 'much publicised and overpraised officer.'[95]

The crossing was led by Major Duncan McKenzie of the Natal Carbineers. McKenzie was a farmer from Nottingham Road, 100km away, and was at home in the area.[96] The crossing at Wagon Drift ran diagonally, upstream against a strong current, and the boulders in the river bed were loose. Private Guiler of the 13th Hussars was washed away and drowned, despite Captain Tremayne's efforts to save him.[97] Tremayne himself almost drowned, and was saved by Trooper Sclanders of the Natal Carbineers. Private Prince was also swept away, but was saved by Lieutenant Wise.[98][99] Sclanders was later awarded the Royal Humane Society's Silver Medal, and Wise and Tremayne were awarded Bronze Medals, as was Major Cooper (Royal Artillery), Captain Parke (Durham Light Infantry), and Trooper Roddy (Natal Mounted Police).[100] Private Guiler was probably buried on Wright's Farm (at GPS 28.66073, 29.47211); when this outlying grave was disinterred in the 1970s, the bodies of four British soldiers were found there.

By 2:00 p.m., ramps to the trestle bridge had been dug, the planks were covered in cut grass, and the artillery began crossing, led by 7th Battery.

They unlimbered near Wright's Farm, which had already been looted by both British and Boers. *Veldkornet* Kemp said: '…and between the two, enormous damage had been wrought. It must be pointed out, however, that the mischief done by our men was in no way authorized.'[101] Lieutenant Charlton of the Lancashire Fusiliers visited the farm to find the furniture smashed and excrement everywhere. His attitude to the Boers changed immediately. He no longer thought of them as a small nation in arms, eventually to be overcome by the might of the

---

94   Wedd, *Letter*.
95   R. E. Stevenson, A Carbineer Remembers in *Military History Journal, The South African Military History Society*, Vol.2, No.2, December 1971, unpaginated.
96   A. G. McKenzie, *Delayed Action* (Pietermaritzburg: Privately published, 1963), p.167.
97   Churchill, *London to Ladysmith via Pretoria*, p.299.
98   J. H. Tremayne, *XIII. Hussars South African War October 1899 – October 1902* (Aldershot: May & Co., 1905), p.11.
99   Blake Knox, *Buller's Campaign*, p.21.
100 Stevenson, *A Carbineer Remembers*, unpaginated.
101 Pienaar, *With Steyn and De Wet*, p.44.

Fig 16: Ammunition wagon crossing the pontoon bridge at Trichardt's Drift. An ammunition wagon, drawn by six horses, resembled two limbers joined together, and carried 104 rounds of 15-pdr shrapnel shells. Numerous ox-wagons are visible on Trichardt's Farm, waiting to cross at the trestle bridge, which is just visible to the right. (Courtesy Neville Constantine)

British Army, but as: '...outlaws who should suffer extermination.'[102] At 7:30 p.m. the first ox-wagons were coaxed onto the trestle bridge, and carts and wagons were brought across all night.[103]

The British Occupy the Nearest Koppies

Buller and Warren had sat together for some hours at the pontoon bridge, watching as Woodgate and Hart's men occupied the koppies opposite. Buller spoke with Woodgate: '... giving also directions to that officer as to his attack.'[104] But that evening, Buller decided that Woodgate's positions were too far east, and wrote a rebuke (Appendix III (a)): 'My dear Warren, ... [Woodgate's] advance from Smith's Farm to-day was all wrong. The one thing if we mean to succeed is to keep our left clear. He was at Smith's Farm [in reality, no such farm existed; this was Wright's Farm]; the Yorkshires had occupied a kopje to the east, and he had advanced northeast; this was wrong.'[105]

This was just the start of spatial confusion that was to recur repeatedly during this campaign. Things which had no name were invariably described relative to something else which was

102 Charlton, *Charlton*, p.102.
103 Maurice, *History of The War in South Africa*, Vol. II, p.356.
104 'Defender', *Sir Charles Warren and Spion Kop: A Vindication* (London: Smith, Elder & Co., 1902), p.72.
105 Maurice, *History of The War in South Africa,1899–1902* (London: Hurst and Blackett, 1907), Vol. II, p.631.

similarly un-named. No feature had a grid reference. Neither Wright's Farm nor the koppies where Woodgate was now bivouacked appeared on the Blue Map, and those koppies were not to the east, but are due north of the pontoon bridge. The habitual use of 'right' and 'left' in place of 'west' and 'east' made communication even more flimsy, as the units often faced in different directions on a zigzag front. To add to these difficulties, the iron-rich soil made compass readings unreliable. The only hill named on the Blue Map was Spioenkop, and it was labelled 2.5km east of where it actually is. But Buller said he was satisfied with his map: '…compiled from all the different farm surveys and made into a map of a scale of one inch to a mile. That was the map we used… Spion Kop, for instance, in this map is in the wrong place; but I think it was good enough to fight by.'[106] [107]

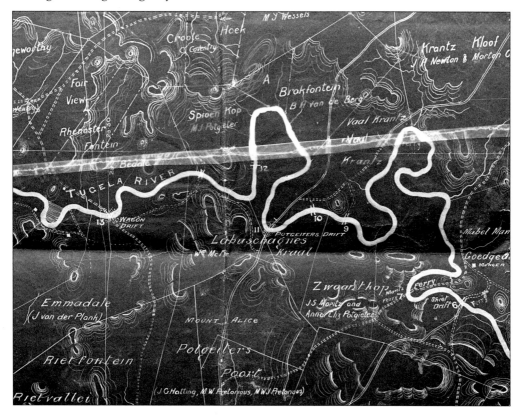

Fig 17: The Blue Map. This copy belonged to Lieutenant Malcolm Riall, the signals officer for the West Yorks. Buller had the map compiled from farm boundaries and copied by the blueprint process at Pietermaritzburg. It has no grid, and no buildings or contours are shown. Spioenkop is labelled in the wrong place but Buller called it 'good enough to fight by.' (Courtesy Nicholas Riall)

106 Commission into the War in South Africa, Vol. II, p.198.
107 Amery, *The War in South Africa 1899–1902*, Vol. III, p.230.

Boer reinforcements could be seen arriving and entrenching but the infantry was practically unmolested throughout the day.[108] Officers could see Boers walking about on Spioenkop, but the summit was out of artillery range and later, when it was within range, the Boers had disappeared. Lieutenant Harrison noted: 'We little thought then that it was so soon to be the scene of a disaster. Outposts were placed around our bivouac and we passed a quiet but very cold night.'[109]

The Inniskillings and Connaughts bivouacked on Wright's Farm, Woodgate's Brigade on the koppies flanking Renosterfontein Spruit, with Hart's Brigade just behind them, and outlying picquets about 1km in front of them. The men with keenest ears and best vision were picked for the hours preceding dawn, when a night attack was most likely. This was their second night sleeping in the open, and their first in Boer territory. Private O'Mahony wrote:

> A Boer being a silent, stalking hunter, the first intimation of his presence would probably be a blaze of rifle fire. We had, occasionally, double sentries on each post who remained standing motionless... What made the ordeal most irksome, no one was allowed to take his straps off during the hours of duty... If the night were wet and top coats worn, straps bound the rain-soaked torturing accoutrements to your groaning backbone and creaking ribs. You can imagine how comfortably we slept with immense pouches of ammunition buttressing our rawny buttocks on either side. Medical men say you should sleep on the right side, but in our case there were seventy-five reasons, or rounds of ammunition, why we couldn't, and when we reversed the medical authorities' dictum, and turned on our left there were seventy-five other, or rounds of ammunition, why we shouldn't...
>
> On settling down for the night each man detached the oil sheet from his belt and laid it on the ground for a mattress... it was summer, and the rainy season, and you often had to improvise another pillow; a helmet ... soon gets flattened out concertina fashion. However, a stone does not do so badly, you must get something to keep your head out of the aqueous matter... it rains nearly every night in the wet season, and as it knows how to rain in this country, we were fairly saturated...'[110]

Warren, Buller and the other generals all greatly overestimated enemy numbers. The British thought they faced 8,000,[111] 10,000,[112] 15,000[113] or even 38,000 Boers.[114] Buller had informed the War Office there were 46,000 Boers in Natal.[115] Warren repeatedly fretted about being cut

---

108 Inniskillings, *The Royal Inniskilling Fusiliers*, p.417.
109 Harrison, unpublished memoir, pp.95—96.
110 O'Mahony, *A Peep over the Barleycorn*, pp.78–80.
111 Blake Knox, *Buller's Campaign*, p.29.
112 Commission into the War in South Africa, Vol. II, p.649.
113 George F. Gibson, *The Story of the Imperial Light Horse in the South African War 1899–1902* (London: G.D & Co, 1937), p.148.
114 Neville Lyttelton, *Eighty Years Soldiering, Politics, Games* (Hodder and Stoughton., London, 1927), p.187.
115 Amery, *The War in South Africa 1899–1902*, Vol. III, p.215.

Fig 18: Frame from an early cine film taken by the Mutoscope Biograph Company, showing an ambulance wagon crossing Trichardt's Drift on 25 January 1900. (Courtesy Neville Constantine)

off and kept an entire brigade, Coke's 10th Brigade, at the Tugela: '...to protect the convoy to the south to prevent an incursion of Boers from Middle Drift...'[116]

The British were not mystified for long as to why the Boers had not opposed their crossing. Louis Botha's intention, as at Colenso, was to draw the British infantry into Mauser range, 2,000 metres, [117] and the British on the lower koppies, and the Boers entrenched on the high ground of Tabanyama and Brakfontein, were still separated by 3,000 metres or more.

The Boer Response to British Crossings of the Tugela

On 16 January, Louis Botha had stayed overnight at General Tobias Smuts' laager near Vaalkrans. During the night, Boer scouts brought news that large numbers of British troops were crossing at Potgieter's Drift. Tobias Smuts telegraphed the news to Colenso, adding that Botha was with him, but that he was not feeling well: 'We view the struggle with confidence,

116 'Defender', *Sir Charles Warren and Spion Kop: A Vindication*, p.73.
117 Barnard, *Generaal Louis Botha op die Natalse Front*, pp.48--49.

relying on our good cause and praying for help from Above. The struggle will be heavy but we will stand firm.'[118] The next morning, 17 January, Botha awoke still feeling ill. A heavy mist obscured the heights, but from lower ground, Botha and Smuts could clearly see Lyttelton's troops on the Maconochie Koppies. At 8:00 a.m. Botha rode over to Schalk Burger behind Twin Peaks, and at 12:15 p.m. the Boer generals learned that the British had also crossed at Trichardt's Drift. Botha went up to Green Hill, watched the British crossing, then rode back to Colenso to pack up his headquarters and summon reinforcements. By evening he was exhausted, lying down on his camp bed while giving instructions and dictating despatches.[119] There was still no clarity about his rank. President Kruger strongly encouraged Botha to command the Tugela Front, which meant the older Generals, Lucas Meyer and Schalk Burger, would become his subordinates. This made Botha uncomfortable. To comply with Kruger's emphatic wishes, he initially agreed to help on the Upper Tugela, but without the status of Commander-in-Chief. This loose arrangement caused a great deal of annoyance to Joubert, who, on the night of 17 January, telegraphed Botha at Colenso, appointing him to command the whole Tugela line. Joubert emphasised that he, too, did not want to offend Generals Meyer and Burger, but he made it clear that they were now Botha's subordinates. In his reply, Botha explained how difficult it was for him to accept the nomination:

> Confidential. Re: your telegram tonight in connection with the General Command here. I am glad that under these critical circumstances that we are currently going through, that telegram did not come into the hands of General Meyer and General Burger, because for me it is not a matter of job title or honour, but duty, as I would prefer to remain without this promotion. Moreover, this telegram puts me in a difficult position, because as you yourself know, I was General Meyer's deputy, and now that he is here himself, he cannot be below me. So, too, with General Burger; and I would much rather be under them before I see any disadvantage to the cause for which we are now in the field. Also, as I said before, I am done in and exhausted by all the worries and tension. The great difficulty now lies at the upper Tugela, four and a half hours on horseback from here, a distance so great that it is impossible for me to manage everywhere at once. I feel so exhausted tonight that I am obliged to do my job lying down. I am glad that Assistant-General Burger is over there and am convinced that he will do everything that can be done in the interest of our great cause ... I know, General, that you have important responsibilities, but let us try to support each other in these times of heavy trials...[120]

In the end, it made little difference. Botha assumed overall command, and the burghers were delighted. *Commandant* Ludwig 'Lodi' Krause of the Zoutpansberg Commando summed up their feelings:

> The influence that Louis Botha had among the burghers at that time was simply marvellous. The mere mention of the fact that Louis Botha was in command and on

118 Barnard, *Generaal Louis Botha op die Natalse Front*, p.47.
119 Barnard, *General Botha in the Spioenkop Campaign*.
120 Barnard, *Generaal Louis Botha op die Natalse Front*, p.86.

the spot was sufficient to inspire the Burgers with courage and confidence, no matter how despondent they may have been before. When we learned that Louis Botha had gone to take over the command at Spioenkop, it was a relief – one felt as if a weight of doubt and care and anxiety had been taken from the mind.[121]

Botha was now senior to Generals Tobias Smuts, Schalk Burger and Andries Cronjé. He assured Pretoria that he would try, with all his might and with God's help, to defeat the enemy. On 17 January, Botha instructed all magistrates in the Transvaal and Orange Free State to send burghers in their districts immediately to their commandos, whether they were at home on leave or for other reasons such as planting crops.[122] Botha and his officers still expected the main attack to fall opposite Potgieter's Drift, and possibly also at Munger's Drift and Skiet Drift. The Boers dug defensive positions opposite these drifts, from Doringkop in the east to Spioenkop in the west. In the Doringkop-Vaalkrans sector were the Johannesburg, Ermelo, Standerton, Krugersdorp and Vryheid Commandos, commanded by General Tobias Smuts and supported by a 75mm Krupp and a pom-pom. Brakfontein was expected to be the focal point of the attack,[123] and in this sector, straddling the road from Potgieter's Drift to Ladysmith, were Free Staters from Vrede, Heilbron, Senekal and Winburg under General Andries Cronjé, with a 75mm Creusot and a pom-pom. Further west, In the Twin Peaks – Spioenkop sector, were Transvaalers from Carolina, Lydenburg, Pretoria, Heidelberg, Wakkerstroom and Piet Retief, under General Schalk Burger. They had two 75mm Krupps, one of which was an old OVS Krupp which fired black powder, and on 17 January, *Commandant* Grobler of the Vryheid Commando reinforced them, bringing a pom-pom.[124] Botha's western flank was dangerously exposed. Tabanyama was manned by only 500 men: Free Staters under *Commandant* Pistorius and Pretoria men under *Veldkornet* 'Red' Daniel Opperman.[125] To remedy this, Botha brought up Transvaalers from Middelburg, Boksburg, Heidelberg, Utrecht and Pretoria, and the German Corps. On the night of 17 January, the first 400 of these reinforcements arrived at Tabanyama, bringing a pom-pom, ammunition, food and shovels. They dug trenches all night, and those not working stayed alert in the dark. Botha was acutely aware of his precarious situation, and, like the British, feared a night attack. By 18 January there were more than 3,000 burghers on the Upper Tugela, of whom 1,800 faced Trichardt's Drift.[126] [127] Among the arrivals were 250 Krugersdorpers under *Commandant* Sarel Oosthuizen and *Veldkornet* Jan Kemp and about 60 Boksburg and Germiston burghers under *Veldkornet* Sarel Alberts.[128]

On 18 January, Botha re-located his headquarters from Colenso to Charles Coventry's abandoned farm, Groote Hoek, just north of Spioenkop. On the same day, the British commandeered John and Harry Coventry's farms, Fairview and Rangeworthy, 5km away. All

121 Ludwig Krause, *The War Memoirs of Commandant Ludwig Krause, War Memoirs, 1899–1900* (Cape Town: Van Riebeeck Society, 1995), p.56.
122 Francois Jacobus Grobler, 'Die Carolina-kommando in die Tweede Vryheidstoorlog, 1899–1902', unpublished thesis, North-West University Repository, South Africa, 1960, pp.39–40.
123 Barnard, *Generaal Louis Botha op die Natalse Front*, p.86.
124 Grobler, 'Die Carolina-kommando in die Tweede Vryheidstoorlog', p.45.
125 Barnard, *Generaal Louis Botha op die Natalse Front*, p.84.
126 Sandberg, *De Zesdaagsche Slag aan de Boven Tugela*, p.86.
127 Barnard, *Generaal Louis Botha op die Natalse Front*, pp.84—90.
128 Kemp, *Vir Vryheid en vir Reg*, p.274.

Fig 19: General Louis Botha (1862–1919). Photographed around the time he was promoted to commander-in-chief on the Tugela, Botha was exhausted but his request for leave was turned down. On the right is Christof 'Sandjie' Sandberg, Botha's military secretary; his aide on the left is unidentified.

three Coventry brothers were trapped in Ladysmith, where their cattle herds were being steadily eaten. Botha slept among his burghers, as was his custom.

Accompanied by his aide and his secretary, 'Sandjie' Sandberg, Botha's headquarters was a green bell-tent, with an orange-painted tent pole; inside was an upturned white wooden box, which served as a desk, and a red-painted chest marked 'Reinbende and Son', on which stood his field telephone. Over the ground was spread a thick layer of cut grass, and along the walls of the tent were rolled up blankets with pillows, where visiting officers would sit. The archives were on the floor in a box marked 'Old Scotch Whisky', and opposite the tent flap was Botha's folding chair and camp bed.[129] [130]

By 19 January, the Boers on Tabanyama had artillery in the form of two 75mm Creusots on the western flank, one 75mm Krupp, and two pom-poms.[131] Though scattered, the burghers and their artillery could move, unseen, to wherever they were threatened. That day, 19 January, Botha cancelled all leave on the Tugela, in preparation for the coming battle.

129 Pienaar, *With Steyn and De Wet*, p.36.
130 Sandberg, *Instantanés uit den Zuid-Afrikaanschen Oorlog*, p.272
131 Hiley and Hassell, *The Mobile Boer*, pp.114–115.

5

18 January, The Ambush at Acton Homes

'Sir C. Warren's nine days' operations, after he crossed the Tugela on
January 17th, 1900, have in a measure been merged under the name 'Spion Kop.'
General John Talbot Coke [1]

Dundonald Rides West

When the sun rose on 18 January, no night attack had taken place. Hart's and Woodgate's brigades awoke on the koppies overlooking Trichardt's Drift; the wagons were still crossing the trestle bridge, and Private Phipps of the Borders wrote that he was: '…sniped at by the enemy but so far no damage has been done. Our artillery has been banging away on the left and small arms fire on the right.'[2] Dundonald's Mounted Brigade had bivouacked 4km to the west, at Venter's Spruit.

Dundonald's orders were straightforward, according to Churchill, who was among them: 'The mounted brigade will guard the left flank of the infantry.'[3] Warren sent two messages to Dundonald, emphasising this role (see Appendix III (b) and (c)). Dundonald, however, was inclined to independent action. He was annoyed that his Mounted Brigade had been depleted by mundane tasks such as squadrons patrolling the flanks and guarding the line of march to Frere, and by the loss of Bethune's Mounted Infantry who stayed at Potgieter's Drift.[4] This left him 1,542 men: 1st Royal Dragoons, 412; 13th Hussars, 260; Composite Regiment, 270; South African Light Horse, 300, and Thorneycroft's Mounted Infantry, 300.[5] They had four Colt .303 calibre machine guns, commanded by Captain Hill, M.P. and mounted on Dundonald's patented 'galloping carriages'. At daybreak, Dundonald ordered the Mounted Brigade to saddle up and probe westward. They were led by the Composite Regiment, comprising A Squadron, Imperial Light Horse and No.5 Squadron, Natal Carbineers – these were the only Imperial

---

1   John Talbot Coke, *Report of His Majesty's Commissioners Appointed to Inquire into the Military Preparations and Other Matters Connected with The War in South Africa*, the Elgin Commission (London: H.M.S.O 1903). Vol. 2, p.442.
2   Phipps, *Diary, 1st Border Regiment*.
3   Churchill, *London to Ladysmith via Pretoria*, p.131
4   Blake Knox, *Buller's Campaign*, p.22
5   Dundonald, *My Army Life*, p.122

Fig 20: Dundonald's Mounted Brigade at the Tugela. Mounted men are moving from right to left, while riderless horses graze on the slope above. The 1st Royal Dragoons, with lances, are coming down to the Tugela. The view is looking north across the river, probably at Wagon Drift where the Mounted Brigade waded their horses across on 17 January 1900. (Courtesy Neville Constantine)

Light Horse (ILH) and Carbineers not besieged in Ladysmith. With them were a mounted infantry company of the 2nd Kings Royal Rifles, a section of mounted Dublin Fusiliers, a squadron of Natal Police, four squadrons of the South African Light Horse, Thorneycroft's Mounted Infantry, two squadrons of the 13th Hussars and the 1st Royal Dragoons. By 2:00 p.m. Churchill said that they: '…formed a line of observation along the lower kopjes by the river…' stretching 8km westwards, and completely out of sight of Warren.[6] They found the countryside quiet, almost deserted. The Natal Carbineers, somewhat familiar with the area, scouted ahead. Dundonald sent a warning back to Warren not to take troops close to Tabanyama, where they would be exposed to Boer fire (Appendix III (d)).

'Danie' Kestell said that when the Boers saw the horsemen going west: 'It was clear that they must be stopped, and some of our men were immediately sent to oppose them.'[7] Botha despatched a large commando, intending to block the westward British movement. They set

6   Churchill, *London to Ladysmith via Pretoria*, p.132.
7   Kestell, *Through Shot and Flame*, p.57.

Fig 21: Lieutenant Friedrich von Wichmann of the Transvaal *Staatsartillerie*. A German, von Wichmann commanded two 75mm Creusot quick-firing field guns from positions near the Acton Homes road. They deterred Dundonald from advancing, and shelled the British on Tabanyama at long range with astonishing accuracy, one victim being Major Charles Childe on Bastion Hill. On 24 January 1900, von Wichmann brought his guns within range of Spioenkop and shelled the summit. In this photograph, taken before Elandslaagte, he wears the dress tunic of the *Staatsartillerie*. On the right is Colonel Adolf Schiel who commanded the German Corps. (Courtesy Neville Constantine)

Ober-Lent. von Wichmann

off from behind Tabanyama, riding along the Acton Homes road, which ran from Ladysmith towards the OVS. (Today, the R616 road follows a similar route.) The Boer commando first came into sight when they emerged through a narrow nek and turned south-west (GPS approx. -28.60630, 29.45417). This nek, and the plain south-west of it, was defended by a Transvaal *Staatsartillerie* 75mm Creusot under Lieutenant Friedrich von Wichmann.

Around 3:00 p.m. McKenzie was observing from a low hill when the Boers rounded the shoulder of Tabanyama and came into view. He immediately saw an opportunity, and said to his British counterpart, Major Graham of the 5th Lancers: 'I can trap these men if you will let me' and Graham replied: 'Do what you like, McKenzie'. McKenzie: ' I gave the order to mount, and my men were in the saddle in a moment. We set off at full gallop'. He had with him 40 Carbineers, and soon 40 men of the Imperial Light Horse joined him, under Lieutenant Barnes. McKenzie: 'I do not know who ordered the ILH to follow me, but they did so.'[8] McKenzie galloped west along a low-lying track. His objectives were two koppies on Peach Tree Farm.

The farm and the koppies are not on the Blue Map, but Acton Homes Farm and trading store 4km north of it was on the map, and the engagement became erroneously named after Acton Homes. The koppies on Peach Tree Farm make up a prominent grassy ridge which straddles the road from the OVS to Ladysmith via Acton Homes. Between the koppies is a shallow saddle through which the road passes, and they overlook a gently rising slope, devoid of cover except for

8   McKenzie, *Delayed Action*, p.167.

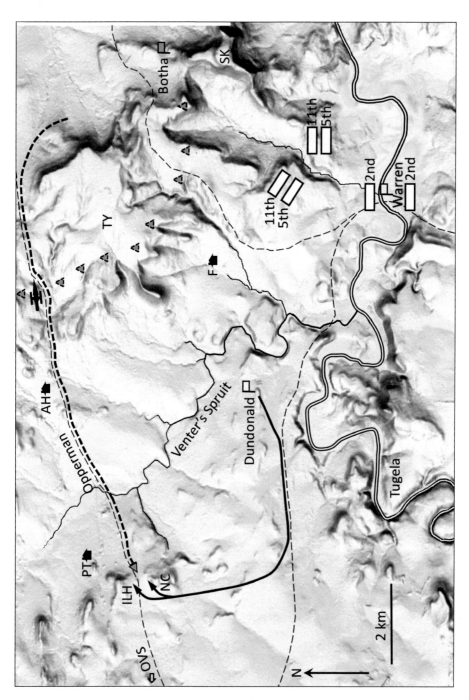

Map 3: Ambush at Acton Homes, afternoon of 18 January 1900. Warren's wagons are still crossing at Trichardt's Drift, protected by the 2nd Brigade. The 5th and 11th Brigades guard the koppies to the north. Dundonald has bivouacked to the west, and Tabanyama (TY) is held by Boer picquets (grey triangles). Mackenzie gallops west with 80 men of Natal Carbineers (NC) and Imperial Light Horse (ILH) to occupy two koppies on the Acton Homes road to the OVS, and ambushes Opperman and Mentz's commando. F = Fairview Farm; PT = Peach Tree Farm; AH = Acton Homes Farm; TY = Tabanyama; SK = Spioenkop; field gun = von Wichmann. Dashed lines indicate wagon roads.

a small knoll 800 metres away, just south-east of the road. About 1km south-east of the road, a deep donga runs parallel to the road. Although the koppies are of no great height, if McKenzie could occupy them unseen, he could dominate the road for about 2km. Because McKenzie kept out of sight of the Boers, he was unable to observe their movements, and he said he: '…hoped we had galloped fast enough to reach the koppies before the Boers.' Among his Carbineers was Trooper Park Gray, a farmer from Cathkin who knew this area intimately.[9] McKenzie ordered Gray to:

> …gallop on as fast as he possibly could to the nek between the two koppies… dismount and peep over and see where the enemy were; and if you found they were close and would get to the position first he was to get back and save himself and I would retire. Otherwise he was to remain there and wave me on. In the meantime, I pulled up and hurriedly told the ILH they would occupy the ground on the left koppie, and not to fire a shot until I gave the order. Trooper Gray did his part splendidly, and I was delighted to see him creep back and remain there waving. We galloped up to him, dismounted, to occupy the position.[10]

The Carbineers were at GPS: -28.63118, 29.39087 and ILH at -28.62688, 29.39074. The rest of the troops were then signalled to come up: 'This they did at the gallop, and, making skilful use of cover, they reached the ridge unobserved.'[11]

The Ambush

As the men took up positions among the rocks, McKenzie sent Lieutenant Barnes back to ask Lord Dundonald for support.[12] About 3:30 p.m., two South African forces were about to clash. Concealed on the crest of the koppie north-west of the road were 40 men, mainly Johannesburgers, of the Imperial Light Horse. Lying in a similar position just south-east of the road were 40 Natal Carbineers from Estcourt and Weenen. Trotting towards them, unaware of the danger, were Pretoria burghers of the Witwatersrand and Elands River *wyke* under *Veldkornet* 'Red' Daniel Opperman, and Free Staters under *Veldkornet* Nicolaas 'Mordechai' Mentz of Heilbron. Estimates of the Boer numbers vary: Barnard writes there were 160,[13] Churchill, who arrived late, estimated 200[14] and Blake Knox reports 300.[15] McKenzie's eyewitness estimate of 320 is probably the most accurate.[16] McKenzie described the scene:

> I only saw one scout a short way in front of them and towards their left flank… They were riding Boer fashion in a very irregular way. About 40 or 50 men were clumped

9   Stevenson, *A Carbineer Remembers*, unpaginated.
10   McKenzie, *Delayed Action* , p.168.
11   Stevenson, *A Carbineer Remembers*, unpaginated.
12   Churchill, *London to Ladysmith via Pretoria*, p.133.
13   Barnard, *Generaal Louis Botha op die Natalse Front*, p.87.
14   Churchill, *London to Ladysmith via Pretoria*, p.132.
15   Blake Knox, *Buller's Campaign*, p.22.
16   McKenzie, *Delayed Action*. p.168.

together in front and they came on in fours and fives, and then another big batch apparently talking and riding in a way as best suited themselves... Seeing this, I made up my mind to let them ride practically onto me... There was a bank which they had to go up, and so they were very close. I did not want to fire until a large number of them were on top of it. I was almost ready to blow my whistle, when one of the ILH could evidently stand it no longer, and fired, and so gave the show away, so I had no alternative but to blow my whistle and everybody fired and continued to do so as quickly as they could.[17]

The Action Begins

The leading Boer scout was about 70 metres away when the ILH opened fire. The ILH and Carbineers were armed with .303 Martini-Enfields, whose smokeless cordite ammunition, sights, and accuracy is identical to the magazine Lee-Enfield. The Martini-Enfield has a slightly slower rate of reloading (up to 10 rounds a minute) but this is no disadvantage for deliberate shooting. McKenzie wrote: 'The enemy was taken completely by surprise and altogether it was a horrible affair. We emptied many saddles, and many of them jumped off while others galloped

Fig 22: Knoll where *Veldkornet* Mentz made a stand. Modern photograph taken from the old Ladysmith-OVS road, facing east. The skyline is made up of Tabanyama (TY), Bastion Hill (BH) 6km away and Spioenkop (SK) 12km away. In the foreground is the knoll where *Veldkornet* Nicolaas Mentz was killed.

17   McKenzie, *Delayed Action*, p.168.

away.'[18] Most of the Boers managed to gallop out of rifle range, down the road they had just come along. Two members of Edwards' *Verkenner Korps*, Slegtkamp and de Roos, galloped to Peach Tree Farm, 900 metres away, and provided covering fire for their comrades.[19] A group of 35 Boers dashed for cover among the boulders of the knoll alongside the road, 800 metres away (GPS -28.62703, 29.40079).

Some were wounded and some had lost their horses, but all were determined to make a stand – among them, *Veldkornet* Mentz. Strangely, many of the riderless Boer horses galloped between the koppies and stood among the British horses behind the ridge.[20] Once concealed behind the rocks it became difficult to identify an individual target at 800 metres. During the prolonged exchange of rifle fire, the unlucky Captain Arthur Shore of the ILH was severely wounded – he'd only just recovered from being shot through the chest at Elandslaagte. Another ILH trooper was lightly wounded. All the men found themselves pinned down. At one point, someone in the Boer ranks raised a white flag for a moment but it was immediately taken down by order of *Veldkornet* Mentz, and the fight continued with even greater fierceness.[21]

Reinforcements

Around 4:00 p.m., Lieutenant Barnes arrived at the Mounted Brigade HQ, requesting reinforcements. Dundonald replied: 'Certainly, every man we can spare.'[22] Off galloped the Mounted Infantry Company of the Kings Royal Rifles, a squadron of the South African Light Horse (including Lieutenant Winston Churchill), followed later by some of Thorneycroft's MI, and later still by Dundonald himself. By now the Boers were tenaciously holding the rocks of the knoll and were quite invisible. The British riflemen curved round them in a half-moon, firing continually at the rocks. A group of SALH worked along the large donga, parallel to the road, south-east of the knoll. This put them almost behind the enemy, and Churchill said: '… every Boer who dared make a dash for liberty ran a terrible gauntlet. Still the surrender did not come. The white flag flickered for a moment above the rocks, but neither side stopped firing. Evidently a difference of opinion among the enemy.'[23]

The shadows were lengthening, and the Mounted Infantry Company of the Rifles in the donga decided to try a bayonet charge. They made the suggestion because they were the only men with bayonets, which are not usually needed by mounted men. A section of the Rifles then crawled forward towards the knoll, described by Churchill sheltering in the donga:

> …there broke out a savage fire from the kopje, and the line of riflemen retreated, wriggling backwards slowly on their bellies, but leaving two brown forms who lay still and hunched in the abandoned position. Then suddenly the retiring Riflemen sprang up and ran for shelter in our donga… "We got to within fifty yards of the Dutchmen,"

18   McKenzie, *Delayed Action*, p.169.
19   Mostert, *Slegtkamp van Spioenkop*, p.33.
20   McKenzie, *Delayed Action*. p.169.
21   Churchill, *London to Ladysmith via Pretoria*, p.135.
22   Churchill, *London to Ladysmith via Pretoria*, p.133.
23   Churchill, *London to Ladysmith via Pretoria*, p.133.

they said; "but it was too hot to go further. They've shot two fellows through the head."[24]

The dead men were Privates Hampshire and Long. The Boers were firing at the donga so determinedly that when a man in the donga raised his helmet on the end of his rifle: '...the bullets whistled round it.'[25]

Around 5:00 p.m. Dundonald and his staff arrived. The intensity of the fire increased, with the British firing from the koppies and the donga. The Boers were under fire from several directions, and again the white flag was raised. A British officer complained to Dundonald: '... the white flag has been up off and on for the last half-hour, but they don't stop firing, and they've just killed two of my men.'[26] Trooper Gray considered that abuse of the white flag was due to genuine misunderstanding and not to treachery.[27]

Dundonald ordered his men to cease fire, and Churchill saw:

> ...from among the rocks [on the knoll] three dark figures stood up holding up their hands, and at this tangible evidence of surrender [the Mounted Infantry] got on [their] horses and galloped towards them waving pocket handkerchiefs and signaling flags to show them that their surrender was accepted.[28]

As they moved forward, they saw the bodies of 10 killed and 8 wounded burghers on the battlefield. Twenty-four burghers surrendered, including the wounded Josef 'Jopie' Fourie. They had run out of ammunition.[29] Among the dead was *Veldkornet* Mentz, aged 53, whose body Churchill described:

> ...with firm aquiline features and a short beard. The stony face was grimly calm, but it bore the stamp of unalterable resolve... Mentz had refused all suggestions of surrender, and when his left leg was smashed by a bullet he had continued to load and fire until he bled to death; and they found him, pale and bloodless, holding his wife's letter in his hand. Next to him was a boy of about 17 years who was shot through the heart.[30]

For many of the British, this was their first opportunity to see their enemy up close, as Lynch described:

> It was curious to notice how the knees and elbows of their clothes showed signs of wear from their favourite shooting attitude, and there were many with buttons missing from their waistcoats that had been scraped off by the stones on the kopjes, or with buttons of different patterns that had evidently been sewn on by the wearers in place of those

---

24   Churchill, *London to Ladysmith via Pretoria*, pp.133–134.
25   Churchill, *London to Ladysmith via Pretoria*, p.134.
26   Churchill, *London to Ladysmith via Pretoria*, p.134.
27   Stevenson, *A Carbineer Remembers*, unpaginated.
28   Churchill, *London to Ladysmith via Pretoria*, p.134.
29   Kemp, *Vir Vryheid en vir Reg*, p.274.
30   Churchill, *London to Ladysmith via Pretoria*, p.134

worn off... all the Boers appear to give up shaving when on the warpath, which adds to the wild picturesqueness of their appearance.[31]

Churchill said the British treated the wounded compassionately:

> The soldiers crowded round [the wounded Boers], covering them up with blankets or mackintoshes, propping their heads with saddles for pillows, and giving them water and biscuits from their bottles and haversacks. Anger had turned to pity in an instant. The desire to kill was gone. The desire to comfort replaced it.[32]

Trooper Gray hated the whole experience; he'd found it hard to shoot to kill.[33] Gray and McKenzie both recognised a wounded man named Moodie, who was an English-speaking Transvaaler who had married a Boer girl. He explained: '...you can't blame me for fighting for my country.'[34] His thigh had been shattered and he was in great pain, and it was he that had waved one of the white flags. Eventually he made a good recovery.

Fig 23: Exhumation of *Veldkornet* Mentz. In 1978, outlying isolated Boer graves were exhumed, and the remains reinterred at the Burgher Monument at Platrand. Mentz was killed in the Acton Homes ambush on 18 January 1900, and originally buried close to the OVS field hospital at Smith's Crossing near Ladysmith. His gravestone indicates he was killed in the battle of Spioenkop, by which was meant all the fighting during the Spioenkop campaign. To deter burrowing animals, Boer dead were customarily buried under corrugated roofing iron, which is being removed in this photograph. (Courtesy Neville Constantine)

31 Lynch, *Impressions of a War Correspondent*, p.64.
32 Churchill, *London to Ladysmith via Pretoria*, p.135.
33 Stevenson, *A Carbineer Remembers*, unpaginated.
34 McKenzie, *Delayed Action*. p.169.

Dundonald sent Lieutenant Silbourne with a white flag to the Boer lines, informing them that they might come in and take their dead. Silbourne observed Boer trenches on both sides of the Acton Homes road. The Boers tied their dead across horses and carried them away for burial.[35] *Veldkornet* Mentz was buried near the OVS hospital at Smith's Crossing near Ladysmith (GPS -28.50961, 29.73061) alongside burgher Francois Lombard of the Boksburg Commando. The remains were reinterred at Platrand in 1978.

The Boer prisoners and wounded reached General Warren's camp about 2:00 a.m. on 19 January, where British doctors attended to them and made them as comfortable as possible.[36]

Fig 24: Boer Prisoners Captured at Acton Homes. 24 Boers were taken prisoner in the Acton Homes ambush. This photograph, taken about noon on 19 January, shows them being escorted past the British camp at Spearman's Farm. (National Army Museum)

35   McKenzie, *Delayed Action.* p.169.
36   Blake Knox, *Buller's Campaign,* p.24.

Towards evening, Warren requested Dundonald to send back 500 men at once, to protect his accumulating park of wagons and oxen, as there were no mounted patrols guarding the camp (Appendix III (b, c, d)). Dundonald was indignant at his men being used as 'cattle guards', but sent back the Royal Dragoons, while Thorneycroft's Mounted Infantry went to guard the line of advance from Venter's Spruit.[37][38]

Nightfall came at 7:00 p.m.; a waning moon rose an hour later. Dundonald remained on the koppies. He exaggerated to Warren the safety of his position and the significance of his success, as the messages between Warren and Dundonald indicate (Appendix III (e) to (k)). In reality, Lieutenant Silbourne, when taking the flag of truce to the enemy lines, had reported the heights on either side of the main road to be very strongly defended.[39] Dundonald requested reinforcements and artillery. He could not advance across the plain without artillery, facing entrenched Boers and, by now, two Boer Creusot guns 6.5km away.[40] Warren was still engrossed at Trichardt's Drift in supervising the crossing of his force. The disappearance of the Mounted Brigade to the west alarmed him. His force could be cut off by a Boer attack and he needed the mounted men to screen the left flank of his infantry. The Upper Tugela valley was becoming a busy place, as described by *The Times* correspondent:

Fig 25: *Veldkornet* 'Red' Daniel Opperman. Daniel Jacobus Elardus ('Rooi Danie') Opperman (1861–1928) led his men carelessly into an ambush at Acton Homes, but fought with extraordinary courage at Spioenkop, where he commanded the Pretoria Commando. (Transvaal Archives)

37   Maurice, *History of The War in South Africa, Vol. II*, p.362.
38   Blake Knox, *Buller's Campaign*, p.23.
39   Commission into the War in South Africa, Vol. II, p.648.
40   Blake Knox, *Buller's Campaign*, p.28.

...villages of men, camps of men, bivouacs of men, who are feeding, mending, repairing, and burying the men at the "front." It is these latter that make the mob of gypsies, which is apparently without head or order or organization. They stretched across the great basin of the Tugela, like the children of Israel, their camp-fires rising to the sky at night like the reflection of great search-lights; by day they swarmed across the plain, like hundreds of moving circus-vans in every direction, with as little obvious intention as herds of buffalo. But each had his appointed work, and each was utterly indifferent to the battle going forward a mile away. Hundreds of teams, of sixteen oxen each, crawled like great black water-snakes across the drifts.[41]

Fig 26: The ambush at Acton Homes. The scene shows the moment before the ILH opened fire. The Natal Carbineers are accurately depicted, wearing Royston webbing and carrying Martini-Enfield Mk I rifles. The steep terrain is misleading. (*With the Flag to Pretoria*)

41   Davis, *Notes of a War Correspondent*, p.143.

The Boers fell into the ambush because they assumed the British were several kilometres southeast of the road. Some blamed one of their scouts, an Austrian: 'It all comes of trusting these cursed foreigners! If we had only had a veldt Boer out we should never have been caught.'[42] The Boers had been carelessly led, but 'Red' Daniel Opperman completely rehabilitated his reputation at Spioenkop a few days later.

The ambush was relatively insignificant, yet, starting immediately and continuing ever since, multiple commentators have viewed the ambush as a lost opportunity. Their notion is that the failure of Warren to follow up on Dundonald's success and use the Acton Homes road led inevitably to disastrous frontal assaults on Tabanyama and on Spioenkop. However, it is often erroneously thought that the ambush took place at the narrow nek on the Ladysmith-OVS road, 6.5km closer to Ladysmith, and this error is shown on some maps, including the map in *The Times* history.[43] Some illustrations mistakenly depict the engagement in the steep terrain of the nek.

Most histories also overlook Warren's failed, large-scale attempt the following day to move westwards to reach Dundonald.

18 January at Potgieter's Drift

While the ambush on Peach Tree Farm was in progress, those at Potgieter's Drift could hear the gunfire in the distance. Lyttelton ordered a dummy attack to draw Boer forces away from Warren and to induce the Boers to reveal their gun positions. At 4:00 p.m. on 18 January, Major Phillips ascended in his hydrogen observation balloon to a height of 365 m, about 80 metres below the summit of Spioenkop. His balloon wagon trundled forwards while the feint attack developed, witnessed by the Bishop of Natal:

> A terrific cannonade began from all the guns and howitzers, and the Boer hillside, with its trenches and rifle-pits and gun emplacements, was spotted all over with the white puffs and columns of smoke from the bursting shells. At the same time the infantry began to advance in extended order – about five yards between each man – all across the plain from the little kopjes. They advanced and lay down, and the shells screamed over their heads. But the hill opposite might have been in the primeval desert; there was hardly a sign of life and not a single shot fired.[44]

The burghers held their fire while the 3rd Kings Royal Rifles moved towards them across the plain. To the east of the Rifles' line, Lieutenant Colonel Buchanan-Riddell reached the farmhouse of Vaalkrans Farm (approx. GPS -28.67365, 29.59408), while 2km further west, Major Bewick-Copley reached a small koppie (approx. GPS -28.66195, 29.57346). They had made a serious miscalculation, and were now within Mauser range. They abruptly came under heavy rifle fire. A Boer pom-pom commanded by General Fourie also opened up, sounding, Baynes thought: 'like a person knocking excitedly and impatiently at your door.'[45] It was

42   Churchill, *London to Ladysmith via Pretoria*, p.133.
43   Amery, *The War in South Africa*, Vol. III, p.300.
44   Baynes, *My Diocese During the War*, p.188.
45   Baynes, *My Diocese During the War*, p.190.

concealed behind a koppie (approx. GPS -28.64576, 29.58899) but the howitzers and naval guns guessed its location and soon it ceased firing. The Rifles were too close to the Boers, and Privates Grady and Jones were killed and 13 men were wounded, including 8 'severely wounded' and 2 'dangerously wounded'. Among the 'dangerously' wounded was Corporal Etheridge, shot through his spine. The Bishop of Natal wrote in his diary: 'He does not seem to know how bad his wound is, and as he may live for some time I did not feel that I was called to tell him plainly that they considered it hopeless.'[46] Lyttelton's men then returned to their positions on the Maconochie Koppies.

Finally, at 10:30pm on 18 January, after 27 hours of continuous activity, Warren's train of ox-wagons completed their crossing.[47]

46   Baynes, *My Diocese During the War*, p.198.
47   Amery, *The War in South Africa*, Vol. III, p.220.

6

19 January, The Failed March West

'Tack-tap, tack-tap, tack, tack, tack, tack, tap – as if the devil was hammering nails into the hills.' George W. Steevens[1]

Tabanyama

Tabanyama, the plateau west of Spioenkop, overlooks the broad Tugela and Venter's Spruit valleys to its south, and the OVS–Acton Homes–Ladysmith road to its west and north. The most important landmark, not shown on the Blue Map, was Fairview Farm – actually two farms, facing each other across a path. John Coventry's farm was Rangeworthy and Harry Coventry's farm was Fairview. Tabanyama, separated from Spioenkop in the east by the Renosterfontein valley, extends 6km from south-east to north-west, its southern crest folded into a line of buttresses and valleys. A deep ravine, which was not named at the time but which is now called Battle Spruit, runs south from the heart of the Tabanyama plateau. Nowhere from the British positions in the valley could the real shape of Tabanyama be discovered, as the Inniskillings noted:

> From our side of the valley could be seen looming above the base of the spurs a broken and irregular crest line, which, in the absence of maps, there was no reason to believe did not mark the top of the range. Actually this was only the false or southern crest, the real crest lying many hundred yards to the northward, at the far end of a gentle slope, destitute of any form of cover.[2]

Inevitably, officers gave contradictory names to the features on Tabanyama (see Map 2). In contemporary accounts, drawings and photographs, and in later publications, these are frequently misidentified. The simplest and best classification of Tabanyama's features was made by the York & Lancasters, who numbered the spurs from 1 to 5, counting from east to west:[3]

---

1   Steevens, *From Capetown to Ladysmith*, p.115.
2   Inniskillings, *The Royal Inniskilling Fusiliers*, p.414.
3   Kearsey, *War Record of the York & Lancasters*, p.14.

Spur 1, between Renosterfontein Spruit and Battle Spruit, is a large, broad and gentle slope, bearing two low koppies called Three Tree Hill and Picquet Hill, the latter of which has a southern extension called Connaught Hill.
Spur 2, west of Battle Spruit, is a long slope rising above Fairview Farm.
Spur 3 is small and undistinguished.
Spur 4 has a double-humped appearance, and is today called Sugar Loaf Hill.
Spur 5 is Bastion Hill.

As far as ease of climbing, Spurs 1 and 2 have a gentle gradient; Spurs 3, 4 and 5 have a very steep, rocky southern face with cliffs in parts. The 'backbone' or 'true crest' of Tabanyama is 1–2km further north and 100–150 metres higher than its southern crest, and was named by the Boers, from east to west, Groenkop (Green Hill), Langkop (Long Hill) and Platkop (Flat Hill). Along this 'true crest' the Boers had entrenched, with scouts on the southern crest. The Boers had allowed the British onto the southern crest of Tabanyama unopposed for the same reason the Boers allowed the British across the Tugela unopposed. That reason being, simply, the range of the Mauser rifle.

Warren Tries to Join Dundonald

Warren needed to re-unite his force with Dundonald's, and to follow Buller's vague instruction to advance westwards to turn the Boer flank (Appendix III (a)). There was no road indicated on the map, but there was a low-lying wagon track, which crossed Venter's Spruit at a drift 3km west of Trichardt's Drift, and which might prove a suitable route to the koppies which Dundonald had captured.[4] This was the track along which McKenzie had galloped for the ambush. At 2:00 a.m. on 19 January, Warren instructed the engineers to make a trestle bridge over Venter's Spruit drift and improve the road for wagons.

Before daylight, at 3:00 a.m. Hildyard's Brigade, with Hart's following, set off westwards. Lieutenant Wedd, with A Company, the Queen's, was in the advance guard, his men in extended order: '…with some idea that a fight might ensue, which it did not.'[5] Woodgate's Lancashire Brigade marched on the northern flank of the column, and part of the infantry and artillery stayed behind to guard Trichardt's Drift, the wagon park, and the line of march. Warren had four days' provisions, and could only be re-supplied as long as he was in communication with Springfield. Buller had requested the pontoons be returned to him as soon as possible. Once Trichardt's Drift was in the distance and the pontoon bridge taken away, Warren would have to achieve the breakthrough and rendezvous in under 4 days. The advance by the Acton Homes road, being much longer, increased the risk of being cut off.[6] At daybreak on 19 January, Warren's artillery and wagons followed the infantry, moving slowly westwards in six parallel columns.[7] As Lieutenant Silbourne had seen the day before, the Boer western flank already extended across the Acton Homes road. The Boer line could keep extending to match the westward crawl of Warren's column; Boer reinforcements were seen taking up positions on the skyline of

---

4   Amery, *The War in South Africa*, Vol. III, p.224.
5   Wedd, *Letter*.
6   'Defender', *Sir Charles Warren and Spion Kop*, p.82.
7   Atkins, *The Relief of Ladysmith*, p.222.

Fig 27: General Warren with Royal Engineers, siting a trestle bridge at Venter's Spruit drift. Taken in the afternoon of 18 January 1900 at Venter's Spruit. Warren, pointing, indicates where a trestle bridge should be built to allow his wheeled transport to move west towards the Acton Homes road. The bridge was built before dawn on 19 January but was not a success. (Cape Archives)

Tabanyama, beyond rifle range.[8] Dundonald had cautioned Warren not to go near Tabanyama, so the columns kept to low ground in the river valleys, which meant the wagons became bogged down, just as they had done on the march from Frere.

The track was nonexistent in many places, and had to be improved by 17th Royal Engineers. Fences and ditches were levelled to allow the passage of the field guns and transport, which were in the centre of the broad advancing mass. Venter's Spruit proved an almost impassable bottleneck, despite the new trestle bridge. The situation was encapsulated by George Crowe of HMS *Terrible*:

> To allow a waggon to leave the track, which was, at any rate, fairly solid under the thick stratum of mud, and attempt to travel on the alluring green veldt, was invariably fraught with disastrous consequences. One experience was sufficient to convince the most sceptic individual, after having both arms stretched for an hour or two on a

8   Romer and Mainwaring, *2nd Royal Dublin Fusiliers in the South African War*, p.47.

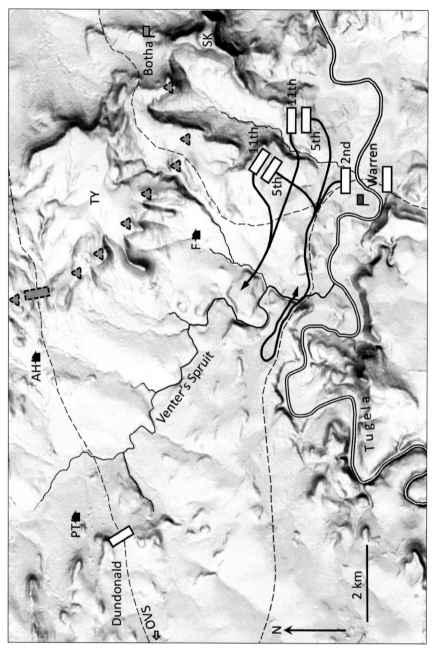

Map 4: The March West, 19 January. The 11th Brigade (Woodgate's) and 5th Brigade (Hart's) march west towards Dundonald. They fail to make progress, turn back in the afternoon, recross Venter's Spruit and bivouac. The 2nd Brigade (Hildyard's) guards Trichardt's Drift and the line of march. F = Fairview Farm; PT = Peach Tree Farm; AH = Acton Homes Farm; TY = Tabanyama; SK = Spioenkop. Boer outposts (grey triangles) are on the southern crest of Tabanyama, while their trenches are being dug on the true crest.

drag-rope trying to extricate a waggon which had gone off its course on to the spongy veldt, that keeping to the track was the safest policy.[9]

The troops halted for hours while the engineers did their best to improve Venter's Spruit drift.[10] Without maps, groups lost sight of each other, got lost and feared they would be cut off.[11] Churchill recalled:

> At any moment two or three thousand Boers could have crossed the river in the intervals between the watching brigades, and riding south might have interrupted the trailing line of communications along which all supplies had to be carried. The nightmare which haunted the Commander-in-Chief was of being cut off from the railway and encircled like Sir George White in Ladysmith without even an entrenched camp or adequate supplies to stand a siege.[12]

An anonymous eyewitness described the difficulties:

> As the wagons marched on the morning of the 19th in four or five parallel columns, in length about three miles or so, the brigades commanded by Major-Generals Hart and Woodgate also kept pace with them until opposite Fair View, where the right of the line was to rest in the attack of the Rangeworthy hills. The two brigades then occupied the slopes of the adjoining hills. This march was a very remarkable one, and it is to be doubted whether there is another instance on record of such a force, forming a length of three or four miles, with wagons four or five deep on the column's reverse flank, being successfully led by a flank march right along the face of commanding hills held by an enemy strongly intrenched and provided with long-range guns, on a road just out of range of effective rifle fire, and with a rapid river on its reverse flank. It was in accordance with [Buller's] instructions, but it was a most hazardous proceeding, and it was owing to the careful management of Sir Charles Warren, as well as the want of initiative or military instinct on the part of the Boer commander, that there was no disaster.[13]

When the British did appear on ridges, they came under Boer artillery fire from von Wichmann's 75mm Creusots, 7km away, as happened to the Dublin Fusiliers about 2:00 p.m. when they halted on higher ground to dry their boots and puttees.

9   Crowe, *The Commission of H.M.S. "Terrible"*, p.136.
10   Blake Knox, *Buller's Campaign*, p.28.
11   Atkins, *The Relief of Ladysmith*, p.221.
12   Churchill, *My Early Life*, p.308.
13   'Defender', *Sir Charles Warren and Spion Kop*, pp.92–93.

Fig 28: British soldiers crossing a tributary of the Tugela. The cattle on the skyline indicate it is not near the firing line. (Arnold van Dyk collection)

Warren Calls off the March

Around midday, with the march in progress, Warren summoned Dundonald to Venter's Spruit. Warren was unhappily watching the wagons struggling to cross. He was unable to make eye contact with Dundonald: 'I want you close to me' was all he repeated.[14] Unlike Dundonald, who was highly mobile, Warren's slow-moving force in the valley was 'a sitting duck'. Dundonald had forced Warren to give up good positions on the koppies to join him. Warren found himself again encumbered with loaded wagons, only hours after unloading them. His entire 5th Division still lacked combat experience against the Boers. The enemy's location, numbers and intentions were entirely unknown, but they were believed to be formidable. Moreover, as Captain Holmes Wilson of the Royal Artillery observed, by protecting the lengthening lines of communication, the numbers available to relieve Ladysmith were rapidly dwindling:

> The whole army had to move to a flank, whilst a covering force was left at Chieveley... The main body had then to be split again, and another covering force left in front of

14   Dundonald, *My Army Life,* p.187.

the enemy's main position at Brakfontein… if the flanking move had been continued to the left… a fresh containing force would have had to have been detached at the point of passage. What would then have remained for the grand encounter? Two brigades had already been left behind, and if the movement had been continued, it would have been necessary to have dropped a third of the six.[15]

By 4:00 p.m. so few wagons had crossed Venter's Spruit that the futility of the westward movement was obvious.[16] Lieutenant George Hyde Harrison of the Border Regiment concluded:

> …Buller's chances of success were repeatedly thrown away owing to the slowness of his movements and by the ridiculous manner in which we allowed ourselves to be tied to our Transport. Both at Pretorius' Farm in the early stages and again at the Venter's Spruit Drift our cumbrous baggage columns alone caused days of delay. This gave a mobile enemy like the Boers ample time to shift their positions and so put up a strong defensive line wherever we chose to attack.[17]

Later that afternoon a heliogram reached Warren from Ladysmith which clinched the decision to turn back: 'A force of 1,500 to 2,000 Boers moved from Clydesdale towards Acton Homes, 5 p.m. to-day, by main road.' (Appendix III (m)) This confirmed to Warren that his column could never outflank the Boers. 'Danie' Kestell wrote: 'The English did not advance any farther [than Acton Homes]. They were prevented from doing so by the presence of numbers of Free Staters and Transvaalers in the road from Acton Homes to Ladysmith, [so] no [more] fighting occurred there.'[18]

Warren called back the troops, the furthest of whom had progressed less than 4km in over 12 hours. As Captain Cecil Romer of the Dublins wrote, they were ordered to: '…re-cross Venter's Spruit and bivouac. The movement by Acton Holmes had been given up… it was not difficult to see that the alternative was a frontal attack on the position which everybody had watched being fortified.'[19]

The men halted close to Venter's Spruit and companies from Woodgate's and Hart's Brigades went forward in the gloom to occupy the low koppies between the river and Tabanyama. Soon, long-range rifle fire was exchanged with Boers on Three Tree Hill and the southern crest of Tabanyama. A long range shot that evening wounded Alex Brand, son of the former president of the OVS, in his left thigh and he lay in no-man's-land for three days. Fortunately, Brand was near water, so he did not die of thirst nor in the flames of the grass fire the next day. Eventually he was found, carried back to the Boer hospital at Modderspruit, and recovered.[20]

Through binoculars the British could see numerous Boers on Bastion Hill, some of whom were riding about leisurely and others industriously digging trenches.[21] Captain Grant, with

---

15   Wilson, *The Relief of Ladysmith*, p.50.
16   Maurice, *History of The War in South Africa, Vol. II*, p.363.
17   Harrison, *Unpublished memoir* p.116.
18   Kestell, *Through Shot and Flame*, p.58.
19   Romer and Mainwaring, *2nd Royal Dublin Fusiliers in the South African War*, p.47.
20   Izedinova, *A few Months With the Boers*, p.50.
21   Blake Knox, *Buller's Campaign*, p.28.

Hildyard's Brigade, feared that the bivouac at Venter's Spruit that evening was vulnerable to attack: '...a chaotic bivouac... a division might have been the prey of a moderately well-educated company, had the Boer army possessed one; men, homes, oxen in one huge muddle at the bottom of a bowl.'[22] During the night the wagons, which had also turned back, eventually caught up with the troops and, Romer recorded: '...the men were thus able to have their great-coats. Not much sleep was, however, allowed.'[23] Lieutenant Alec Kearsey of the Yorks & Lancasters reflected: 'Fearfully hot day, nothing to eat; rum and biscuits served out at 8 p.m. ...'[24]

The Boers Expect an Attack

The Boers had no doubt that Warren would attack Tabanyama the following day. Dr Raymond Maxwell, an English doctor with the Ermelo Commando Ambulance behind Tabanyama, wrote on 19 January:

> The English are now trekking for Acton Homes, and have occupied Mount Alice [Spearman's Hill], on which they have posted artillery to cover the advance. A patrol from the Pretorian commando was surprised and cut off – forty-eight killed, wounded, and missing. The two forces are now getting into touch, and the English are evidently going to try and obtain the Thaba Mjama [Black Mountain] ridge.[25]

'Sandjie' Sandberg, Louis Botha's secretary, wrote:

> ...the enemy began to bring infantry as close to our positions as possible, probably to determine where they were located, and whether further upstream there would be an opportunity for out-flanking... to our joy they realized that out-flanking was impossible. It was not long until they returned to their camp without them succeeding in making us betray the placement of our guns. That day the enemy contented himself with bombarding us heavily with artillery; and Saturday [20 January] the attack began in earnest.[26]

That night, Buller recalled: 'I debated with myself whether or not I should relieve Warren of his command... It is true that I disapproved of his first two days' work in the first command that he had ever held under me, but I did not think that this was sufficient justification for his removal.'[27]

22   Linesman, *Words by an Eyewitness*, p.39
23   Romer and Mainwaring, *2nd Royal Dublin Fusiliers in the South African War*, p.47
24   Kearsey, *War Record of the York & Lancasters*, p.13.
25   'Defender', *Sir Charles Warren and Spion Kop*, p.120.
26   Sandberg, *De Zesdaagsche Slag aan de Boven Tugela*, p.89.
27   Commission into the War in South Africa, Vol. II, p.178.

The 13th Hussars Reconnoitre

While Warren's column was struggling westwards, Lieutenant Smythe's troop of 13th Hussars scouted the approaches to Three Tree Hill as an objective for the coming attack. They came into rifle range and were pinned down, with Corporal Coghlan and Private Findlay being severely wounded. Infantry went forward at 5:30 p.m. to extricate them. Fortunately, the Hussars had gathered good information about the approaches to Three Tree Hill and Picquet Hill, both of which would conceal troops approaching from the south.[28]

That evening, General Warren held a council of war, attended by his staff, brigade commanders, and the commanders of the engineers and artillery. Dundonald was excluded. The officers discussed, and rejected, the road via Acton Homes, as 'Defender', possibly Warren himself, later wrote:

> There was only one road leading to it, and the wagons could only go singly. The force could not possibly watch a front of fifteen miles occupied by the enemy. The result would be that each day's march must be limited by the length of road that could be watched. The force was to be provisioned for only four days, and, even if everything went successfully, it would take three days to get from Venter's Spruit by Acton Homes to the point near Groote Hoek. It was therefore evident that the road could not be used, even if it were not so strongly held by the enemy… such a route in the circumstances was impossible.[29]

Buller heliographed the day's news to Ladysmith, and acknowledged that he would have to supply Warren for a longer campaign: 'Warren is meeting with great difficulties regarding roads, and his progress is very slow. I am sending him three more days' supplies.'[30]

Meanwhile at Potgieter's Drift the naval guns and howitzers continued to shell the Boer positions at Brakfontein. The Boer 'Official War News Bulletin' reported: 'The enemy kept up bombarding our positions on the upper Tugela without doing us any damage. In the meantime the enemy was using a balloon to observe our positions.'[31]

28   Tremayne, *XIII. Hussars South African War*, p.13
29   'Defender', *Sir Charles Warren and Spion Kop*, pp.94, 96
30   Commission into the War in South Africa, Vol. II, p.163
31   Anon., *The Bulletin of Official War News*, Heidelberg, Transvaal Field Press, 19 January 1900

7

20 January, the Battle of Tabanyama – Morning

'We would, therefore, almost passively, have to endure the enemy's artillery fire, until we could engage him with rifles.' Burgher Roland Schikkerling, Pretoria Commando[1]

The Plan of Attack

At the council of war on the evening of 19 January, Warren and his generals acknowledged they could not outflank the Boers. As Atkins, the *Manchester Guardian* correspondent, observed: 'It had been discovered that after all there was no way round to the back of Spion Kop through open country. The hills in which the Boers are, in fact, a spur of the Drakensberg Mountains; wherever Sir Charles Warren might go, he must go through mountains.'[2] The longer route to Ladysmith via Acton Homes had been rejected, so the objective was the direct route, the Fairview-Rosalie road. This road rises from Trichardt's Drift, and has a wide base of sandy red soil and stones, and it still exists today as a farm track. It ascends an easy gradient east of Fairview Farm, between Three Tree Hill and Piquet Hill, over the *wapadnek* on Green Hill, and descends to the foot of Spioenkop at Groote Hoek Farm, where it turns eastwards to Ladysmith. Warren telegraphed his intentions to Buller, saying that he would adopt 'special arrangements', which would involve his remaining at Tabanyama for 2 or 3 days (Appendix III (n)). These 'special arrangements' can be understood as: first, continual artillery bombardment to weaken the Boers' morale. Second, to attack up both sides of Battle Spruit, or 'the long ravine',[3] by independent commands, which Warren later called Left Attack and Right Attack. Finally, once the Boer line had broken, for the infantry to march to their next battle without wagons. They would be a true 'flying column', with 3 or 4 days' food in their haversacks.[4] The attack was planned by Major General Sir Cornelius Francis Clery, aged 61 (Appendix IV(a)). Clery was renowned for his tactical skill but he was eccentric, and for some unknown reason, he dyed his prominent 'Burnside' whiskers blue. Woodgate's 11th (Lancashire) Brigade would

---

1   Schikkerling, *Commando Courageous*, p.47.
2   Atkins, *The Relief of Ladysmith*, pp.222–223.
3   Amery, *The War in South Africa*, Vol. III, p.230.
4   'Defender', *Sir Charles Warren and Spion Kop*, p.180.

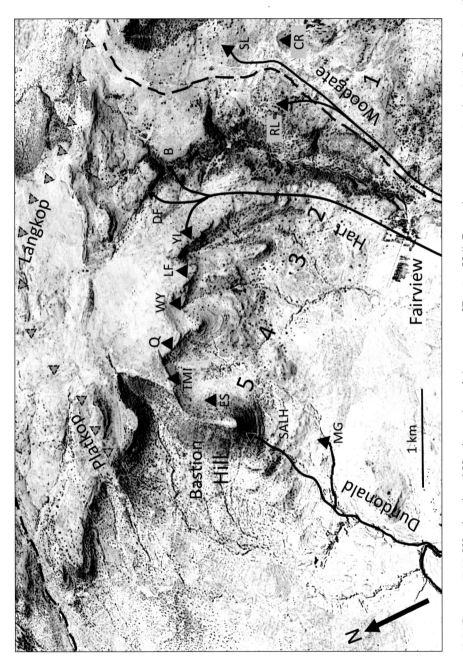

Map 5: 20 January 1900: Woodgate's and Hart's attacks and the capture of Bastion Hill. Boers shown as grey triangles. 1–5 = Spurs 1 to 5; B = Borders; CR = Connaught Rangers; DF = Dublin Rangers; ES = East Surreys; LF = Lancashire Fusiliers; MG = machine guns; Q = Queen's; WY = West Yorks; YL = York & Lancasters; RL = Royal Lancasters; SALH = South African Light Horse; SL = South Lancashires; TMI = Thorneycroft's Mounted Infantry.

attack first, on Spur 1, in the east. Hart's Irish Brigade, Dublins, Inniskillings, Connaughts, and Borders, would attack next, on Spur 2, in the centre. Hildyard's Brigade, the Queen's, East Surreys, West Yorks and Devons, would remain near Venter's Spruit, to support as needed. The western flank would be guarded by Thorneycroft's Mounted Infantry, now removed from Dundonald's command.

Woodgate's task was predicted to be the easier one, and this turned out to be accurate. His objectives, on Spur 1, were Three Tree Hill and Picquet Hill. These objectives were overlooked by Boer trenches, but they were also in clear view of the lower slopes and would be within rifle and artillery range from the start. They would be taken in the dark, and once these two koppies were secure, the artillery would unlimber on Spur 1 and bombard Spur 2, allowing Hart to attack. Hart's attack would be trickier, he would advance in broad daylight in front of Boer trenches. Hart's objectives were not visible from the south, were not on the map, and there had been no reconnaissance. To those on low ground, Hart's front line would disappear from sight, though Three Tree Hill would have a good view of his front line. Consequently, two of Woodgate's battalions – the Lancashire Fusiliers and York and Lancasters – were lent to Hart to strengthen his force. Once Hart's objectives were reached, Hildyard and Hart would jointly occupy the whole southern crest – Spurs 2, 3, 4 and 5. The Inniskillings and Devons would be Hart's and Hildyard's reserves, respectively.

General Woodgate's Attack

The Royal Lancasters and South Lancashires had bivouacked near Venter's Spruit after the aborted westward march the previous day. At 2:00 a.m. on 20 January they packed their greatcoats onto wagons, and without eating breakfast or receiving rations, marched off to the north–east. In the dark, they advanced in open order, their objective being Three Tree Hill.

This was a low koppie named for three large paper-bark Acacia trees growing on its summit. The three trees would not last long; the artillery thought them too prominent a landmark for Boer artillery, so they were cut down the following day.[5] As day broke, the surgeons laid out their boxes of instruments and bandages in anticipation of casualties.[6] The South Lancashires and Royal Lancasters reached the slopes of Spur 1 before daylight came. They advanced unopposed, apart from occasional long range rifle shots, because the Boers had already withdrawn to their main trenches on Langkop and Green Hill. The Royal Lancasters occupied Three Tree Hill, and at 6:00 a.m. the South Lancashires occupied Piquet Hill. That afternoon, both hills were strengthened by the Connaughts, who divided themselves between Three Tree Hill and Connaught Hill (a low ridge just south of Picquet Hill). Thereafter, the only safe access to Picquet Hill in daylight was from the south; crossing from Three Tree Hill was dangerously exposed. On the reverse slopes of the koppies the soldiers built lines of stone *schanzes* (sangars). On the crest of the hills were the firing lines, where the men lay behind *schanzes* and fired at the Boer trenches about 2,000 metres away. On the reverse slope the men rested behind *schanzes* which gave partial protection against stray bullets.

5   Burleigh, *The Natal Campaign*, p.319.
6   Blake Knox, *Buller's Campaign*, p.10.

The Royal Field Artillery Comes into Action

At dawn, the 78th Battery came up the Fairview-Rosalie road, unlimbered near Three Tree Hill, and came into action.

Fig 29: 15-pdr Field Gun of 78th Battery in action on the Fairview-Rosalie road. The skyline shows Langkop ahead and, to the right, Green Hill and Conical Hill. This photograph was taken at approx. GPS -28.64583, 29.48412 by the artist Rene Bull, just east of Three Tree Hill, on 20 January 1900. The epaulements in front of the gun have not yet been fully built up. (*Black and White Budget*)

Three further batteries soon trotted up the road, unlimbered, and were manhandled north-west onto Three Tree Hill, which became the main British artillery position. At first, they pointed their gun barrels outwards defensively, like the spokes of a wheel, but when no counter-attack came, they took up positions on three terraces on the reverse slope.

Furthest south was the 73rd Battery (The GPS of No. 1 gun of the 73rd Battery is -28.64603, 29.48380) 100 metres up the slope, and slightly to the east, was the 63rd Battery; 100 metres north-east of them was 7th Battery.

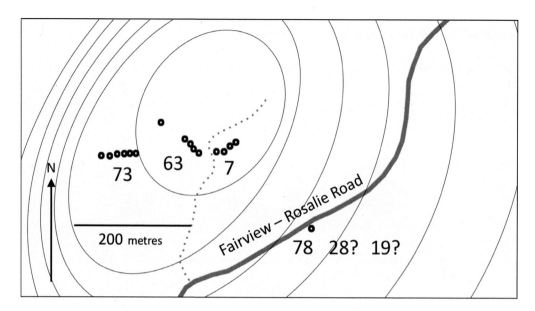

Fig 30: Sketch map of field gun positions on Three Tree Hill. The gun positions were confirmed by T-Friction Tubes behind epaulements, except for 19th and 28th Batteries whose positions are assumed. South of the 73rd Battery are many protective *schanzes* of the infantry who guarded the guns.

Each battery of 15-pdrs, including its limbers and ammunition column, comprised about 87 horses and 170 men – 5 officers, 9 sergeants, 6 bombardiers, 6 corporals, 76 gunners, 59 drivers; trumpeters, farriers, saddlers, wheelers, and rangefinders.[7] The sheltered reverse slope of Three Tree Hill immediately became crowded, while the forward slope was already swept with long range Mauser bullets. Soon, a mass of *schanzes* were built on the reverse slope, behind which the Royal Lancasters lay. Their *schanzes* are still visible about 25 metres behind the gun positions, for example GPS -28.64627, 29.48302 to -28.64663, 29.48390, and can be seen on satellite images. With a mass of infantry and artillery on the slope, there was no room for the remaining batteries, which unlimbered in more exposed positions in a maize field just east of the wagon road. Nearest was the 78th Battery (GPS: -28.64709, 29.48677), 28th Battery in the centre, and 19th Battery to the east. The artillery selected their targets on Green Hill and Langkop at ranges of 1,900 to 3,500 metres. Each battery comprised six 15-pdr, seven hundredweight, breech-loading guns. They fired 3-inch shrapnel shells, propelled by bags of cordite, which were ignited by T-Friction Tubes.

Each shrapnel shell had a time fuse, expertly adjusted so that on its downward trajectory the nose cone would blow off 5–8 metres above the target, ejecting 200 lead shrapnel balls.[8]

7   Hall, *Halt! Action Front!* pp.3–4
8   Darrell D. Hall, 'Ammunition', *South African Military History Society: Military History Journal*, Vol.3 No.4, Dec 1975.

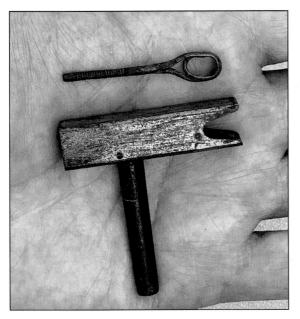

Fig 31: T-Friction Tube. The friction wire was pulled out sharply with a lanyard, igniting gunpowder in the tube which fired the cordite charge in the breech of the field gun. 15-pdr field guns and 50-pdr howitzers used the same system.

Fig 32: 15-pdr shrapnel shell. The time fuse was adjusted so the shell would detonate about 5 to 8 metres above the ground, blowing 200 lead shrapnel balls onto the target. This example was reassembled from fired components as a souvenir.

The time fuse allowed a maximum of 13 seconds of flight, and the maximum elevation of the gun barrel was 16 degrees; these factors limited the range of shrapnel to 3,750 metres. The fuse could also be set to percussion. This allowed ranges up to 5,120 metres, but the meagre bursting charge of 43 grams of black powder imparted very limited explosive effect. When firing shrapnel, the gunners removed both pins so that, if the time fuse failed, the shell would detonate on percussion as a back-up. The gunners opened fire with shells set to percussion to find the range, timing the flight of the shell with stopwatches, then they switched to timed shells, to burst in the air above the target.[9]

Typically, the six guns of a Royal Field Artillery battery went into action at the trot, and on the command: 'Halt! Action Front!' the guns unlimbered in a line, in sight of their targets. The guns were about 10 metres apart, the right-hand gun becoming No.1 Gun. On the Upper Tugela, however, the 15-pdrs were stationary. Their gunners built them into defensive positions from which they did not move for several days.

9   H.M.S.O., *Infantry Drill Manual 1896* (London; Harrison and Sons, 1896), p.153.

Boer Artillery

In contrast to the British batteries, Boer artillerymen, who were often German or German-trained, used their guns singly or in pairs.[10] Schikkerling, a Pretoria burgher, wrote:

> The Boer, finding the long-range magazine rifle the most effective weapon, sets little store when on the move, by artillery which might only divide his attention and hamper his mobility; yet when he has cannon they are not clustered in batteries, but spread about and hidden like his men.[11]

The Transvaal *Staatsartillerie* guns fired smokeless ammunition, like the British guns, but had longer ranges. Creusot 75mm guns fired percussion or shrapnel shells to 6,200 m, and Krupp 75mm gums fired shrapnel to 3,520 metres or percussion to 6,000 metres.[12] The Boers also used pom-poms, made by Vickers, Sons & Co. and Maxim in England.

Fig 33: Boer pom-pom in action. This posed scene from the western front shows a *Staatsartillerie* pom-pom firing from behind an empaulement of sandbags concealed by branches of thorn bush. *Commandant* Jacobus Frederick ('Tollie') de Beer is in the centre; to the right an artilleryman is ready with a belt of ammunition. (Courtesy Neville Constantine)

10   L. Jooste, 'Foreigners in the Defence of South Africa', *South African Journal of Military Studies*, Vol.16, Number 2 (1986).
11   Schikkerling, *Commando Courageous*, p.209.
12   Hall, *Halt! Action Front!* pp.27–31.

Pom-poms fired 1-pound, 37mm shells which exploded on impact. They were belt-fed, 25 shells in a belt, like an enormous machine gun. The Boer gunner would fire a burst of 3 to 5 rounds and watch their explosions, before adjusting aim. The pom-pom had a range of 2,750 metres, and Atkins thought they sounded like: '…a post-man rapping on the door of an empty house.'[13] Pom-pom shells flew at low velocity, so soldiers could dive for cover – if cover existed – once they heard the gun firing. Boer guns on the Upper Tugela were invariably sited where they were invisible to their target. Often, they would move to duplicate gun emplacements if they came under fire. Amery described the Boer artillery on Tabanyama as being posted: '…in the same line as the riflemen…' but this is erroneous; careful examination of the Boer trenches indicates that all the massive trenches and parapets were built for riflemen, not artillery.[14] *Commandant* Krause described how the Boers built epaulements to protect their guns:

> We obtained bags and filled them with loose soil. We set to work and packed a strong stone wall, 4 ft thick, in a semicircle around the cannon on the summit of the kopje. This wall we covered with earth. Then we placed two rows of sandbags three feet from the stone wall, and filled in the space between with loose soil. An opening was left in the middle for the muzzle of the cannon.[15]

Fig 34: Krupp 75mm QF Field Gun. Commanded by Lieutenant Heinrich Grothaus, the gun is dug in behind epaulements of stone and earth, disguised by cut branches. A tarpaulin under the gun barrel prevents the muzzle blast from raising a cloud of dust. *Staatsartillerie* men, armed with Mauser carbines, are laying the gun; two hold a round of timed shrapnel and one of percussion shell. Among the onlookers is, extreme right, Dr Elsberger of the German Corps ambulance. Photograph taken near Ladysmith. (Courtesy Neville Constantine)

13   Atkins, *The Relief of Ladysmith*, p.175
14   Amery, *The War in South Africa*, Vol. III, p.229.
15   Krause, *War Memoirs*, p.27.

Under the muzzle they spread animal hides or tarpaulins to prevent the muzzle blast raising a dust cloud which might disclose the gun.

The Boer gunners, being out of sight of their targets, used heliograph signallers to direct their fire.

The Sounds of Battle

Everyone on Tabanyama was struck by the absence of visible Boers. Treves wrote: 'The country, although occupied by thousands of Boers, appeared to be absolutely deserted.'[16] Lacking anything to see, the sounds of the battlefield made a strong impression on correspondents like Lynch:

> An innocent, harmless-looking hill it seemed, with not a Boer visible on it, yet the bright summer air simply sang with the notes of Mauser bullets – clear and musical notes when they pass high overhead, but with a sharp and bitter ping when they pass close.'[17]

Soldiers, on first hearing long range Mauser shots, noted a double report, unlike their own rifles that gave a single sound. Lieutenant Blake Knox described the sound as: 'pit! pot!'[18] Lieutenant Charlton as: 'pock 'em!'[19] and O'Mahony as: 'ping pong.'[20] At first, they mistook this as a property of Mauser ammunition, but soon learned it was the echo off the hills around them. Steevens in Ladysmith described the sound of Mausers: 'Tack-tap, tack-tap – each shot echoed a little muffled from the hills. Tack-tap, tack-tap, tack, tack, tack, tack, tap – as if the devil was hammering nails into the hills.'[21]

Boer Entrenchments

The Boers were invisible because they were standing in trenches, later described by Treves: 'The [Boer] trenches were wide and beautifully made, and were nearly neck deep.'[22] The British had watched them: '…digging for dear life, their labouring figures showing up plainly on the skyline.'[23] Boer trenches were dug by spade, pick and crowbar, sometimes using African labourers.

The Boer trenches ran in short sections for 5.5km from Green Hill in the east, along the ridge of Langkop, to Platkop in the west. Their massive stone parapets can be clearly seen today. Schikkerling wrote that the trenches were as narrow as possible: '…so as to present the slenderest target to shell and shrapnel, and so constructed that they could hardly be seen, by

16   Treves, *British Medical Journal*, 1900, p.471.
17   Lynch, *Impressions of a War Correspondent*, p.55.
18   Blake Knox, *Buller's Campaign*, p.18.
19   Charlton, *Charlton*, p.95
20   O'Mahony, *A Peep Over the Barleycorn*, pp.120–121.
21   Steevens, *From Capetown to Ladysmith*, p.115.
22   Treves, 'The War in South Africa,' in *British Medical Journal*, 7 April 1900, p.863.
23   Linesman, *Words by an Eyewitness*, p.39.

Fig 35: Boers Making a Trench on the Upper Tugela. A group of Boers and *agterryers* move boulders into place, using crowbars. The stone parapet is visible behind them, and would later be camouflaged with cut branches. On Tabanyama, each trench ran for 10 to 25 metres, and housed 10 to 20 men. (Cape Archives)

hiding all new earth or covering it with grass… The trenches were usually so out of line that they could lend slant fire to a neighbour, and not be enfiladed or raked by artillery.[24]

Veldkornet Kemp and *Commandant* Sarel Oosthuizen of Krugersdorp helped Botha select the positions, and Kemp later reflected with satisfaction:

> Though I say it myself, our officers knew damn well what they were doing when they chose the positions… for the enemy to try to charge over those thousand yards means suicide, because the open ground they had to move on could be covered by crossfire.[25]

Each trench on Tabanyama was about 10–25 metres long, and held 10–20 men, rather than a continuous trench such as those dug on Brakfontein, which attracted British artillery. The Tabanyama trenches were slightly below the skyline, to avoid silhouetting the burghers. About 500 metres further back, cut into the steep reverse slopes of Tabanyama, were a number of shelters in which they rested during bombardments; one example is at GPS -28.63551, 29.50468. These were safely below the trajectory of shrapnel and bullets, though they could not protect against howitzer shells, which dropped almost vertically.

24   Schikkerling, *Commando Courageous*, p.209
25   Kemp, *Vir Vryheid en vir Reg*, p.278

Fig 36: Boer shelter behind Tabanyama. On the steep reverse slope, about 500 metres behind the fighting trenches, the Boers built shelters below the trajectory of bullets and shrapnel. They could not protect against howitzer shells which fell almost vertically. In this photograph a group of Boers, *agterryers* behind, pose with Mausers, a Lee-Enfield, and two Guedes rifles. Sandbags on the roof protect against stray shots. (Wellcome collection)

Every man was supposed to complete at least three metres of trench – one and a half for his own use and the remainder for the use of any man; this limit was generally exceeded, as it was good to have plenty of room. Some of these trenches were a curious sight. Here, a man had made a comfortable seat in the side, so as to allow him when sitting, to see across the parapet in front. There, another fashioned an incline, sloping up to the embankment, so that he could recline in the trench, and fire at his ease over the top, while next to this the trench had been hollowed out inwards, forming a small underground chamber where no shell could reach him, and where, under the cool earth, he could take shelter from the burning rays of the hot Natal sun. Some cut little square holes in the sides of the trenches, in which they were able to store away hundred rounds of ammunition, water bottles, and even food – and in some cases little wooden doors on hinges secured with padlocks were added. In cases of emergency, the owner needed only run to the trench with his rifle, and there he would find everything ready for a long stay. Corrugated iron was also used to roof the trenches in some parts.[26] Fresh hay was

26   Krause, *War Memoirs*, p.47.

brought in to make the trenches more comfortable, though latrines were lacking, and water was scarce.[27] The Tabanyama trenches provided a superb field of fire for the Boers facing Warren on Tabanyama.

There were 1,400 Transvaalers from mixed units: Pretoria, Krugersdorp, Ermelo, Middelburg, Boksburg, Utrecht, Bethal, Piet Retief, Zoutpansberg, Wakkerstroom, Heidelberg, Johannesburg and the German Corps. There were also 400 Free Staters, mainly from Heilbron, Winburg and Senekal. On Spioenkop and Twin Peaks were outposts of the Vryheid and Carolina Commandos.[28,29]

The Royal Field Artillery Comes into Action

At 7:00 a.m. the six batteries around Three Tree Hill opened fire, and for two hours, shelled the Boer trenches. Private Phipps of the Borders noted the Boer guns did not reply: 'The Boers appeared to have no big guns, not a shot being answered to our gunners magnificent practice.'[30] Lieutenant Blake Knox observed the 15-pdr shrapnel shells fired from Three Tree Hill:

> The shells were invisible till they exploded. We could see them tearing great holes in the hillside, and sending up clouds of red dust when they burst [on] the ground. When time shrapnel was used, it exploded some 20 feet in air, over the target aimed at; all one could see was a flash, not always visible except against a dark background, or as a small convoluting globe of pure white smoke. If the ground under the 'cone of dispersion' of the shrapnel bullets is visible, little clouds of dust thrown up by the individual pellets as they strike the soil can be perceived. The shells went through the air with a scream that reminded me of rockets…[31]

At first, the British gunners were unprotected against Mauser fire. Lieutenant Blake Knox noted: '…the coolness of the gunners, standing by their guns with absolutely no cover, was admirable, although they were subjected during all the afternoon to a continuous long-range rifle and shell fire.'[32] That night, the gunners built protective epaulements, crescent-shaped walls of soil or sandbags about 1.25 metres high, on stone foundations which are still visible on Three Tree Hill today. Horses, ammunition wagons and limbers were under cover in the gully of Battle Spruit, about 500 metres back.

The gunners: 'bivouacked nightly by guns, dug epaulements in front of guns to save men from continuous sniping, men very comfortable & happy all meals cooked by wagons & sent up to guns. Battery very well behaved under fire.'[33] The British gunners could only guess where enemy fire was coming from: 'You might say that in this war the object of the Boer gunners is to kill an enemy who cannot see them; that of the heroic British gunners is to be killed by an enemy

27   Pretorius, *Life on Commando During the Anglo-Boer War* p.130
28   Barnard, *Generaal Louis Botha op die Natalse Front*, *p.*90.
29   Kemp, *Vir Vryheid en vir Reg*, p.266
30   Phipps, *Diary, 1st Border Regiment.*
31   Blake Knox, *Buller's Campaign*, p.39.
32   Blake Knox, *Buller's Campaign*, p.39.
33   Anon, *78th Battery Digest of Service 1900.*

Fig 37: Royal Field Artillery Officers on Three Tree Hill. Seven officers with RFA flashes on their pugarees in discussion behind a *schanz* on the reverse slope of Three Tree Hill, approx. GPS -28.64663, 29.48390. Behind them, an ammunition wagon is on the Fairview-Rosalie road; the skyline is the Spioenkop ascent spur. (National Army Museum)

whom they cannot see.'[34] Lieutenant Charles Holmes Wilson, a gunner on Three Tree Hill, was frustrated:

> The view was barred in front by a ridge, [Langkop] the average range of which was about 2600 yards. On this the only visible traces of the enemy were a few patches of newly turned-up earth, which were indistinctly outlined against the darker colour of the remainder of the ridge. The lie of the enemy's position could, however, only be generally defined by the outline of the ridge, and it was against this indefinite target that the artillery had to open fire. As to "observation," there was practically nothing to observe. The fire effect could only be gauged by the information received from the attacking infantry. When any particular spot was shelled, and the enemy's rifle fire from it slackened, information to that effect was signalled back by the infantry to the artillery. In the same way, if the Boer rifle fire became troublesome in any particular direction, the officer commanding the artillery was notified of the fact, and asked to turn his guns on to the spot indicated.'[35]

34   Atkins, *The Relief of Ladysmith*, p.240.
35   Wilson, *The Relief of Ladysmith*, p.62.

Unlike the Boer artillery, who had heliographers for each gun, the Royal Field Artillery had done away with signalling shortly before the war. On Three Tree Hill, they borrowed flag-signallers from the infantry. On occasions, the signallers became bored and careless, as Atkins noticed:

> Some signallers were at work there. One stood, at one time, outside the shelter of the breastworks with his flag in his hand. An excellent target, the Boers seemed to think. The singing of a bullet came more frequently over-head, one or two struck the ground near. "Better mind where you stand," said another signaller. "I'm all right."...but at last he had exhausted his chances and he fell. He was only hit in the foot, but he spun round before he fell. Another signaller at the end of his spell of signalling dashed off to join his regiment in the firing line. "Where am I going?" he said, "Going to give 'em a 'undred and fifty of the best. That's for my pal who was killed at Willow Grange"[36]

Around noon, the shellfire ignited the long grass, which had not been grazed for months nor burnt in the spring, as is the custom in Natal. Blake Knox wrote: 'The grass blazed furiously, sending up dense volumes of smoke, through which friend and foe emptied their magazines. Some of the wounded suffered in the flame.'[37] The Boers' perspective was seen by Penning: 'The amphitheatre of the hills caught fire, and great clouds of smoke drifted off in the direction of the

Fig 38: 15-pdr Field Guns on Three Tree Hill. Taken before the batteries had lined up on the terraces of the reverse slope, the guns face outwards like the spokes of a wheel. The camera is facing west, with Battle Spruit ravine in front and Spur 2 beyond. The air is hazy with smoke from grass-fires on Tabayama, Spur 2 being partly burnt. (National Army Museum)

36   Atkins, *The Relief of Ladysmith*, pp.232–233.
37   Blake Knox, *Buller's Campaign, p.36*.

Boer sharp-shooters.'[38] Captain Grant said: 'All over the battlefield, as if sent by telegraph-wire, ran the rumour that twenty wounded Boers were burnt in the flames...'[39] Fortunately, there were very few Boers wounded that day. The fire burnt all afternoon, and into the night.

General Hart Attacks Spur 2

Major-General Arthur Fitzroy Hart, commanding the Irish Brigade, never ducked away from bullets, thus his nickname became 'General No-Bobs'.[40] Private Harry Phipps of the Borders had witnessed Hart's personal courage at Colenso: 'a shell came bounding along the ground & jumped right over Gen. Hart; it did not explode but lay on top of the ground. Gen. Hart went up to it, carelessly poking it with a stick, exclaiming that "if this was the sort of stuff they fire they had better go home."'[41] Hart's advance from Venter's Spruit began in the dark, at 3:00 a.m. It was led by the battalions lent by Woodgate: the Lancashire Fusiliers and York and Lancasters. Hart recalled: 'I said I would not deprive them of the privilege of front place, and arranged that they were to attack abreast, followed by my three battalions... in three successive lines.'[42] Lieutenant Charlton of the Lancashire Fusiliers had never before been in combat. That morning he ate nothing so: '...there would be less chance of a stomach injury proving fatal; so, at least, he had heard somewhere from someone.'[43] Charlton extended his company into a line five paces apart. They lay down in the dark, and awaited the order to advance. As the sky began to lighten, Charlton noticed a curious and sinister sound: 'a sort of mechanical chuckle, accompanied sometimes by a shrill noise overhead.' The sounds came in little spurts and then at intervals from the skyline opposite, and it only gradually dawned on him that these were notes of rifle fire from the Boers, and that the whistle in the air above was a bullet too near for comfort: 'As they moved forward the light of day grew clearer and with it an intensification of those malignant sounds opposite. A few men were hit, though not in his immediate vicinity, and he saw from the corner of his eye that the stretcher-bearers were plying their trade.'[44] Hart's battalions at first marched too far east in the dark, and once it was daylight they moved to the west in line of quarter-columns, as if on parade. Captain Romer of the Dublins disapproved of this display:

> It was a hot day, and the men, who had eaten nothing that morning, suffered some discomfort from such a close formation. The ground, too, was broken and covered with long grass and scrub, so that it was no easy matter to satisfy the General's injunctions in the matter of "dressing." The brigade moved in full view of the enemy and the compact body of men must have been a great temptation to the Boer gunners, who, however, were either not ready or exercised much self-restraint.[45]

---

38   L. Penning, *De Oorlog in Zuid-Afrika* (Rotterdam: Daamen, 2nd edition 1901), p.478.
39   Linesman, *Words by an Eyewitness*, p.42.
40   Wilson, *The Relief of Ladysmith*, p.601.
41   Phipps, *Diary, 1st Border Regiment*.
42   Hart, *Letters*, p.312.
43   Charlton, *Charlton*, p.103.
44   Charlton, *Charlton*, p.104.
45   Romer and Mainwaring, *2nd Royal Dublin Fusiliers in the South African War*, p.48.

After scrambling through Battle Spruit valley, Hart's Brigade halted on Fairview Farm, where Rangeworthy Military Cemetery stands today (GPS -28.65018, 29.46847). They were out of view of the Boers, and relatively safe from overshoots falling nearby. They waited, drinking water from the *spruit* they had crossed, while the artillery on Three Tree Hill bombarded the trenches on Langkop, above Spur 2. At about 11:00 a.m., when the bombardment had been in progress for about 3 hours, the Lancashire Fusiliers and York and Lancasters were ordered to stand up and move forward as the 1st line, the Lancashire Fusiliers on the right. They advanced onto the start of Spur 2, with the Dublins and Borders in the 2nd line and the Inniskillings in support.

Fig 39: The 1st Border Regiment on Tabanyama. Originally captioned 'The Borders below Spion Kop' this shows fighting on Tabanyama. Some men have removed their foreign service helmets to shoot prone. (From *The Border Regiment in South Africa 1899–1902*)

Hart himself led, waving his sword. Captain Henry Jourdain of the Connaught Rangers thought his men: '...were fascinated by the gallant bearing and bravery...' of Hart.[46] At first, as they started up the gradual slope of Spur 2, they were out of sight of the Boers, and the bullets flew overhead. They halted about 2,250 metres from the Boer trenches, forming three attacking lines. The first line, the York and Lancasters and the Lancashire Fusiliers, was itself subdivided into three rows: the firing line, the supports, and the reserves. The firing line, about 300 men,

46   Jourdain, *Ranging Memories,* p.100.

was in extended or 'skirmishing' order, at least 10 paces apart. Behind them came about 300 men in support, slightly closer to each other in a row. Further back were the reserves to the first line. Following them at distances of about 700 metres and 1400 metres were the second and third lines.[47] The second line was itself made up of two rows, 200 metres apart, of the Borders and Dublins, the Dublins on the left. Behind the second line was the third line, the Inniskillings. 'Sandjie' Sandberg was at Botha's side when the attack began:

> That Saturday morning early [20 January], as soon as our furthest forward posts on the ridge came into view, the enemy concentrated the fire from five batteries of field guns, i.e. thirty guns, at one point, while the other …batteries tried to silence our guns. A true storm of shells and shrapnel descended on the doomed spot on the edge of the mountain plateau above the river, and as a persistent rumbling of thunder swept the sound of the bursting, screaming projectiles over it. The ground became red, as if raised by a gust of wind; little dust clouds rose with jerks from the balls that come out of the exploding shrapnel shells. Soon there were several of us injured, and those positions had to be abandoned; they were absolutely untenable. Three times we attempted to re-occupy the abandoned posts; three times we had to give up. And now, in open order they came: - here one; a pace or four or five to his right another; a pace or ten one behind him; next to him on the left still at a considerable distance one; and so on – the khakies walked up the slope, seeking cover whenever possible, or laying flat on the ground shooting, so that even for the sharp eye of a Boer, they temporarily became invisible.[48]

Schikkerling of the Pretoria Commando frankly described how:

> …the minutes preceding a fight, after the enemy comes into view, and until the strife commences, are, for me, full of a nervous excitement. I know it cannot be fear; rather an intense anxiety to begin. Yet, at the same time, no farther from fear than red is from purple, sweet from sour, or tears from laughter. It is one's sense of honour that upholds one, or perhaps, more often, the fear of being called a coward. It is not a clean-cut fear of death so much as a vague terror in the air. I can understand that a nervous man, to be rid of the trial of suspense, would willingly take his own life at such a time.[49]

Hart's First Line Stalls

The Lancashire Fusiliers, on the right of the first line, advanced in skirmishing order, the York and Lancasters parallel with them on their left. As they moved up the slope, the ravine of Battle Spruit limited their extension to the right, and they crowded together. Hart ordered Colonel Blomfield, commanding the Lancashire Fusiliers, to move his men to the left, and during this movement two companies came under severe fire at about 1,400 metres range: 'Six or seven

---

47   H.M.S.O., *Infantry Drill Manual 1896*, p.134.
48   Sandberg, *De Zesdaagsche Slag aan de Boven Tugela*, p.90.
49   Schikkerling, *Commando Courageous*, p.47

Fig 40: Burgher Roland Schikkerling (1880 - 1944) fought to the bitter end with the Pretoria Commando, and wrote *Commando Courageous*. Some Boers like him vowed not to cut their hair until the war was over. (Arnold van Dyk collection)

casualties occurred as they crossed a patch of white flowers, which was evidently a range mark to the enemy.'[50] When they found cover, groups in the first line stopped to shoot, loading their rifles singly from their pouches and saving their eight or ten round magazines for a critical moment. At this distance, they fired in volleys on command, the officers controlling their fire by whistles. Independent fire was kept for 'decisive ranges' of under 450 metres.[51] Behind the first line the Maxim machine guns on their heavy wheeled carriages were dragged up and came into action.[52] Their contribution cannot have been great, as no Boer accounts mention machine gun fire. The Boer artillery remained silent, but a vigorous rifle fire was directed on the skirmishers of the Lancashire Brigade.[53] Without cover, the pace of advance slowed down. Lieutenant Charlton of the Lancashire Fusiliers recalled:

> Before long, owing to the roughness of the surface, to fatigue and faint heart, the line became disordered, and an uncontrollable tendency asserted itself to collect in pockets of the ground for shelter, for breathing space, and for the summoning of resolution for further advance. On the first few occasions the halt was momentary, but the impulse to linger ever grew until finally, as the sense of physical danger overpowered the mental resolve, and as the hills loomed more threateningly ahead, the laggard progress stopped for good and all, and the tired and dispirited attackers longed only for dark.[54]

The York & Lancashires, to the west of the Lancashire Fusiliers, came under intense fire, from Boers about 1,500 metres away. From 1:00 p.m. they could only advance slowly from one small patch of cover to the next, building *schanzes* as they went. Around 2:00 p.m., Hart sent two companies of the York and Lancasters, A company under Captain Cobbold, and B Company under Captain Walshe, to occupy the southern crest of Spur 3, to clear any Boer sharpshooters from his western flank and to give covering fire.

50   Blake Knox, *Buller's Campaign*, p.34.
51   H.M.S.O., *Infantry Drill Manual 1896*, pp.131, 138.
52   Amery, *The War in South Africa*, Vol. III p.232.
53   Anon., *Connaught Rangers Regimental Records*, p.48.
54   Charlton, *Charlton*, p.104.

8

20 January, the Battle of Tabanyama – Afternoon and Evening

'The enemy knew what they were about when they let the British army plant its foot on Taba Myama ridge.' Lieutenant Ernest Blake Knox[1]

Bastion Hill

The capture of Bastion Hill was an entirely separate action, which took place while Hart's advance on Spur 2 was slowing down. Bastion Hill (Spur 5) is very distinctive, and named after its resemblance to an Anglo-Saxon earthwork. It extends 1,000 metres south from Tabanyama, its flat top is 200 metres above the Tugela plain, and its slopes so steep that they provide shelter from riflemen above. Spurs 4 and 5 had been allocated to Hildyard's Brigade, to be attacked when Hart had secured Spur 2. Lasham noted that the Queen's started 'subduing' the crest of Spurs 4 and 5 from Fairview Farm while it was still dark: 'Fire was opened by the battalion (who formed the attacking party) at 3:00 a.m., and from that time up to dusk a continuous fusilade was kept up at the foot of the hill.'[2] Soon after sunrise, the Boers withdrew from the southern crest of Spurs 3, 4 and 5, and evacuated Bastion Hill, taking up positions in their trenches on Platkop and beyond. This line of defence was already well-prepared in all areas except the west (Platkop) but there was nothing but an open plain behind it. If the line were broken anywhere, the Boers would have to withdraw to Ladysmith.

At 5.20 a.m., while Woodgate was taking Spur 1, Warren messaged Dundonald, in triplicate to prevent misunderstandings: 'You must take care that you are not cut off, and must keep touch with the main force' (Appendix III (m)).[3] Dundonald could not disobey this direct order. Leaving the Composite Regiment to guard the Acton Homes road, 500 of Dundonald's mounted men returned to their camp 3km south of Bastion Hill. From there, they could see Hart's advance up Spur 2 and Hildyard's Brigade firing volleys at Spurs 3 and 4. Dundonald and Colonel Julian 'Bungo' Byng of the South African Light Horse were keen to play their part, and discussed attacking Bastion Hill. Atkins reported that Dundonald encouraged Byng: 'Go a little way

---

1   Blake Knox, *Buller's Campaign*, p.47.
2   F. Lasham, *Some Notes on the Queen's Royal West Surrey Regiment, Together with an Account of the 2nd and 3rd Battalions in the late South African Campaign* (Guildford: Privately published, 1904), p.38.
3   Dundonald, *My Army Life*, p.189.

Fig 41: Lieutenant Winston Churchill (1874–1965). After his capture and escape from Pretoria, Churchill returned to the front and enlisted in the SALH, continuing to file stories for the Morning Post. His bespoke uniform has two pockets for his C96 Mauser pistol ammunition, which is under his right arm (he was left-handed). Ostrich feathers have been substituted for the sakabula feather plume of the SALH.

up it. See what sort of place it is and who is there. If it is strongly held, come back; but if it is not, go on, take it, and hold it.'[4] The assault was led by Captain Shepherd's A Squadron, SALH. They rode out from their camp at about 12:30 p.m., at first concealed by the banks of Venter's Spruit and by an Acacia forest (which has since been cut down). Once the horsemen emerged from the forest, the two 75mm Creusots under von Wichmann, still in their positions on the Acton Homes road, began to shell them. The SALH galloped forward and dismounted in a dry tributary of Venter's Spruit, which leads to the foot of Bastion Hill.

Lieutenant Winston Churchill brought up three of the Mounted Brigade's .303 machine guns – the 13th Hussars' Maxim under Lieutenant Clutterbuck, one of Dundonald's 'galloping' Colts under Captain Hill, M.P., and the SALH Maxim, under Major Villiers.

They set them up on the bank of a donga (approx. GPS -28.63934, 29.44839) and opened fire on the skyline at 2,000 metres. Churchill noted how their noise attracted the attention of the Boer gunners, and shell after shell dropped: '…with remarkable accuracy into the wood… another shell fell within a yard of the leader, a moving target at 7,000 yards showing the accuracy of the enemy's fire.'[5] At 1:00 p.m. Hildyard ordered the Queen's to advance from Venter's Spruit to support the SALH attack. Lieutenant Wedd described how A Company, the Queen's, waded waist deep through Venter's Spruit towards Bastion Hill then: '…lay down to watch the Cavalry [SALH] being shelled.'[6]

4   Atkins, *The Relief of Ladysmith*, p.229.
5   Churchill, *London to Ladysmith via Pretoria*, p.322.
6   Wedd, *Letter*.

Fig 42: Captain Hill M.P. and his Colt machine gun. Captain Hill was in charge of four Colt Model 1895 machine guns, mounted on Dundonald's patented 'galloping carriages'. Warren had 14 Vickers-Maxim and Colt machine guns, but they over-heated and their carriages were cumbersome. The wheel of this carriage has already had three spokes repaired. (Arnold van Dyk collection)

As the SALH, now on foot, reached Bastion Hill, Atkins wrote: '...they drew open like a fan into their line of advance'[7] and began scaling the steep slope.

Colonel Pink of the Queen's was speaking to Colonel Thorneycroft when they noticed the SALH climbing Bastion Hill. Thorneycroft rushed his Mounted Infantry forward while Colonel Pink took F, G and H Companies of the Queen's to the base of Bastion Hill, and their fire drove the last few Boer riflemen from the skyline of Spurs 3, 4, and 5. Lieutenant Claude 'Shruby' Du Boisson had a lucky escape when a Mauser bullet struck his pocket knife, as Wedd saw: 'The knife was shattered and the small blade was missing, believed to have gone with the bullet into this thigh. Luckily it had not hit a bone or artery...'[8] The Boers were by now further back on Platkop, away from the southern crest, so the SALH climbed unseen. Atkins watched Trooper Tobin lead the way: 'Up he went hand over hand, up an ascent like the slope of a bell-tent. Everyone who watched held his breath for a man to fall – not from the steepness, but from a bullet. Ten minutes before all the others he reached the top...'[9] The crest of Bastion

7   Atkins, *The Relief of Ladysmith*, p.229.
8   Wedd, *Letter*.
9   Atkins, *The Relief of Ladysmith*, p.230.

Fig 43: Bastion Hill. Modern photograph, looking north from 19th and 28th Batteries' positions.
Bastion Hill is on the skyline; the SALH advanced on foot up the donga from the left of this picture,
and set up their machine guns on the lip of the donga.

Hill was being swept from the south by the Colts and supporting squadrons of SALH, and from the east by TMI and the Queen's.[10] At 2:50 pm Tobin was on the summit, and waved his *Sakabula*-plumed hat upon his rifle to signal those below to divert their fire from the summit.

Lord Tullibardine said to Atkins the next day: 'No Boer was there, and the hill in a few minutes was ours... It was splendid to watch. It was a V.C. thing, and yet, if you know what I mean, it wasn't.'[11] Tobin was erroneously reported to have been killed by a shell the next day; he was uninjured and was awarded the Distinguished Conduct Medal. The flat top of Bastion Hill proved a very dangerous place, as it was overlooked by Platkop, 1.5km away and 30 metres higher, and soon came under shell fire from von Wichmann's Creusots. *Veldkornet* Kemp of the Krugersdorp Commando observed: 'Bastion Hill was occupied by the enemy, a position that we regarded as unimportant, as it extended too far, and those on it could easily be cut off. Here the enemy was exposed to our fire.'[12] Thorneycroft's Mounted Infantry and A and C Squadrons 13th Hussars occupied the eastern slopes, keeping below the crest and away from the western

10   Dundonald, *My Army Life*, p.187.
11   Atkins, *The Relief of Ladysmith*, p.230.
12   Kemp, *Vir Vryheid en vir Reg*, p.277.

Fig 44: Trooper Tobin, SALH, signals from the summit of Bastion Hill. (*With the Flag to Pretoria*)

slope which was exposed to Platkop.[13] Corporal Smith and Private Servey, the signallers of 13th Hussars, tried sending semaphore messages from the summit of Bastion Hill but came under intense fire. Servey's signal flag had seven bullet holes through it; he was awarded the Distinguished Conduct Medal for his plucky behaviour under fire.[14] Later that afternoon, Major Charles Childe, SALH, was sitting on the summit, partly sheltered by rocks, when one of von Wichmann's shells struck. Dundonald had been with Childe, but had left him for a few minutes to explore the summit. On his return, he found Childe dead with blood pouring: 'from a fearful wound in his head.'[15] Kemp saw the fatal shell explode:

> The first couple of shells which we aimed at the Kop were over-shoots. They were, however, followed by one that burst on the Kop. Now our artillerymen had the range and fired a timed shell which exploded neatly behind the enemy schanzes, and wounded

13   Tremayne, *XIII. Hussars South African War*, p.12.
14   Dundonald, *My Army Life*, p.191.
15   Dundonald, *My Army Life*, p.190.

half a dozen men and killed Maj. Childe, their officer. Theoretically, the enemy won ground that day, but the occupied positions were only exposed to more of our fire.[16]

Childe was carried under fire down Bastion Hill by Surgeon-Major Hind, and bearers Burgess, Maddox, Penfold, and Phister of the Queen's.[17] Dundonald had been at school with Childe and that night read the burial service, recalling: '...we buried him close to a field of Indian corn. His men buried him affectionately and reverently in his clothes just as he was...'[18] The *Daily Telegraph* reporter wrote: 'there were sobs and tears in that sad last farewell.'[19] Childe had come out of retirement to fight in South Africa, and the night before he had confided to his comrades a premonition of his death. He asked them, as a favour, to put on his grave the epitaph 'Is it well with the child?... It is well.' (2 Kings iv. 26.)[20] Childe was buried near the Mounted Brigade camp (GPS -28.6592, 29.4364) and later reinterred at Rangeworthy Military Cemetery.

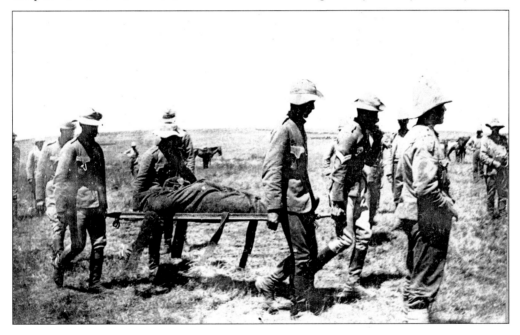

Fig 45: A wounded soldier is carried down from Tabanyama by four men of a bearer company. (National Army Museum)

16   Kemp, *Vir Vryheid en vir Reg*, p.277.
17   Blake Knox, *Buller's Campaign*, p.38.
18   Dundonald, *My Army Life*, p.191.
19   Burleigh, *The Natal Campaign*, p.317.
20   Burleigh, *The Natal Campaign*, p.317.

The Afternoon on Spur 2

A and B Companies of the York and Lancasters had occupied Spur 3, while the remainder of their battalion formed the eastern half of the first line on Spur 2. At 2:00 p.m., E Company, under Major Scholes, stood up to advance, followed by the remaining companies. Lieutenant Kearsey, of the same battalion, extended his firing line to 10 paces between the men, and they doubled forward from place to place of shelter. They got under cover about 1,000 metres from the enemy, when they were ordered to lie down and fire at the skyline. He wrote: 'Firing at an invisible enemy seemed tame, but the request for permission to charge was met by an order to advance no further.' There was so little cover that the York and Lancasters were packed six deep on the kopje, and suffered severely. As the first line slowed down, the second line – the Dublins on the left and Borders on the right – closed up with them. The first line had fortified their koppies, and when the second line came up, the first line advanced to the koppies beyond and fortified them, as Lieutenant Kearsey described: 'This kopje then became very crowded, and it seemed to afford but slender cover from the enemy, who, attracted by the bigger target, now gave it their special attention.'[21] Kearsey could see no Boers: '...though the effect of their fire was very telling... and though we could not see them it was good to be able to fire at the hills, which the guns were shelling and where we hoped the Boers were lurking.'[22] Lieutenant Brandreth, Private Savage and Lance Corporal Grove carried away wounded men under fire, Grove himself already being wounded. Further advance seemed impossible – the first line was thoroughly pinned down. Behind them, the Borders and Dublins fired over their heads, Lieutenant Kearsey noting: 'The volleys of our men sounded as if their bullets were coming very close to us, and the Boers, when not employed in answering, filled in their spare time in trying to finish us off.'[23] Private Phipps of the Borders ran to warn his comrades that their fire was endangering the firing line. As he ran back, he: '...realised the meaning of having a place marked, for on my crossing a piece of ground which had a rock on it, the bullets fairly rained about me, but fortunately I did not get hit. I delivered my message all right and started to return when a bullet hit me in the leg...'[24] Wounded men lay where they were till dark, as it was too dangerous to retrieve them. Lieutenant Kearsey was hit at about 4:00 p.m. The bullet struck his ammunition pouch, entered below his left breast and exited beneath his right collar bone. He wrote: '...we were told to advance although only 1,000 yards from the position & on to an absolutely open plain with no cover... of course our advance drew a tremendous fire & before we had gone 300 yards most of us were shot down...'[25] Lieutenant Kearsey lay among the wounded:

> Most of us were lying out wounded, and those who had escaped were occupied in looking after their disabled comrades. The sun, which had burnt us all the morning, was obscured by clouds during the afternoon and sharp showers ensued. At night it

21   Kearsey, *War Record of the York & Lancasters*, p.14–15.
22   Kearsey, *War Record of the York & Lancasters*, p.17.
23   Kearsey, *War Record of the York & Lancasters*, p.18.
24   Phipps, *Diary, 1st Border Regiment*.
25   Alec. H. C. Kearsey, *Letter dated 29 January 1900*, National Army Museum 1999-12-15.

was very cold, especially so for those who could not move, and who were weak from loss of blood.[26]

Colour Sergeant Stewart stayed with Lieutenant Kearsey until darkness came, and then went for a stretcher.

Hart's Second Line Advances

With the first line, the Lancashire Fusiliers and York and Lancasters, pinned down, Hart himself led the second line. This consisted of the right half-battalions of the Borders and Dublins, the Borders being on the right. It was followed at a distance of about 200 metres by the left half-battalions.[27] Hart disregarded the rule about swords, which was, as Davis noted: 'with this column every one, under the rank of general, carries a rifle...'[28] Burleigh saw Hart lead his men: '...in rather close formation...' with his sword drawn.[29] When they reached the first line, the Dublins and Borders marched straight through them. Private Phipps of the Borders recalled this with pride:

> It was thought the enemy were not in strong force but on commencing the attack we were soon undeceived. They were in exceptional numbers & also had splendid cover amongst the rock at the top of the hills... We commenced advancing in extended order and on leaving the cover, we realized what a stiff job lay in front of us... The valley we had to advance over was practically devoid of cover with the exception of a small hill about five hundred yds away. Our firing line consisted of the Lancashire Fusiliers & the York & Lancasters. The Dublin Fusiliers & the Border Regt. was supports, with the Inniskillings in reserve. As soon as we started to advance the bullets began to fly, but we took no notice of this; when, imagine our surprise to see our firing line cuddled up in a heap behind the small hill I have mentioned. When we got to them we could plainly see they were in a state of blue funk, the officers were as bad or worse than the men. Our men indignantly told them what they thought about their action, & after a lot of persuasion (one way or another) they commenced to advance like a pack of frightened sheep. All of a sudden an automatic Maxim Nordenfeldt [pom-pom] began to play upon us. That stopped the firing line, for flat on their faces they fell & devil of a move would they make at all. Then the effects of discipline was exhibited. Our officers, equal to any emergency shouted, "advance & leave the cowards there", and to a man the Dubs & Borders responded, walking along like men on parade... Our men began to fall rapidly now, being only eight hundred yards from the [Boer] position... We commenced blazing away at the rocks we knew the Boers lay hidden behind. The General [Hart] gave us orders to hold the place where we were...[30]

26   Kearsey, *War Record of the York & Lancasters*, p.18.
27   Romer and Mainwaring, *2nd Royal Dublin Fusiliers in the South African War*, p.48.
28   Davis, *Notes of a War Correspondent*, p.149.
29   Burleigh, *The Natal Campaign*, p.314.
30   Phipps, *Diary, 1st Border Regiment*.

The koppie behind which the first line huddled is likely at GPS -28.64195, 29.47823.

Hart led the Borders on the right, while Colonel Cooper led the Dublins on the left.[31] Captain Charles Hensley of the Dublins knew: '...they must advance in open order formation, take advantage of all cover, and fire independently when they could see anything to fire at.'[32] Soon five men of the Dublins were killed, including Captain Hensley and Lance-Sergeant Taylor; and 20 were wounded including Major English.[33] Hensley was sorely missed. A Canadian, he had recently married Agnes Wylde of Pietermaritzburg. Churchill praised him: '...one of the smallest and bravest men in the Army.'[34] Hensley had observed, after Colenso: 'I have come to the conclusion that men are just like sheep; where one goes – especially in time of fright – the rest will follow'[35] but despite their extraordinary courage, by late afternoon all of Hart's Brigade were pinned down behind rocks. Men were getting hit at random, because the Boer position on Langkop formed a crescent around them. Lieutenant Charlton saw one of his Lancashires Fusiliers killed while sitting behind a rock:

> Suddenly, for no apparent reason, a dark blue spot appeared in the centre of his forehead. An expression of utter bewilderment passed across the man's face, and he was seized with a slight shivering. The next instant death came.[36]

At 5.30 p.m. Captain Woolley-Dod of the Lancashire Fusiliers was hit in the hand but he continued in action until dark, and was back in the firing line the next day.

Private Sprague of the Borders felt advancing through the zone of fire was: '...like being out in the rain, the bullets whistling uncomfortably past our ears and giving you the sensation of having upset a beehive.' When he reached cover, Sprague took careful notice of every man's face near him: '...each one bore the same resolute expression, pale, and with eyes brighter than usual with excitement, the only way one could see they were affected by what was going on... I went through it all as one in a dream, knowing nothing of fear or nervousness, and my brave comrades were all the same.'[37]

Now in the front, the Dublins and Borders still had 1,000 metres of open ground between them and the Boer trenches on Langkop. The intensity of rifle fire can be deduced from Surgeon George Makins' observation: 'On the top of Tabanyama... the whole ground was littered... at the time of my visit with shattered mantles [the steel jackets of Mauser bullets] and leaden cores, deformed almost past recognition.'[38]

31   Amery, *The War in South Africa*, Vol. III, p.232
32   Charles A. Hensley, 'Letters of Capt. C.A. Hensley to his Father,' *Military History Journal, The South African Military History Society*, Vol.6 No.6, December 1985.
33   Romer and Mainwaring, *2nd Royal Dublin Fusiliers in the South African War*, p.48.
34   Churchill, *London to Ladysmith via Pretoria*, p.331.
35   Hensley, *Letters*.
36   Charlton, *Charlton*, p.105.
37   Aubrey Sprague, Letter to his father of 27 January 1900, *The Smethwick Telegraph*, 31 March 1900.
38   Makins, *Surgical Experiences in South Africa*, p.89.

The Boer Heroes of Platkop

During the afternoon of 20 January, a remarkable episode took place which became an Afrikaner legend. It happened during the afternoon, after the SALH had taken Bastion Hill. Hart's men, pinned down, requested permission for a bayonet charge. Clery denied this request, thinking they might be cut off by a commando of 500 Boers on their left.[39] In fact, there was no such commando. The firing from the west, from Platkop, came from just three Boers: Hendrik 'Henri' Slegtkamp, Oliver 'Jack' Hindon and Albert de Roos. Hindon, a Scotsman, had joined the British Army as a drummer at the age of 14, and after later being sent to Zululand, he had deserted. He gained Transvaal citizenship after fighting Jameson's Raiders. He had served with the Middelburg Commando, then the *Zuid Afrikaansche Republiek Politie* (ZARP) and was now serving on the Upper Tugela with Edwards' *Verkenner Korps*. Hindon later specialised in train wrecking. Albert de Roos was a Hollander, as was Slegtkamp, and they had both served in the Middelburg Commando before joining Edwards' *Verkenner Korps*.

When Bastion Hill fell to the SALH, the defences on Platkop were still incomplete. Under bombardment from Three Tree Hill, the Middelburgers on Platkop under General Christiaan Fourie fell back, leaving a gap on the Boer western flank. Slegtkamp, Hindon and de Roos arrived as reinforcements. They dismounted behind Tabanyama and climbed the reverse slope of Platkop. There they spoke to General Fourie and *Veldkornet* Johann Vercueil, who were trying to rally the Middelburgers. Vercueil said: 'I can't take anymore, I don't see a way to get the burghers to make a stand.' The three scouts called for volunteers, and a group of about 20 came forward. They all began climbing, but by the time they reached the summit of Platkop, only Hindon, de Roos and Slegtkamp

Fig 46: Hendrik Slegtkamp (1873–1951), a hero of Platkop, kept this photograph in his wallet. He holds the homemade *vyfkleur* unity flag. (Courtesy Henk Loots)

39   Burleigh, *The Natal Campaign*, p.317.

remained.[40][41] Hindon carried with him a 'unity flag' which his girlfriend had sewn. It was the Transvaal flag, known as the *Vierkleur* (four-colour), with a diagonal orange stripe added to represent the Orange Free State becoming a *vyfkleur*.

They suspended this flag prominently on a discarded rifle, to simulate a Commando headquarters. Hindon noticed that the stock of the Mauser was beautifully carved with the Boer surname 'Buitendag'.[42] With their flag flying, the three scouts then crept forward to reconnoitre the ravine south of Platkop (GPS -28.62296, 29.46802). Seeing no British approaching, they returned to the Platkop *schanzes*, where they moved about and fired furiously, so as to give the impression of a large force.[43] The ruse succeeded, as the Inniskillings recorded: 'Hart ... was on the point of ordering [his men] to close and sweep the enemy from the hill when a peremptory message arrived from General Clery to stop all further advance.'[44] The artillery turned their guns to face Platkop, which was at the limit of shrapnel range, and shelled the target with shrapnel for half an hour.[45] Sandberg, standing near Louis Botha on Langkop, described the scene:

> Some British had already reached the plateau [Bastion Hill]; the enemy cannons hadn't bombarded that point for a while, then suddenly with renewed anger the storm burst forth, though against a position, about a few hundred yards to the right of the position we had abandoned... For a long time we could not determine the target the enemy had chosen: we had, we believed, entirely abandoned that spot. Suddenly a rider approached the General at high speed on his horse and breathlessly called out "General, general! look there!" "What is it?" asked Botha. "General, the cheeky English are already on top of that kop and they've planted their flag, look right in front of us; why should we just look at that? Let's shoot it to ribbons because that's really taunting us." The messenger sat on his horse pointing with his arm outstretched. The General peered through his binoculars, and from those around came exclamations of "yes", "that's right", "there it is". "No chaps, that's not an English flag." "Yes, look at it," "Can you not see?" they interrupted each other. The whole group was agitated. "But chaps, can't you see that isn't the English flag," says the General calmly now, the binoculars still in front of his eyes: "That's our flag, I can see it clearly!"[46]

Botha initially wondered if the enemy had captured a Boer battle flag, then dismissed that possibility; this flag was clearly the target of British artillery.

> For more than half an hour our Vierkleur flapped proudly, under a shower of enemy bullets; only then was she taken down. The enemy did not advance further as long as

40   Mostert, *Slegtkamp van Spioenkop*, p.34.
41   Gustav S. Preller, *Kaptein Hindon – Oorlogsavontuur van ń Baasverkenner* (Nasionale Pers, Cape Town. 1942), p.82.
42   Preller, *Hindon*, p.84.
43   Kestell, *Through Shot and Flame*, p.60. Preller, *Hindon*, p.82.
44   Inniskillings, *The Royal Inniskilling Fusiliers*, p.419.
45   Sandberg, *De Zesdaagsche Slag aan de Boven Tugela*, p.92.
46   Sandberg, *De Zesdaagsche Slag aan de Boven Tugela*, pp.90–91.

she flew; when she disappeared there commenced almost simultaneously a deafening bombardment. After about twenty minutes the news quickly spread among our men that in the position where the flag flew, three, just three, men were lying; they remained in position when the others were forced to evacuate. And as soon as the Englishmen appeared on the plateau, the three welcomed them with such a fierce, well-maintained and well-directed fire that they suddenly came to a stop. All their guns and Maxims were aimed at them, but they never dared to advance before that flag disappeared and the firing stopped. And the firing ceased and the flag disappeared when these three brave warriors ran out of cartridges. Then they returned under cover, back to our lines.[47]

Slegtkamp himself recalled: 'Us three men, who were just five yards apart, couldn't see each other at all because of the dust. Only at intervals could we shout to each other... and so it went on for a full half hour. Then the bombardment subsided.'[48]

Fig 47: Heroes of Platkop. After the battle, Slegtkamp (Left), Hindon (Centre) and de Roos (Right) re-enacted their heroism for the photographer. (Courtesy of Neville Constantine)

47   Sandberg, *De Zesdaagsche Slag aan de Boven Tugela*, p.91.
48   Mostert, *Slegtkamp van Spioenkop*, p.35.

Fig 48: Major Jan Francois Wolmarans (1873–1929) commanded the Boer artillery on the Upper Tugela, from Botha's HQ near Spioenkop. (Transvaal Archives)

Kestell recalled that, while Slegtkamp and his comrades were holding the position, two of Fourie's burghers, Smit and Du Toit '...went to acquaint General Botha with the state of affairs... General Botha once more persuaded the burghers to return to their positions; and the English did not approach any nearer there.'[49]

The pause in the British advance gave Major Jan Francois Wolmarans of the *Staatsartillerie* an opportunity to position a pom-pom behind Langkop.

Kemp said:

When the ... pom-pom started pumping, the brave three returned intact to their commando. If then the enemy knew how unprotected and poorly defended that koppie was, they would surely have charged and taken it; and if they did, then our right flank would have been in a bad position, and the enemy could have taken the road, exposed us to a heavy flank attack, taken Tabanyama, and trapped us on Spioenkop.'[50]

According to Penning and Preller, the three Boer heroes were congratulated by General Botha: '*Fluks gedaan, jongens!*' (Well done, lads!)[51] and Fourie's men reoccupied their positions on Platkop during the late afternoon.[52]

Boer Artillery Comes Into Action

At 1:15 p.m. two Boer field guns opened fire towards Three Tree Hill, scattering the spectators. Captain Grant described Boer shells: 'A high whistle, like an escape of gas in the air, a heavy thud upon the ground... an appalling crash and a leap into the air of clods of earth, and a whirring and groaning of fragments of jagged iron, these were the signs amidst which the faint

49   Kestell, *Through Shot and Flame*, p.60.
50   Kemp, *Vir Vryheid en vir Reg,* pp.278–279.
51   Penning, *De Oorlog in Zuid-Afrika,* p.479.
52   Preller, *Hindon*, p.84.

boom of the gun responsible for them was almost unnoticed.'[53] One of the first shrapnel shells caused half a dozen casualties.[54] For 20 minutes Wolmarans bombarded the British batteries, and then turned his attention to Hart's advance, raking the assaulting lines with pom-poms and bursting their shrapnel accurately among them. The gun positions moved from time to time to avoid counter-battery fire. The effect of the artillery and the rifle fire on Spur 2 caused the advancing second line, by then in advance of the first line, to swing round to the east, into the shelter of the deep valley of Battle Spruit.

Captain Grant wrote that, about 3:00 p.m., Hart's force:

> ...rushed the two right gorges [the ravines of Battle Spruit] with a dash that was positively startling in its unexpectedness. The artillery preparation was a mere form. There was a hasty bang, bang, bang, from the artillery position on Three Tree Hill, a terrified crackle of musketry from the occupants of the re-entrant, and up from the shadows burst the Irish and North-Countrymen with a typhoon of yells... a tremendous fire broke out from the ridge behind, as the cheering soldiers flowed over the level above the re-entrants. The foremost men fell in heaps, the rearmost were stopped, as all should have been stopped, at the crest-line. "Thus far, and no farther,' sang the Mausers.[55]

At 3:15 p.m. a 75mm *Staatsartillerie* Krupp under Lieutenant Heinrich Grothaus, sited behind Tabanyama, came into action, soon joined by a pom-pom. At 5:00 p.m. two 75mm Creusots under Lieutenant von Wichmann began firing from the Acton Homes road to the west, and Captain Grant noted: 'The ground in front of Hart soon becomes a whirlwind of dust as the shrapnel beats upon it.'[56] The artillery fire killed Driver Beaseley of the 63rd Battery, and 9 horses were hit.[57] The Boer guns behind the ridge could neither see, nor be seen by, the British gunners; their fire was directed by forward artillery observers with heliographs. The British batteries which had been in action since the morning had fired on an average about 450 rounds apiece.[58] During the afternoon, Lieutenant Blake Knox observed the Royal Lancasters, nonchalant on the reverse slope of Three Tree Hill:

> [With] a perfect hail of bullets whistling over... Some, those on the crest, were firing their rifles from behind lightly-constructed sangars; others, lying below the crest in the blazing sun, were playing cards, smoking, and chaffing each other. Occasionally one would rise and walk up to the crest line, and, though warned, recklessly expose himself to the full view of the enemy, for no other reason than to see what was going on... I saw a sergeant walk up with a canteen of tea in his hand; while standing up there, open to

53   Linesman, *Words by an Eyewitness*, p.8.
54   Blake Knox, *Buller's Campaign*, p.35.
55   Linesman, *Words by an Eyewitness*, p.41.
56   Linesman, *Words by an Eyewitness*, p.42.
57   Anon, *63rd Battery Digest of Service 1900*.
58   Anon, *63rd Battery Digest of Service 1900*.

the aim of hostile marksmen, not 2,000 yards away, he was shot through his stomach when in the act of finishing his drink. This unfortunate man died that evening.[59]

Late Afternoon

After the SALH had taken Bastion Hill, a 1.5km section of the Tabanyama southern crest still remained unoccupied, namely Spur 4 and the isthmus of Spur 5. Spur 3, around 2:00 p.m., had been taken by A and B Companies of the York and Lancasters. At 5:00 p.m. the West Yorks scaled the steep slope of Spur 4 under shell fire, but they found no Boers remained on the southern crest. Captain Mansel Jones, West Yorks, was leading D Company when a shell burst just in front of the right-hand man, scattering shrapnel, but fortunately, nobody was hit. Once on the crest, they built *schanzes* and maintained a vigorous fire, which gradually died away as the light failed.

Fig 49: Infantrymen among rocks on Tabanyama. They shoot their Lee-Metford Mk 1* rifles with rear sights set to about 1,100 yards. Three of the men have reversed their helmets to get the low brim out of their eyes. (Cape Archives)

59   Blake Knox, *Buller's Campaign*, pp.43–44.

When darkness came, the Queen's rushed the crest between Spur 4 and 5, completing the British line.[60] The men behind the firing line built shelters on the steep slope of Tabanyama, among them Private O'Mahony: '…in the very wet night every man built for himself a sangar of stones with front and side walls, and lived as it were in 'his own castle.' … At Rangeworthy [Tabanyama] we [made sangars with] a front and two complete sides… a semi-circle.'[61]

Lieutenant Blake Knox recalled: '[The] continuous swish of bullets passing overhead forbade any further advance. Most of the enemy's shells either failed to burst or passed over into the valley… the gorges under the steep crest were literally packed with the battalions who were acting as supports. Fortunately, these were not visible to the enemy.'[62] O'Mahony wrote that on the crest line: '…it was a dangerous matter to stand up even for a minute. Stone sangars were built and the companies relieved each other by the men crawling up the slope… When not in the firing line, we lay behind the slope in column, each company being protected by a parapet of earth or stone.'[63]

Fig 50: Soldiers firing from *schanzes* on the crest of Tabanyama. The nearest soldier has his rear sight leaf elevated for long range, and has reversed his helmet. (Davitt, *The Boer Fight for Freedom*)

60   Lasham, *Notes on the Queen's Royal West Surrey Regiment*, p.38.
61   O'Mahony, *A Peep Over the Barleycorn*, p.142.
62   Blake Knox, *Buller's Campaign*, p.37.
63   Romer and Mainwaring, *2nd Royal Dublin Fusiliers in the South African War*, p.51.

A storm broke at about 4:00 p.m.[64] and further British advance on Spur 2 was suspended around 4:30 p.m. When night came, five and a half companies of the Border Regiment under Captain Bellamy, and about 100 men of the Dublin Fusiliers, remained far in advance of the rest of the line. They sheltered in a Y-shaped ravine at the head of Battle Spruit, directly below the Boers on Langkop, only 800 metres away (GPS -28.63308, 29.48838). Captain Bellamy requested permission to attack at night, but this was declined.

Captain Grant reflected on the day's fighting from his bivouac at Venter's Spruit:

> '...the crest-line is ours, and our men cling to it all night, whilst the [grass] fire in front of them burns fiercely, and we of the reserve brigade lie chilly out on picket behind the newly won position, watching the red glow in the sky, and wondering who has been killed, and what the morrow will bring forth. Up on the hill-side all is comparatively quiet; only an occasional flare of musketry shows how many pairs of eyes and ears are straining through the darkness watching for the slightest movement, all alert even at the rustling of the grass-tufts in the fitful night-wind. It is a lifetime, that clinging to a position won at nightfall throughout the night... there was no movement on either side... the only sleepers were the British dead, which lay like seaweed marking the high tide-line of Hart's onset, and the poor charred corpses of the Boers lying hideously on the burnt black grass.'[65]

Casualties

Lieutenant Blake Knox set up his dressing station in a recess near Battle Spruit, behind Three Tree Hill. In the operating tent of the 11th Brigade bearer company, the wounds were examined and the field dressings checked. The wounded were given Bovril, coffee, and something to eat; the badly injured got hypodermic injections of strychnine as a stimulant, or morphine if they were in pain. No operations were done there, owing to the close proximity of the 11th Brigade Field Hospital, under Major Moir. As Lieutenant Blake Knox recorded: 'Major Moir had commandeered the entire buildings of the deserted spacious homestead known as Coventry's Farm on the 19th, and had set up his full complement of tents in the surrounding grounds...' Lieutenant Blake Knox found the surgeons extremely busy: '...as General Hart's wounded were also arriving at the time'[66]

The day after being hit, the seriously wounded were sent to No.4 Stationary Hospital at Spearman's Farm, which as Lieutenant Kearsey experienced, was an 8km journey: '...along roads that were not roads, and in an ambulance wagon without springs, so that the jolting caused the wounds to open afresh.'[67]

Private Phipps of the Borders was shot in the leg that day:

---

64   Burleigh, *The Natal Campaign*, p.319.
65   Linesman, *Words by an Eyewitness*, p.43.
66   Blake Knox, *Buller's Campaign*, p.45.
67   Kearsey, *War Record of the York & Lancasters*, pp.18–19.

Fig 51: Wounded being brought to ambulance wagons. The photograph was taken on the site of the Rangeworthy Military Cemetery (GPS: -28.65018, 29.46849). Bastion Hill is on the skyline, and stretcher-bearers carry a casualty to ambulance carts, which will take him to No.4 Stationary Hospital at Spearman's Farm. (*Black and White Budget*)

> Never in my life shall I forget the ride. We were put on trek wagons and had to come over very rough ground for 5 miles. The jolting of the wagon affected the wounds and half suppressed shrieks issued from our lips at every jolt. One poor fellow next to me had his leg splintered by a shell; big tears streamed down his face with the agony which he was undergoing, but never a complaint passed his lips.[68]

The wagons stopped at the halfway point to allow the wounded refreshments. Some who succumbed on the journey were buried beside the track. Private O'Mahony of the West Yorks described the 'Body Snatchers' bringing the wounded from the battlefield:

> Occasionally someone came down and the shout went up: pass the word for the stretcher-bearers. The civilian stretcher corps located a few hundred yards down the hill approached the wounded man, in the firing line or out of it, carrying a large white flag with a red cross in the centre. There were four bearers to a stretcher, and a leader

68   Phipps, *Diary, 1st Border Regiment.*

who carried the flag. The flag, though meant as a signal to the enemy to cease fire, had always an opposite effect... Getting wounded soldiers away is, and always will be, a difficult puzzle where quick-firing rifles are engaged. It is indeed a ticklish job...'[69]

Night of 20 January 1900

By nightfall on the British occupied the whole zigzag southern crest of Tabanyama, a front of 7km. One or two companies of each battalion formed the firing line, peeping across the plateau. The remaining six or seven companies sheltered on the steep slopes, below the arc of Boer shells and bullets.

Warren reflected: 'After fighting for twelve hours we were in possession of the whole part of the hills, but found a strongly intrenched line on the comparatively flat country before us.'[70] When Buller rode over to see Warren that evening, he seemed satisfied – though later he would re-interpret the day as one of missed opportunities, seemingly unaware of the failed march west the previous day:

> [Warren] had that day attacked the salient and taken it, but instead of supporting Lord Dundonald, he had induced him to fall back from the position which he had occupied on the 19th... General Warren was evidently not carrying out the orders which he had received from me, and in which he had signified his full concurrence. I saw, for my own part, that the advantages for which I had hoped from his crossing had been let slip, and that my own plan of operations had been hopelessly wrecked... It was possible that Warren might work more kindly for a plan of his own than he had worked for mine... In any event, whether successful or not, the troops would spend some little time under fire in fairly close contact with the enemy, and would thus gain comparatively cheaply that battle training in which I knew them most deficient.'[71]

Hart was, predictably, annoyed at being restrained from charging the Boers; he proudly named Spur 2 as '20th Hill' and Spurs 3 & 4 as 'Hart's Hill', but the names didn't catch on. Hart recalled his losses without flinching: 'I fought on the 20th, and took a strong hill position successfully from the Boers at a cost of 365 officers and men... I was sent repeatedly positive orders not to advance without orders on any account, but simply to hold my ground. I did so.'[72]

The Boer guns ceased firing around 7:30 p.m.[73]

Dr Maxwell, with the Ermelo Commando Ambulance behind Tabanyama, wrote in his diary:

> The English have got on to the ridge, and have put up schanzes all along it, and at some points are only eight hundred to nine hundred yards from our trenches. Our

69   O'Mahony, *A Peep Over the Barleycorn*, p.148.
70   Kearsey, *War Record of the York & Lancasters*, p.15.
71   Commission into the War in South Africa, Vol. II, p.178.
72   Hart, *Letters*, p.311.
73   Blake Knox, *Buller's Campaign*, p.45.

men are beginning to get very jumpy and nervous, as their trenches are lying mostly in open rolling country, and, according to many of the Burghers, could be rushed. There has been continuous rifle fire from the various schanzes and trenches all day. Two Ermelo men have been killed and five wounded. Total Boer casualties up there [on Tabanyama], so far, are sixty. The English artillery is magnificent, so much so that our guns can only be worked at intervals.'[74]

Lieutenant Blake Knox: 'With bursts and lulls the battle continued until it dropped to sleep about sunset.'[75] In the dark, small groups of men, including those wounded on the plateau, withdrew to the southern crest. About 8:00 p.m. the men received tinned rations; some, like Wedd, also had 'an odd bit of biscuit' in their haversacks.[76][77] The cooks set up field kitchens in the ravines between the Spurs, though usually the men had tinned food, and, as Lieutenant Kearsey noted: '...an issue of rum being served out to do duty for both food and drink.'[78] The gunners on Three Tree Hill slept by their guns. The Dublins and Borders remained in the Y-ravine of Battle Spruit, received rations at 8:00 p.m., and slept where they were.[79]

It had been Lieutenant Charlton's first day in action; for him it had been like a waking dream or sleepwalking, from which he emerged at intervals into consciousness. The whole thing, he felt, was unreal: '...it was not he who had been present under that glaring sun, striving to reach the hill crest ahead. Certain scattered incidents lodged themselves in his brain, but time had ceased to operate as normal.'[80] The Lancashire Fusiliers withdrew in little groups when it got dark. When they returned to their starting-point near Venter's Spruit, which they had left before dawn, they threw themselves down and slept. Mounted picquets protected both flanks against a Boer night attack – the Composite Regiment in the west, and the Royal Dragoons in the east. All night the Boers' *brandwagte* stayed on the alert, fearing a night attack, and firing into the dark.[81] The Inniskillings noted the Boers: '...worked feverishly at [their] entrenchments on the true crest, over which [they] frequently burst star shell.'[82] Star shells burnt a magnesium compound, brightly illuminating the plateau for a few seconds.

Potgieter's Drift, 20 January

During the afternoon, General Lyttelton's force at Potgieter's Drift made another feint attack. The 61st Battery (howitzers) and the naval guns covered the advance, while Bethune's Mounted Infantry protected the eastern flank. About 3:00 p.m. the balloon of No.2 Balloon Section, Royal Engineers, ascended to survey the Boer trenches, Captain Phillips in the observation basket. The balloon was hit in several places and slowly began to leak gas, and Phillips was

74 'Defender', *Sir Charles Warren and Spion Kop*, p.121.
75 Burleigh, *The Natal Campaign*, p.317.
76 Anon., *Connaught Rangers Regimental Records*, p.49.
77 Wedd, *Letter*.
78 Kearsey, *War Record of the York & Lancasters*, p.14—15.
79 Romer and Mainwaring, *2nd Royal Dublin Fusiliers in the South African War*, p.49.
80 Charlton, *Charlton*, p.105–106.
81 Nicholas Riall, *Boer War: The Letters, Diaries and Photographs of Malcolm Riall from the War in South Africa 1899–1902* (London, Brassey's, 2000), p.4.
82 Inniskillings, *The Royal Inniskilling Fusiliers*, p.420.

Fig 52: Star shells. To reveal a night attack, both British and the Boer gunners frequently fired magnesium shells to light up the battlefield for a few seconds. The Boer photographer has enhanced the effect on this photograph. (Cape Archives)

grazed in the forehead by a bullet.[83] The Bishop of Natal overheard the telephone conversation between Phillips and his ground crew:

> "Why don't you move the cart to the east? I can't see over this hill, and I am getting horribly sea-sick."
> "If you are sea-sick, why don't you go to the leeward of the balloon instead of leaning over this way? Or better still, why don't you come down and let me go up?"
> "Here, I say, lower away; these beggars have just hit me in the head with a Mauser bullet."[84]

The balloon was a disappointment. At the altitude of the Upper Tugela it had insufficient buoyancy to rise higher than Spearman's Hill, and once Mauser bullets had perforated the envelope it was no longer useful. One of the naval 12-pdr guns had been hit by a Boer shell, its trail smashed. With help from the Royal Engineers it was later repaired with a new pair of gaudily-painted iron wheels from Durban, which earned it the name of the 'Circus Gun.'[85]

83   Burne *With the Naval Brigade in Natal*, p.32.
84   Baynes, *My Diocese During the War*, p.169.
85   Burne *With the Naval Brigade in Natal*, p.32.

9

21 January, The Battle of Platkop

'Some companies of the Queen's and West Yorkshire, ordered to essay what to every eye was the most hazardous of experiments, did rush up over the crest-line onto the naked flat.' Captain Grant.[1]

Before Dawn

Captain Grant of the Devons described the start of his fourth day across the Tugela:

> The dawn of Sunday, January 21, was greeted with crash after crash of volleys from the hill crest. It is a curious thing, but in battles which extend over days there is often a kind of hesitation as to which side is to say "Good morning" to the other first on any particular day, even though the situation is perfectly well known to both... The reason why the Boers had allowed the British to take the southern crest so easily is not, I think, so much of a mystery as it is made out to be. The Boer main position, an immensely strong one, lay along higher ground about 1200 yards in rear of the summits of the spurs and gorges, ...and separated from them by a nearly flat plateau... the main body [of Boers] lay all ready for the acres of slowly moving Britons they expected to see roll across the intervening plateau.[2]

During the night of 20 January, the Dublins and Borders slept in their position, in advance of the British line, in the Y-shaped ravine at the head of Battle Spruit.

Hart's Brigade held the crest of Spurs 2 and 3, and Hildyard's Brigade the crest of Spurs 4 and 5.

Having been in reserve on 20 January, Colonel Walter Kitchener made plans for an assault on Platkop the following day. Platkop (Flat Hill) was known to the British only as 'the hill north of Bastion Hill.' Kitchener commanded one battalion, the 2nd West Yorks, yet planned to attack with three of Hildyard's battalions: the Queen's, West Yorks, and East Surreys, with Hart's battalions providing support. Kitchener did not have the rank to command an attack this big,

---

1   Linesman, *Words by an Eyewitness*, p.46.
2   Linesman, *Words by an Eyewitness*, pp.43–45.

but he was well connected. His older brother, Herbert Horatio Kitchener, was the most famous soldier in the world, and he had just arrived in South Africa as Lord Roberts' Chief of Staff. General Hildyard apparently approved Kitchener's attack, but it was exactly what Warren and Clery had decided against on the evening of 20 January: 'I quite concur that a frontal attack is undesirable, and that a flank attack is more suitable... frontal attack, with heavy losses, is simply playing the Boer game' (Appendix IV (b)).

The events of 20 January had proven that charging Boer trenches in daylight over an exposed plateau would be disastrous. But north of Bastion Hill, Kitchener had spotted an exception. Just east of Spur 5, or the isthmus of Bastion Hill, a spring trickles in summer over the edge of the plateau, forming a marshy depression. This area was already filled with *schanzes* and had become the firing line of the Queen's (GPS -28.62831, 29.46709). In this position, they were closer to the enemy than any other unit – only 1,100 metres from the Boers on Platkop. It would be slaughter to advance directly across the plateau, but there was shelter halfway across, in the form of a large donga. This donga is the bed of a second, larger, seasonal stream which runs south from the Tabanyama plateau, and which tumbles as a miniature waterfall over the crest just west of Spur 5. The donga runs from GPS -28.62104, 29.47182 to GPS -28.62285, 29.46824, and on the exposed Tabanyama plateau it provides a trench 400 metres long and 2 metres deep. At its closest, the donga was 650 metres from the position held by the Queen's, and only 450 metres from the Boers on Platkop.

Kitchener's plan was for two companies of the Queen's to dash forward early in the morning to occupy the donga. Those in the donga, and the remainder of the force on the crests of Spurs 3, 4 and 5, would then fire volleys at Platkop. Under cover of this fire, Colonel Harris, with four companies of the East Surreys, would work round on the slopes below Platkop to the west, out of sight below the crest. Two further companies of the East Surreys would advance on each side of the ravine west of Bastion Hill. Then, about 8:00 a.m., two more companies of the Queen's would join the two companies already in the donga. Once Mauser fire from Platkop was suppressed, all the units on Spurs 3, 4 and 5 would simultaneously converge on Platkop – the East Surreys climbing from the plain west of Bastion Hill, the Queen's from the donga, and the West Yorks from Spur 4. The Lancashire Fusiliers and York and Lancasters on Spur 3 would provide covering fire until they advanced. Once Platkop was taken, a general advance would follow, and the Boer trench line would be rolled up from west to east.

Kitchener's plan had some merit. There was excellent shelter in the donga, and Colonel Harris might well be able to climb the steep slope unseen from the plain below to reach Platkop. But the plan had three glaring weaknesses. First, it would be a daylight attack: the only cover was the donga, and men going to and from the donga would be exposed at close range. Second, the three attacking regiments would be unable to see each other: they had no method of signalling apart from runners, who would themselves be in full view of the Boers. Third, there could be no artillery preparation. The 36 guns on Three Tree Hill could not see Platkop fully, because it was partly obscured by Spur 2, and could see none of the plateau in front of Platkop. At a distance of 3.5km Platkop was close to the limit of shrapnel range, and shells falling short would land among soldiers on Spurs 3–5. The artillery could not see the southern slopes of Platkop, nor the donga, and would not know how far the British attack had advanced. For these reasons, the Three Tree Hill batteries could not support the attack. Warren and Buller had, on 20 January, arranged for 19th and 28th Batteries of 15-pdrs to move to a new position south-west of Bastion

Hill (GPS -28.64245, 29.45025).[3] From there, they would fire up the west side of Bastion Hill directly onto Platkop. The two batteries would be in position by midday, but Kitchener did not wait. In the absence of an artillery bombardment, Kitchener's idea was to precede the assault by a small arms fusilade of continuous machine gun and rifle fire. This tactic had not been tried before, and it was not used subsequently. To add firepower to the fusilade, the West Yorks and Queen's dragged their two Maxim machine guns up to the crest behind Spur 4, and Hart lent Kitchener the Dublin Fusiliers to fire volleys from Spur 4.

Fig 53: Maxim gun of the Queen's. The cumbersome wheeled carriage of British machine guns meant they could seldom be placed in the firing line. This Maxim machine gun of the 2nd Queen's (Royal West Surreys) was manhandled onto the southern crest of Tabanyama to support Colonel Kitchener's attack on Platkop, 21 January 1900. (Cape Archives)

The East Surreys led the attack.

3   Commission into the War in South Africa, Vol. II, p.649.

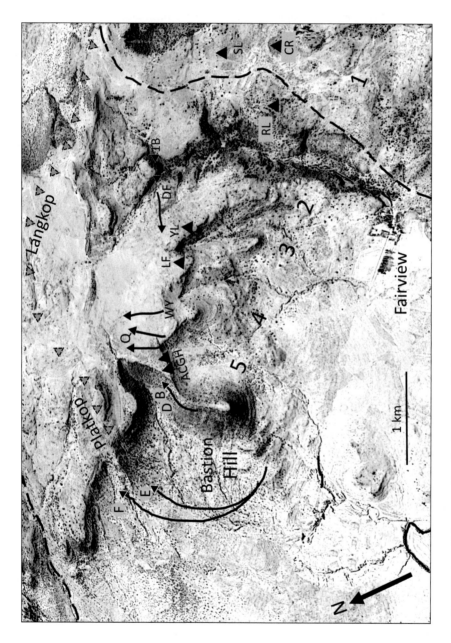

Map 6: Attack on Platkop 21 January 1900. Satellite view of Tabanyama, showing Colonel Walter Kitchener's attack on Platkop. Boers shown as grey triangles. A to H: Companies of East Surrey; 1–5 = Spurs 1 to 5; 1B = 1st Borders; CR = Connaught Rangers; DF = Dublin Fusiliers; ES = East Surreys; LF = Lancashire Fusiliers; Q = Queen's; WY = West Yorks; YL = York & Lancasters; RL = Royal Lancasters; SALH = South African Light Horse; SL = South Lancashires; TMI = Thorneycroft's Mounted Infantry.

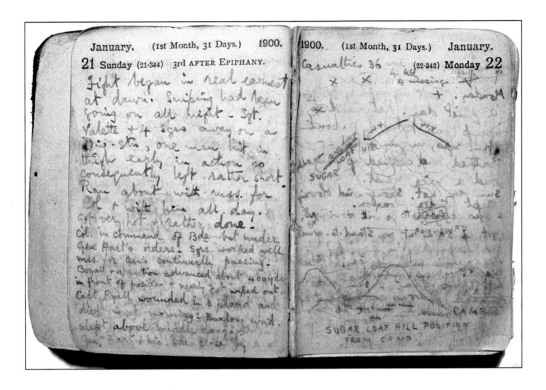

Fig 54: Diary of Lieutenant Malcolm Riall of the 2nd West Yorkshire Regiment. On 21 January, his unit was on Tabanyama: 'Fight began in real earnest at dawn…', this was Colonel Kitchener's failed assault on Platkop. On 22 January, Riall sketched, from Fairview Farm, the crest of Tabanyama Spurs 2–4. (Courtesy Nicholas Riall)

Before sunrise, F and E Companies marched west in the plain below Bastion Hill, and began to climb the lower slopes south-west of Platkop. As soon as it was light the Queen's Maxim gun opened fire, while the infantry on Spurs 4 and 5 fired volleys, as Wedd of the Queen's wrote: '… to get ranges and prepare for business.'[4]

Around 8:00 a.m. B and D Companies, the East Surreys, began to move in open order towards Platkop along the flanks and summit of Bastion Hill. A, C, G and H Companies of the East Surreys provided support by firing across the isthmus of Bastion Hill. The small arms fusilade ceased when the Queens and the West Yorks formed up to advance.[5] Lasham wrote: 'A company and a section of E company the Queen's rushed towards the donga… but no sooner were they in the open than the enemy's murderous fire practically annihilated them. In saving the wounded of these sections great bravery was shown by Private Godwin, who crept out under a terrible fire and rolled the wounded in under cover (he dare not carry them).'[6] A Company

4   Wedd, *Letter.*
5   Pearse, *East Surrey Regiment: Digest of Service*, p.11.
6   Lasham, *Some Notes on the Queen's Royal West Surrey Regiment*, p.38.

advanced in two sections – the left section under Captain Arthur Raitt, the right section under Lieutenant Laurie Wedd. As soon as they stood up the Boers saw them and one man fell dead immediately. Lieutenant Wedd's section of A Company, the Queen's dashed forward about 30 metres to find:

> ...the bullets kicking up the dust all round. There was no cover at all and after a short pause we made another rush about the same distance [30 metres] and lay down again. The man next to me was badly hit and I was just having a look for the wound when my leg got an awful bang. I spun round and sat down... and found myself hit below the knee crosswise behind the bone. It did not hurt much. Poor old Raitt was hit about the same time and died next morning, he was hardly conscious at all. One of our Company was hit five times and is doing well, no bones broken. I crawled back slowly under cover, hoping sincerely to get back without another hit, and was tied up by some fellows in B Company. Shortly after, our Company was told to retire again as quick as possible and they fairly legged it you can be sure. Both the officers of E Company, [Captain] Warden & [Lieutenant] Smith were hit, Warden in the arm and Smith above the heart, just touching his lung. They are both going strong. We lost six killed and 20 wounded in ten minutes – not bad.'[7]

About 9:00 a.m., E Company, the Queen's, dashed forward, followed by men of C and G Companies. They sprinted to the donga and ducked into it. They fired over the lip of the donga at Platkop, while, invisible to them, the leading company of the East Surreys slowly pushed up the ravine below. The Queen's made an attempt to charge from the donga, but this was checked before they had advanced 50 metres across the plateau. The Queens' Digest of Service records: 'Some 35 men of C & G companies got into the donga in front at 9 am and the attack being stopped, remained there till dusk 6 pm when the East Surrey companies arrived at the lower end of the ravine. Orders had been given for a retirement so all returned round the foot of the hill.'[8] When darkness came, B and D Companies of the East Surreys reached the donga and led the men back.

The Queen's had advanced close enough for their officers to be picked off. Captain Raitt was mortally wounded and Captains Bottomley, Sillem, and Warden and Lieutenants Du Boisson, Smith, Mangles, and Wedd were all wounded. Lieutenant Smith of the Queen's had almost reached the donga when he was shot through the chest, the bullet coming out through his back. Smith lay down behind cover nearby until 3:00 p.m., when the fire slackened and he crawled into the donga, where he remained until dark.[9] Colour Sergeant Kingsley's company of the Queen's was caught in a cross-fire; both his officers were hit but Kingsley steadied the men and led them to cover. He was awarded the Distinguished Conduct Medal and received a scarf knitted by Queen Victoria.

The East Surreys were, perhaps fortunately, unable to get close to the Boers, and sustained lighter casualties: 5 men killed and 23 wounded, including Lieutenant Porch 'very severely

7   Wedd, *Letter*.
8   Anon., Battle of Venter's Spruit 21 Jan 1900, *Digest of Service, 2nd Bttn Queen's*, (1900). Surrey Infantry Museum. QEWS 3/5/1 21 Jan 1900.
9   Blake Knox, *Buller's Campaign*, p.48.

wounded' in the leg. Some had lucky escapes – among F Company, the East Surreys, Lieutenant Colonel Harris and Captain Packman were both shot through their uniforms.

Dr Maxwell, with the Ermelo Commando Ambulance, described the attack:

> For some reason the English would jump out from the schanzes in batches of twenty-five or thirty men, and make a run for the kloof [donga], and it was while doing this that most of the English were shot. If they had waited till dark, as many men as required could have got into the kloof without any risk, and then a night attack or a rush on the trench could have been made at daylight. This was what the Boers were afraid of for five or six days.[10]

At 9:30 a.m., while the attack was in progress, the Boers sent reinforcements to Platkop, and Kitchener received a reported of a Boer force moving towards them from Acton Homes to counter-attack.

By late morning, the sun was blisteringly hot. The West Yorks attempted to advance, and immediately had to take cover. Officers of the Queen's and West Yorks called for volunteers, fixed bayonets, and tried to charge. Lieutenant Blake Knox watched: 'They were greeted by a deadly hail of Mauser bullets, followed by a steady roll of fire. The rush was disastrous; it could not succeed.'[11] Captain Ryall, West Yorks, was mortally wounded and 5 men were killed; Lieutenant Barlow and 42 men were wounded. Lieutenant Boyall led a section of 16 men of E Company, West Yorks, to within 450 metres of the Boer trenches, and they were pinned down in the open. Private Morant was wounded while running back with a message from Boyall. Private Powell was hit while bringing water to wounded men. The West Yorks Digest of Service records: 'An advance... was attempted but found to be perfectly impossible as it was an absolutely open Glacis leading up to their entrenchments... as many as 300 rounds per man were fired, and the MG [Machine Gun] fired 7,500, rounds during the day.'[12]

The attack had been impossible to coordinate. Charging a concealed enemy, across open ground and without artillery preparation had been slaughter. Yet despite this experience, drummer Goodwin of the West Yorks wrote a few days later in his diary: 'Tommies favourite was the Colonel F W Kitchener and he knew it, and when leading his men he knew no fear; the troops would follow him anywhere.'[13]

The Boer Response

Veldkornet Kemp, with his Krugersdorpers on Platkop, faced Kitchener's attack:

> Early the next morning, Sunday, January 21st the battle resumed. Gen Hildyard sent three battalions [from] east of Bastion Hill into a ravine, in order to reach the crest and,

10   'Defender', *Sir Charles Warren and Spion Kop*, pp.166—167.
11   Blake Knox, *Buller's Campaign*, p.48.
12   West Yorkshire Regiment, *Extract from Digest of Service of the 2nd Battalion in South Africa, 1899–1902* (York: Yorkshire Herald, 1902), p.11.
13   H. Goodwin, 'Diary of 4412 Drummer Goodwin, 2nd Bn West Yorkshire Regiment', National Army Museum 1976-07-47, 30 Jan 1900.

like a wedge, split our position. However, this bunch got stuck exactly where I was; because at the top of the ravine, that is, on the plateau, lay our prepared positions about a thousand paces further behind the crest and at the next summit, and for the enemy to try to storm those thousand steps meant suicide, because the open ground they had to move on could come under cross-fire... Some of the enemy tried to storm our position with the bayonet. However, less than half of them made it back to their mates.[14]

Dietlof van Warmelo of the Pretoria Commando was on Langkop, above the donga:

Towards morning, while we were still digging at the trenches, fire was opened across the whole line of battle. We imagined that we were being attacked, and jammed ourselves in the narrow trench. But as the attack did not come off, and the bullets flew high over our heads, we went on digging until daybreak. Then we noticed that the enemy were lying in a ditch [donga] about 800 paces ahead of us. We fired a few shots at them, but saved our ammunition for an eventual storming.[15]

Captain Grant of the Devons watched the attack with dismay:

Some companies of the Queen's and West Yorkshire, ordered to essay what to every eye was the most hazardous of experiments, did rush up over the crest-line onto the naked flat. The roll of fire which greeted them told the result plainly enough, without the line of bloody stretchers which straggled back across the valley, with here an arm stiffly uplifted like a little mast between the stumbling bearers, or a leg flexed in pain or death.[16]

Even seasoned newspaper correspondents like Burleigh, who were usually eager to witness action, could not bear to watch the disaster unfold: 'A companion who was lying low said to someone who wished to use his field-glasses, "Oh, you may have them altogether. I don't want to look any more"'.[17] Lieutenant Blake Knox described the battle from Three Tree Hill:

The aspect of the troops massed on the slopes was that of a great body of ants, large and small, the latter being men, the former animals and vehicles; for some ammunition mules, Maxim mules, and even ambulances, had climbed up. Outside the main body the specks grew thinner and thinner, and in the firing line they became invisible, except at times, when a thin, scattered line of khaki-coloured specks, almost particles, might be seen springing into sight from some cover, then flitting rapidly forward, and disappearing with the same rapidity as they threw themselves prone on the ground to recommence firing... Each time the infantry became visible, it was possible through field-glasses to distinguish the dust thrown up in little clouds all round them as the enemy's bullets struck the ground... Over the black plain, the grass of which had been

14   Kemp, *Vir Vryheid en vir Reg*, p.278.
15   Dietlof van Warmelo, *On Commando* (London: Methuen, 1902), p.27.
16   Linesman, *Words by an Eyewitness*, p.46.
17   Burleigh, *The Natal Campaign*, pp.320—321.

burnt the day before, stream the three battalions, their khaki visible against the dark ground; another blast of musketry, and a shell or two, and figures fall; but the rush is not for a moment checked; a charge, a scuffle, and the ridge is reached, and a portion of it is British property. But this is of little use; another ridge, with an intervening plateau some 1,200 yards wide, is now seen for the first time. It is the Boer main position, and is immensely strong. To reach this… that glacis-like plateau must be crossed. It is commanded by the heights, with their lines of low rock and earth redoubts, and trenches carefully prepared with overhead cover, so placed as to command all approaches with converging fire, and here and there with a cross-fire. The enemy knew what they were about when they let the British army plant its foot on Taba Myama ridge.'[18]

Fig 55: Fighting on Tabanyama. Painted in London based on sketches and photographs from the field, it captures the spirit of the fighting on Tabanyama. Wounded soldiers are walking or being carried down from the crest, where a shell is bursting. Ammunition mules make their way up, while lines of men wait to go into action. (Painting by Sidney Paget for *The Sphere*, March 1900)

18   Blake Knox, *Buller's Campaign*, pp.41 & 47.

Casualties and Stretcher-bearers

By 11:00 a.m. the number of casualties had reached 100, and Lieutenant-General Clery, who outranked both Kitchener and Hildyard, ordered Kitchener to stop.

Throughout the day the NVAC 'Body Snatchers', together with regimental stretcher-bearers, found the wounded and carried them to safety. Lieutenant Blake Knox watched them through his binoculars:

> Very soon I noticed other specks, solitary ones and slightly larger, moving out. My glasses showed these to be stretcher-bearers, who had their work cut out for them on that hill. Throughout the day these stretcher-bearers, the majority of whom were... civilians... went forward, solidly and unflinchingly, to the very firing line, and could be seen bending over the fallen, tending and removing the wounded... unfortunately many paid dearly for their self-sacrifice.[19]

The risk in four men carrying back a wounded man was, as Lynch wrote: '...immensely greater than remaining in the firing line or advancing more or less on one's stomach.'[20] Two NVAC bearers were wounded while bringing in Captain Raitt of the Queen's; two more were killed, including an ex-coffeehouse-keeper from Durban named Robertson. Burleigh wrote that, while calling to his comrades: 'Come on, and never mind the Boers!' Robertson was shot through the head.[21]

Corporal Lewis of the Queen's was one of the wounded: 'I first of all had my arm dressed, and then went back to the field hospital [on Fairview Farm] about two miles to the rear of where the fighting was taking place.'[22] Lieutenant Laurie Wedd of the Queen's, his leg bandaged, came down sitting on a rifle held by two of his men, and was handed over to the NVAC who carried him to hospital. After a day at Major Moir's Field Hospital at Fairview Farm, Wedd travelled by ambulance wagon to No.4 Stationary Hospital at Spearman's Farm. Wedd wrote that, in his wagon there were: '...three arms, one sitting-up leg, and two lying-down legs,' and on arrival they were delighted to be greeted by: 'Beds, sheets, fresh milk, tents, nurses, pyjamas and water...'[23] Within a few days the wounded were moved to hospital in Frere, then by ambulance train to Mooi River or Pietermaritzburg. Gandhi's Natal Volunteer Indian Ambulance Corps carried the wounded for long distances with great care, and the wounded men found this method of transport to be the most comfortable. The NVIAC comprised 34 leaders, 300 free Indians and 800 indentured labourers. They were led by an attorney, Mohandas K. Gandhi, later Mahatma Gandhi, the celebrated Indian leader. Gandhi had lived in Natal since 1893, had founded a political group called the Natal Indian Congress, and had become the editor of a periodical, the *Indian Opinion*. Gandhi, a strict Jain, asked if his volunteers could join the white stretcher-bearers of the NVAC, then being recruited in Durban. This was declined; in Natal, unlike the Cape, racial mixing was unacceptable. Undeterred, Reverend Dr Lancelot Parker

---

19   Blake Knox, *Buller's Campaign*, p.41.
20   Lynch, *Impressions of a War Correspondent*, p.4.
21   Burleigh, *The Natal Campaign*, p.318.
22   Edward M. Spiers, *Letters from Ladysmith*. (Barnsley: Pen & Sword 2010). p99.
23   Wedd, *Letter*.

Booth, a missionary in Durban, went ahead and trained them anyway, and when Buller himself intervened, the NVIAC was formed. Two days after Colenso, Gandhi's NVIAC was abruptly disbanded, but it was re-formed on 7 January 1900. Gandhi embellished the role of the NVIAC on the Upper Tugela in his memoir *Adventures with the Truth*:

> The authorities did not want us to be within the range of fire. The situation, however, was changed after the repulse at Spion Kop, and General Buller sent the message that, though we were not bound to take the risk, Government would be thankful if we would do so and fetch the wounded from the field. We had no hesitation, and so the action at Spion Kop found us working within the firing line. [24]

The reality was less glamorous: the NVIAC were far away from danger on Tabanyama or Spioenkop, and sustained no casualties.

The Transvaal 'Official War News Bulletin' reported Boer casualties for 21 January as 4 killed and 10 wounded.[25] British casualties that day were 24 killed, 223 wounded, and 4 missing.[26] Treves' hospital received the severely wounded the next day: 'Many of the wounded who were brought in between the 18th and the 24th of January came in after sundown. The largest number arrived on the night of Monday, the 22nd.'[27]

Hart Withdraws his Advanced Units

While Kitchener's attack on Platkop was in progress, Clery ordered Hart to withdraw the Borders and Dublins from their advanced positions in the ravine at the head of Battle Spruit. The men needed to move to Spur 3 to re-unite with their battalions. Hart withdrew them reluctantly: 'I wanted to go on, all my men did too, and finish the job by crowning the heights now but a few hundred yards before me, with pretty easy going in front of me, and all the difficult ground now behind me; but my hands were tied.'[28] Hart sent his staff officers back to safety, southwards down the sheltered valley of Battle Spruit. Then, rather than withdrawing the Borders and Dublins the same way, Hart led his men westwards out of the sheltered valley onto the open plateau. They then marched 1,000 metres directly across to Spur 3, parallel to the Boers' trenches 800 metres away, and in clear sight of the enemy:

> General Hart ordered Colonel Cooper [commanding the Dublin Fusiliers] to move by the straightest line, first down a ravine across a spruit, and then over a hill. While climbing the latter, the battalion was in full view of the enemy, who at once opened fire with guns and rifles. Each company extended in succession, and doubled, so far as possible, over the exposed ground. Once over the hill a region of comparative safety

---

24   Gandhi, *The Story of My Experiments with Truth*, p.499.
25   Anon., *The Bulletin of Official War News*, (Heidelberg, Transvaal Field Press, 22 January 1900).
26   Blake Knox, *Buller's Campaign*, p.51.
27   Treves, *The Tale of a Field Hospital*, p.64.
28   Hart, *Letters*, p.311.

was reached, and General Hart finally formed up his command behind a rocky ridge overlooking the position held by the 2nd Brigade.[29]

Captain Grant observed:

> There is nothing apologetic or doubtful about General Hart to start with, gallant fiery Irishman, too hot with the *ignis sacer* [holy fire] of fighting to see anything ridiculous in a sword angrily brandished at an enemy a thousand yards away. Soldiers under the eye of a man like this do not fire dropping shots, the rifles blaze and bellow and volley as soon as there is light enough to charge the magazines, their owners ready to speed after that waving sword, forgetting that it is as much an anachronism as the dare-devil recklessness of its owner...[30]

In a few minutes, Hart's withdrawal cost the Borders and Dublins 37 casualties. Burleigh met an Irishman who was shot through his face: 'It took my left eye out, carried it into my mouth, and I spat it out with three teeth... But we gave it to them Boers, this time, and I am content.'[31]

The rest of the day on Tabanyama was spent in long-range rifle fire, described by Captain Grant of the Devons:

> All along the ridge ran the steady roll of fire, from behind low sangars, big boulders, from little depressions, sometimes dying away in portions of the line, sometimes redoubling in intensity throughout its length, as if by common impulse. Now a company would top the orchestra with rhythmic volleys, whilst the thousands of freelances on either side stayed their hands for a moment as if to listen: then the independent firing would recommence, rifle by rifle, until the rhythm of the volleys was drowned in the tremendous rattle: then two or three Maxims would chime in, and the whole ridge resounded from end to end, peak calling to peak, ravine to ravine.[32]

The Royal Field Artillery Changes Position

In the late morning of 21 January, 19th and 28th Batteries arrived at their new positions, coming into action against Platkop at 12:10 p.m. By then, Kitchener's attack had been called off.

Lieutenant Kearsey of the York and Lancasters noted:

> [The Boers] had not wasted their time during the past three days, and had evidently made themselves bomb-proof shelters, behind which they were now safely resting, not disclosing their position till it became necessary for them to hold their trenches against the attacking infantry.[33]

29   Anon., *Connaught Rangers Regimental Records*, p.50.
30   Linesman, *Words by an Eyewitness*, p.44.
31   Burleigh, *The Natal Campaign*, p.320.
32   Linesman, *Words by an Eyewitness*, pp.48.
33   Kearsey, *War Record of the York & Lancasters*, p.16.

The Boers were becoming accustomed to shelling, although they hated it. 'Lodi' Krause noted that, when the shell came directly towards him: '...the shrieking and screaming would grow louder and louder, then for a few seconds this would be succeeded by a rushing sound, the air would feel depressed and heavy.'[34] Hofmeyr, another Boer, thought: 'Every bombardment weathered with a modicum of self-respect adds some iron in the blood and manliness to the personality.'[35] Reverend 'Danie' Kestell visited the battlefield on 21 January and noted the bombardment: '...had often been so intolerable that the burghers were driven out of the earthworks and compelled to seek shelter behind the hill slopes. But they had always returned and kept up a continuous fire on the advancing soldiers.'[36]

21 January. Evening Comes

At 6:00 p.m. Warren inspected the western flank, and discussed with Clery the possibility of a renewal of the attack. Clery, having called off Kitchener's disastrous assault, was firmly opposed, especially as the Boers were reinforcing this sector. Warren agreed, and informed Buller: '...I am under the impression that with continuous fighting we shall clear the range of hills we are now attacking...' (Appendix IV (d)). At 6.30 p.m. Warren ordered General Talbot Coke to join him with his 10th Brigade as reinforcements, and in the night, they crossed Trichardt's Drift. Three of Coke's battalions – the 2nd Somersetshire Light infantry, 2nd Dorsetshire, and 2nd Middlesex – were regular units, though as yet un-tested in South Africa. Coke's fourth battalion, the Imperial Light Infantry, was 'green'. The ILI were a brand-new volunteer unit, composed mainly of South Africans. They were still at Frere, and set off that evening for the Upper Tugela. Warren requested heavy guns, and was promised four howitzers from Potgieter's Drift. He also requested naval guns, but they were not granted.[37] With these reinforcements, Warren considered the best chance of success would be a frontal attack on Langkop up both sides of 'the long ravine' of Battle Spruit.[38]

About 6:30 p.m. it began to grow dark, and men who had been lying out on the plateau and in the donga crept back to the firing line, attracting what Pearse of the East Surreys called: '... heavy but ineffective fire...'[39]

In the gathering darkness, Captain Grant of the Devons climbed the steep hillside of Spur 5 to relieve the Queen's:

> Evening was just falling when we entered the deep gorge, at the top of which lay the battalion we had come to relieve. It was a curious and depressing spectacle... Imagine a huge basin of blackish-brown earthenware, with sides so steep that your neck is strained as you look up from your position at the bottom of it. From the encircling rim are darting innumerable spurts of flame, looking almost scarlet against the darkening

34   Krause, *War Memoirs*, p.25.
35   Nico J. Hofmeyr, *Zes Maanden bij de Commando's*, ('s-Gravenhage: van Stockum & Zoon, 1903), p.108.
36   Kestell, *Through Shot and Flame*, p.59.
37   Amery, *The War in South Africa*, Vol. III p.237. Maurice, *History of The War in South Africa, Vol. II*, p.372.
38   Commission into the War in South Africa, Vol. II, p.650.
39   H. W. Pearse, *2nd Battalion East Surrey Regiment: Digest of Services in South Africa 1899–1902* (London: Medici, 1903), p.12.

sky: these are from the rifles of the men clinging like flies to the crest-line. All around a casual "whit! whit!" more felt than heard, as the Mauser bullets whisk down at the end of their flight and plop into the soft earth, or strike with a crisp spit upon a boulder. There are not very many of them now, for the Boers are 'easing off' after a hard day, and we are sending them ten Lee-Metfords for one Mauser across the plateau... We climb up the stony wall, the released battalion [the Queen's] stumbles wearily past us, and disappears in the gloom behind to its well-earned rest, all save one of its officers, who refuses to go until he has found some of his dead still lying out upon the plateau. He pokes about in the darkness in front of us, at the hazard of his life, finds the horrors he is looking for, and on his return joins us in a hasty candlelight dinner, with as much unconcern as if he had been out mushroom-picking.[40]

General Buller struck a positive note when he telegraphed to the Secretary of State for War at 9:00 p.m.: 'Warren has been engaged all day, chiefly on his left, which he has swung round about a couple of miles. The ground is very difficult, and, as the fighting is all the time up-hill, it is difficult exactly to say how much we gain, but I think we are making substantial progress.'[41]

Buller also heliographed Ladysmith, informing White that Warren was making slow progress up the hills, and asked whether they knew the strength of the Boer force. White replied: 'I believe there are more than 10,000 facing you, or in position to face you rapidly.' In fact, there were probably only around 1,800 Boers on Tabanyama.

The night of 21 January passed quietly, with what Captain Grant called: '...only an occasional spasm of firing from our crest-line.'[42] The Boers remained in their trenches, alert for a night attack, and used the darkness to improve their trenches.[43] Mostert recalled: 'The fighting continued almost day and night. The men had to sleep in their firing line. There was no such thing as going to cook meat over a fire.'[44]

40   Linesman, *Words by an Eyewitness*, pp.49–50.
41   Commission into the War in South Africa, Vol. II, p.649.
42   Linesman, *Words by an Eyewitness*, p.50.
43   Kemp, *Vir Vryheid en vir Reg*, p.279.
44   Mostert, *Slegtkamp van Spioenkop*, p.33.

10

22 January, Bombardment

'The bombardment was fearful. Never for eight days long was there a pause.'
Reverend John 'Danie' Kestell[1]

Warren and Buller Confer

At 5:00 a.m. Buller telegraphed Warren, expressing his overnight worries: 'I think it possible the enemy may try a counter-stroke; they are concentrated, while your troops are widely extended, and do not support each other. I should be cautious how I attempted any enterprise further on the left [Bastion Hill to Acton Homes] at present.'[2]

Warren had come to the same conclusion the day before; he saw no alternative to a direct assault on Langkop. Buller met with Warren at 10:00 a.m. Warren laid out his plan to capture the Fairview-Rosalie road; this meant attacking Langkop, which in turn meant first occupying Spioenkop, which overlooked Spur 1. Buller agreed: 'Of course you must take Spion Kop.'[3]

Exchanges of Fire

Lieutenant Blake Knox described how, at first light on 22 January, rifle and artillery firing resumed, for the third continuous day of battle:

> The preceding night was occupied by both sides entrenching; now and again rifle-fire created alarms, for sometimes in the darkness the smallest sound will set a position ablaze with spluttering flame. As soon as light allowed, the Boer guns which the enemy had mounted on their right the evening before, and which had been brought up with reinforcements from Spion Kop, set to work. Though they made most accurate

---

1   Kestell, *Through Shot and Flame*, p.59.
2   Commission into the War in South Africa, Vol. II, p.650. Maurice, *History of The War in South Africa, Vol. II*, p.372.
3   Commission into the War in South Africa, Vol. II, p.650.

shooting with their shell-fire, the slopes, behind which our men were taking cover, like flies on the side of a wall, were luckily too steep for effective results.[4]

Captain Grant of the Devons described the start of the day's fighting:

...as before, the first glint of dawn on the 22nd was fairly roared at from all along the line. During the night the enemy had got a couple of guns in position on our left front, and these, accurately ranging with shrapnel, cracked and splashed their rain of bullets over our heads all day, though the slope was luckily too steep for effective results. Then another gun opened from the invisible right, also a pom-pom, whose procession of little shells raced across the flat below us at intervals, sometimes amongst the ambulance or the mules, once causing a universal catch of the breath by plunging straight into the midst of men, drivers, bearers, ration-carriers, etc.[5]

Grant, in the absence of visible Boers, observed the sounds resonating among the hills:

I became aware that the note permeating a battle is one endless E flat. How it sings and drones throughout the long days, audible, or rather sensible, amid the many-toned hubbubs around, dropping occasionally a third of a tone, but always re-ascending to its endless semibreve...[6]

The noises of battle also fascinated Lieutenant Blake Knox:

Varied were the sounds the missiles made, some whistling, others humming, some ending their course in a dull thud; others, probably ricocheting ones, passing by, purring or screaming. The rifle reports also varied, the individual Mauser discharge, with its double report, "pit! pot!" contrasting markedly with the more solid and duller 'bang' of the Martini rifle [probably the Guedes rifle, which was used on the Upper Tugela]; the pom-pom, with its hyena-like laugh of five notes; the Maxim, with its deadly spitting fire – its report can be well simulated by rapidly drumming one finger on a table; and, last but not least, the fire of our Lee-Metfords, which can be imitated by similarly drumming all fingers at once.[7]

Mausers sounded very distinctive to Private O'Mahony:

At ranges over 500 yards you would imagine the rifle articulates distinctly the words: ping pong. The further away the more distinctly you hear this peculiar sound, and at long range there is a good interval between ping and pong. When on the trek and the skirmishing line moves off in the morning you immediately hear this familiar sound, the snipers "God speed"; and on the whole route to the next bivouac your march is

4   Blake Knox, *Buller's Campaign*, p.52.
5   Linesman, *Words by an Eyewitness*, p.50.
6   Linesman, *Words by an Eyewitness*, p.49.
7   Blake Knox, *Buller's Campaign*, p.169

punctuated with ping pongs. From the kopje on the right, ping pong; from the rock on the left, ping pong; from the donga on the right rear, ping pong; the drift on the left rear, ping pong; the reed-covered river bank, ping pong; from the hole in the ground, ping pong; from the farm house flying the white flag, ping pong; and often in your bivouac at night, star gazing, or dreaming, perhaps, of home and beauty from the dark would ring out the eternal ping pong. The man in the street would ask how it was those snipers were not blown off the earth. The man on the veldt would say:- "What a pity he did not come out and try.'[8]

British Shelling

Four howitzers of the 61st Battery, commanded by Major Gordon, came under Warren's command early in the morning of 22 January.

Fig 56: Howitzer and Gun Crew. Four 5-inch howitzers of the 61st Battery were brought across Trichardt's Drift to shell the Boer trenches on Tabanyama. They fired 50-pound percussion shells filled with Lyddite high explosive. (Cape Archives)

Buller arrived about the same time and personally directed one section of two howitzers to join 19th and 28th batteries on Fairview Farm, and one section to Three Tree Hill, where they opened fire on the enemy's trenches at 2,500 m, and kept firing slowly all day.[9] Their targets

8   O'Mahony, *A Peep Over the Barleycorn*, pp.120–121.
9   Anon, '61st Battery Digest of Service 1900,' Royal Artillery Institution Archives.

were the concealed Boer guns, but they were unable to locate them. Lieutenant Blake Knox was disappointed by the howitzers, which he thought:

> …frightened the enemy considerably, but could not range their guns. As the large 50-pound lyddite shells burst on the opposite ridge, throwing up great clouds of red dust, mixed with their dark brown or canary yellow fumes, according as this explosive detonated completely or otherwise, the Boers could be seen running from place to place to escape the effects of the missiles. Neither the howitzers nor the 15-pound field-guns could reach the enemy [guns], and there were no long-range naval guns available.'[10]

The howitzers brought Sandberg, on Tabanyama, his first experience of Lyddite shells: '[they] burst with a violent storm – red dust, black and yellow smoke in an inverted cone shape, rising up.'[11] At first, the yellow fumes were alarming, but John Blake found Lyddite to be relatively ineffective: 'The whole atmosphere was fairly laden with the yellow, sulphurous-looking, lyddite fumes, and the Boers who finally emerged from their trenches… were yellow about the eyes, nose, mouth and neck, and their clothes were yellow too; but when they washed their faces they were Boers again, and very lively ones at that.'[12]

It seemed to 'Lodi' Krause that:

> …artillery fire caused more dust and smoke and noise than harm. The shell on striking the earth would explode straight down, like dynamite. It tore a good-sized hole in the earth, and then the whole force of the explosion seemed to be broken, and it expended itself further straight up into the air, so that, should such a shell strike the ground say two or three yards from a recumbent man, no effect would be produced on him beyond the shock and the nausea of the lyddite fumes… I have even seen a lyddite shell exploding with thunder, smoke and dust not five yards from an erect Boer – we measured the distance – and doing him no further harm other than throwing him to the ground with the shock.'[13]

General Ben Viljoen described a near miss from a Lyddite shell: 'It seemed to me as if a huge cauldron of boiling fat had burst over us and for some minutes I must have lost consciousness… I felt a piercing pain in my head, and the blood began to pour from my nose and ears.'[14]

'Danie' Kestell described the bombardment:

> Shells of every sort and size fell fast and thick on our positions… great clouds of dust and smoke arose whenever one of these huge shells came in contact with the earth. The ground was torn and ploughed up when the lyddite shells burst with a terrific crash, and their yellow smoke gave the burghers headaches and made the water in their flasks bitter. The bombardment was fearful. Never for eight days long was there a pause.

10   Blake Knox, *Buller's Campaign*, p.51
11   Sandberg, *De Zesdaagsche Slag aan de Boven Tugela*, p.96.
12   John Y.F. Blake, *A West Pointer with the Boers* (Boston: Angel Guardian Press, 1903), p.118.
13   Krause, *War Memoirs*, p.24.
14   Ben Viljoen, *My Reminiscences of the Anglo-Boer War* (London: Hood, Douglas, & Howard, 1902), p.92.

Fig 57: Soldier standing in a Lyddite shell hole. Lyddite shells contained a new high explosive made from picric acid and gun cotton. However, they seemed to explode vertically and were relatively ineffective, though they produced a cloud of yellow smoke. Here a soldier in Natal stands in a deep but narrow Lyddite crater. (National Army Museum)

Clouds of smoke constantly rose from the earth, where the shells burst, and one could continually see the hundreds of vanishing cloudlets in the air where the shrapnel burst over the positions.[15]

Dr Maxwell, with the Ermelo Commando Ambulance, doubted the Boers could go on much longer:

> All eyes are now directed to the Upper Tugela, and there is no doubt affairs there are becoming critical. The strain of the continuous fighting is beginning to tell on the Burghers, more especially as there are every day more or less casualties in the trenches. The Burghers get into the trenches before daylight, and then have to remain in them till they are relieved the next morning before daybreak. The country is too open and exposed for them to leave the trenches, unless it is dark. Moreover, they are expecting a rush some morning early, or a night attack.[16]

Despite the shelling, Wilson, with the Royal Field Artillery, found the Boers kept up heavy rifle fire:

15   Kestell, *Through Shot and Flame*, p.59.
16   'Defender', *Sir Charles Warren and Spion Kop*, pp.121—122.

Crack-crack-crack-and then a continued spluttering which swelled in intensity until it resembled shipwrights hammering at the iron plates of a budding battle-ship. Then it died away; then a solitary crack started it again, then it died away afresh, and all was quiet for a time. So on day after day, from daylight until dusk. Sometimes at night the smallest sound would set the hills alight with a spluttering flame...[17]

Atkins noted that the shelling did not keep the Boers inactive for long:

...generally, the lyddite and the shrapnel battened the enemy down in his works. He was quiet. Then our guns would become quiet too, and no sooner did that happen than the Boer marksmen would pop up again. Ping, ping, ping! round the very gunners who had scarcely had time to settle themselves behind the smoking guns. Bullets that missed the ridges could do nothing but drop over into the plain; the whole field was under fire.[18]

As long as they lay behind *schanzes*, soldiers in the firing line were relatively safe, as Private O'Mahony recalled:

We had made our position impregnable to rifle fire. On our right front across the plateau, between 1,200 and 1,800 yards away, the Boers had done likewise, so from daylight till dark a continual sheet of lead passed between the two forces. Sit tight in your sangar and you were as safe as if the rifle fire were a thousand miles aloof. What was the good then of exposing yourself to fire at all? Well, the fighting instinct that could not sit still and listen to the pings of passing bullets must give back tit for tat to the enemy, so a stream of lead spat and hissed across the valley incessantly... If you are ever in the firing line at long range, keep there unless much better cover can be secured in the rear... you were much safer in the firing line.[19]

Warren's Council of War

Having conferred with Buller that morning, around 1:00 p.m. Warren summoned Clery, Hildyard, Hart, Coke and Woodgate to discuss the tactics for the strategy that Buller had just approved.[20] Hart loathed the meeting: 'Warren called a council of war. I have never had anything before to do with such an institution, and hope I may not again...'[21] Clery and Hildyard, having watched the previous day's disaster on Platkop, were opposed to a repeat attempt on the western flank. This left only three alternatives. The first was a frontal attack, possibly at night, against the Boer trenches. A night attack could end badly, as had happened at Magersfontein. Moreover, the Boers seemed to stay awake, sniping all night, and regularly fired star shells, which would

---

17   Wilson, *The Relief of Ladysmith*, p.64.
18   Atkins, *The Relief of Ladysmith*, p.232.
19   O'Mahony, *A Peep Over the Barleycorn*, p.146.
20   Maurice, *History of The War in South Africa*, Vol. II, p 373.
21   Hart, *Letters*, p.315.

reveal the attack. The second option, a variation of the first, was to occupy Spioenkop by night, entrench, and enfilade the Boer position on Green Hill, assisting a frontal assault up Spur 1. It may even be possible to drag field guns up Spioenkop after dark. Apparently, Spioenkop summit was undefended, but there was no information about its north-eastern slopes and it was unclear how it could withstand a counter-attack.[22] The third option was to withdraw across the Tugela, and look elsewhere to break through. The generals chose to attack Spioenkop. Battle Spruit cut Tabanyama into two battlefields – men could only cross the ravine with difficulty, and forces on either side would not be able to communicate or even see each other during an attack. Just as he had split his artillery into two on 21 January, Warren now split his infantry into two independent commands, to function on each side of Battle Spruit (Appendix IV (f)).

Left Attack would be under Hart, Right Attack under Coke. Coke and two of his newly-arrived battalions would occupy Spioenkop that night. Coke decided not to lead the assaulting column in person: '…it being such a small portion of my force.'[23] Coke selected Colonel Hill of the Middlesex to lead the column, which would comprise the Middlesex, Dorsets, and a few of Thorneycroft's Mounted Infantry. However, by then it was already 5:00 p.m. and Coke and Thorneycroft both requested that the attack on Spioenkop be deferred, so the battalion commanders could reconnoitre and sketch the route.[24] Warren agreed, and the attack was postponed for 24 hours, to the night of 23 January.

In preparation, Coke moved the Middlesex and Dorsets from Venter's Spruit onto Connaught Hill and Picquet Hill, to be ready for the next night's attack. The Somerset Light Infantry and TMI were moved to Wright's Farm. By then it was pitch dark. Coke did not yet have his bearings on Tabanyama, and got lost trying to find his new headquarters on Connaught Hill. He had to sleep out on the veldt.[25]

The Boers Reinforce Tabanyama

During the night of 21 January, some of the Johannesburg and Heidelberg Commandos abandoned their trenches.[26] The next morning, Botha telegrammed his misgivings to Joubert.

Despite this isolated incident, the Upper Tugela defences were not collapsing, and in fact, the Boer forces were growing. Around Ladysmith, they could see that White's garrison, though still able to resist an attack, had become too feeble to break out from Ladysmith, or even take offensive action. A steady stream of Boers took the opportunity to saddle up for Tabanyama.[27] Kestell wrote how Botha '…rode from position to position, and whenever burghers were losing heart and on the point of giving way under the awful bombardment, he would appear as if from nowhere and contrive to get them back into the positions by "gentle persuasion," as he expressed it, or by other means.'[28]

22   Blake Knox, *Buller's Campaign*, p.53.
23   Commission into the War in South Africa, Vol. II, p.442.
24   Blake Knox, *Buller's Campaign*, p.53.
25   Commission into the War in South Africa, Vol. II, p.442.
26   Johan H. Breytenbach, *Die Geskiedenis van Die Tweede Vryheidsoorlog in Suid-Afrika, 1899–1902* (Pretoria: Staatsdrukker, 1971) Part 3, Chapter 5, section 7, p.49.
27   Commission into the War in South Africa, Vol. II, p.649.
28   Kestell, *Through Shot and Flame*, p.60.

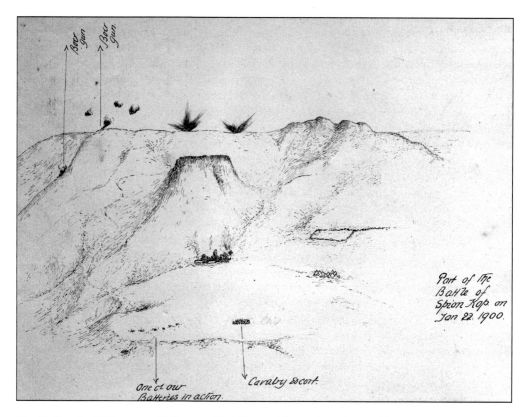

Fig 58: Sketch of Tabanyama 22 January 1900. Entitled 'Part of the Battle of Spion Kop on Jan 22 1900' this sketch by Lieutenant J. G. Browne, 14th Hussars shows the British artillery below Bastion Hill shelling the Boer position at Platkop. On the left skyline, two Boer Creusots under Lt Friedrich von Wichmann are firing from near the Acton Homes road, 4.5km away. Thorneycroft's Mounted Infantry are in the foreground, as is Fairview Farm. Bastion Hill is the flat-topped hill below the skyline and Spur 2 makes up the skyline on the right. (Arnold van Dyk collection)

Reverend Kestell, riding from Tabanyama towards Ladysmith on 22 January, was struck by the way the burghers were pouring in from all directions as reinforcements:

> I saw persons of every age going to the positions. There were amongst them boys and middle-aged men; there were even grey-beards. And the most remarkable thing about this was that all these men had not been ordered to the battle. They came of their own accord. I thought of a text in the Bible which, when separated from its context, was applicable here, "Thy people shall be willing [on Your day of battle]" (Psalm 110 verse 3).[29]

29   Kestell, *Through Shot and Flame*, p.60.

There were also moments of comedy. Louis Botha and 'Sandjie' Sandberg were riding behind the Boer lines near Spioenkop when they spotted a burgher with a long grey beard behind a big boulder. He was leaning back, legs outstretched, rifle across them, quietly smoking his pipe. As soon as he was discovered, the old fellow diligently began to polish his rifle. 'Old comrade,' Botha called out, 'from what Commando are you? Why are you not with your people at the front? Don't you hear how heavily they are fighting? What are you doing here?' The old Boer replied: 'No, General, I'm reinforcing.'[30]

General Ben Viljoen at Vaalkrans sent two batches of reinforcements from the Rand Commandos, making 200 Johannesburgers on Tabanyama, including the red-bearded Bernardus Rudolph Buys. Buys, aged 49, was without fear. When the battle was raging fiercely on Tabanyama, Willie Pohl said:

> Buys would climb onto the trench wall and presenting his buttocks to the enemy would invite them to do their worst; and when, as sometimes happened, a bullet covered him with dust or whined past his ears, he would make faces jeer and at what he called "the rottenest shots in creation." Then he would empty the magazine of his rifle at the enemy before snatching someone else's with which to fire. This fooling went on for six days and during that time he got not a scratch.[31]

Reinforcements were sent from every commando around Ladysmith, the 17-year-old Deneys Reitz among them: 'From the Pretoria laager fifty volunteers were asked for, and more than three times that number immediately offered themselves.' The men left after dark, riding all night until they reached the rear of Spioenkop at daybreak. 'As we rode, we could hear the sound of heavy gun-fire from the forward hills, and it never ceased for any length of time although we were still too far back to be in danger.' After a short halt to rest their horses and cook breakfast, they were ordered to Tabanyama to dig a reserve trench. A mule-wagon had accompanied them from Ladysmith carrying provisions, ammunition and a supply of pick-axes and shovels. When they had dug for some time, *Veldkornet* Zeederberg, who was always kind to Reitz, said that as he was the youngest he need not dig any longer and could go down to the wagon for a rest. 'I made haste to reach the halting-place, and, leaving my horse in charge of the mule-drivers, I started out to see what was going on in the front positions, which were out of sight from where we had been digging.' Since sunrise, there had come the unbroken boom of guns and the rattle of small arms, and Reitz decided to walk across the koppies to the firing line.

> As I went, the gun and rifle-fire grew louder, and before long I reached a point from which I could see the Boer front strung out along the top of the next rise. Black mushrooms of earth and smoke hung along the course of the positions from the heavy shells flung across the Tugela, and puffs of shrapnel flecked the air above. From the noise I judged that a battle was in full progress and, after some hesitation, I hurried on and reached the line in safety. The spectacle from here was a fine one. Far below on the plain the Tugela wound shining in the sun, and the bank beyond was alive with

30 Sandberg, *Instantanés uit den Zuid-Afrikaanschen Oorlog*, p.273.
31 Victor Pohl, *Adventures of a Boer Family* (London, Faber & Faber, 1944), p.20.

English foot and horse. From the wooded hills farther back came the flashes of the British guns, and in the din I asked myself more than once why I had been foolish enough to come.'[32]

The Twin Peaks sector had been relatively quiet, so *Commandant* Hendrik Prinsloo sent 60 Carolina burghers to reinforce Tabanyama, the focus of Warren's attention.[33] *Commandant* Krause brought men of the Zoutpansberg Commando as reinforcements from Colenso. They assembled at 4:00 p.m. and set out. At 7:00 p.m. they off-saddled in the veldt a short distance from Spioenkop, and slept in the open. British searchlights were sweeping the open country, so Krause waited behind a hill for a favourable opportunity, and then dashed across the space that the searchlight had swept the moment before. 'But both because it was safer, and because we wished to conceal our movements, we generally did this by night…' They received orders to station themselves 'on the extreme right of the Boer positions, where the big road coming up from Acton Homes sweeps up towards Ladysmith through a break in the mountain chain. On arrival there we left our horses at the base of the mountain, and climbed the heights above on foot.'[34]

Boer Difficulties

Boer casualties were slowly accumulating, and on 22 January 6 Boers were killed and 30 wounded.[35] While Botha was striving to inspire his men, the charismatic OVS President, Marthinus Steyn, visited the Free State laagers for the same purpose.[36] But the Boers were becoming exhausted from continual shelling and lack of provisions. Their commissariats were further than 45km away at Elandslaagte and Modderspruit, and supplies were intermittent. Large-scale pilfering had caused a lack of salt, coffee, sugar, flour, soap, matches, paraffin, oats and clothing. Botha complained to the War Commissioner: 'As things stand at present the commandos closest to the source get everything and those who are in real need get nothing.'[37] On Christmas Day, the Middelburgers, now located on the western flank, had gone hungry because another officer had claimed all supplies for his burghers, including 80 bags of bread. Danie Theron's scouting corps regularly sent their wagon to the commissariat, but it invariably returned without vegetables – everything had been carted off by the laagers around Ladysmith. The Upper Tugela was 35km from the railway line, so the burghers on Tabanyama often had no coffee or flour. The Apies River *wyk* of the Pretoria Commando, under *Veldkornet* Pretorius, went without meals for 72 hours. Only under cover of darkness could they leave their positions to draw water from a spring, and even that was exposed to fire. Although their *agterryers* could bring meat to the trenches at night, the Boers were forbidden to light fires, like the British troops in their firing line.[38] The howitzers added to the strain. Schikkerling wrote: 'The enemy… soon

---

32   Deneys Reitz, *Commando* (London, Faber and Faber, 1929), pp.71–72.
33   Grobler, *Die Carolina-kommando in die Tweede Vryheidstoorlog*, p.44.
34   Krause, *War Memoirs*, p.58.
35   Anon., *The Bulletin of Official War News*, (Heidelberg, Transvaal Field Press, 23 January 1900).
36   Amery, *The War in South Africa*, Vol. III, pp.243–244.
37   Pretorius, *Life on Commando During the Anglo-Boer War*, p.29.
38   Pretorius, *Life on Commando During the Anglo-Boer War*, p.30.

brought out a lyddite gun and commenced to feel all along the crest of our hill. The shells fell among us with terrific concussions, sending pieces of hot iron, big and small, whistling and whirring through the air.'[39]

Men dreaded the howitzer: '...for with its shell dropping almost vertically, nothing was wanted to complete your grave-head but tombstone.'[40] Yet the bombardment did not dislodge the Boers, one of whom wryly observed: 'In the rifle's jurisdiction, the casting voice is not with the artillery.'[41]

22 January at Potgieter's Drift

While Coke's Right Attack was preparing for the following night's ascent of Spioenkop, at Potgieter's Drift, Lyttelton's Brigade kept up a steady bombardment and 'demonstrated' in front of Brakfontein to draw Boer forces away from Warren. 'Flip' Pienaar, the Boer telegraphist, counted 60 shells a minute: 'Looking down upon the plain before us, we could see the British regiments drilling on the bank of the river, about two thousand yards away, probably to draw our fire, but in vain.'[42]

39 Schikkerling, *Commando Courageous*, p.54.
40 O'Mahony, *A Peep over the Barleycorn*, p.132.
41 Schikkerling, *Commando Courageous*, p.209.
42 Pienaar, *With Steyn and De Wet*, p.30.

11

23 January, Stalemate

'You will not kill us with your Lee-Metfords: you will make us.' Olive
Schreiner[1]

The garrison in Ladysmith could see a stream of Boers riding westwards to the Upper Tugela, and at dawn on 23 January they shelled the Boer positions, trying in vain 'to call them back'. Believing his weakened garrison would need its stamina to support Buller, that day White issued full rations to his troops, who had been on half rations for some time. White announced: '...the relief of Ladysmith may now be held to be within measurable distance.'[2]

Stalemate

Atkins observed that, from afar, Tabanyama appeared deceptively peaceful: 'Only the piping song of a bullet tells you that you have come within the zone of fire; you can no more see the enemy than you could when you stood on the quiet veldt miles away. This green hill is under fire, that green hill is not; but both have the same innocent appearance.'[3] The infantry had made themselves masters of all the edge of the plateau, and clustered in the steep valleys, Churchill describing them: '...like flies on the side of a wall.'[4]

Hart recalled that, when Boer shells struck the boulders on the crest: '...large pieces of rock were flung down the slope, and were greeted with shouts of "Look out!" Casualties occurred at intervals, but by careful precautions and the great help of our artillery from elsewhere, we managed to keep them down to an average of about ten to fifteen a day.' One young officer of Hart's 'was killed by shrapnel, three bullets of it entering his head, when he was far down the rear slope of the horseshoe.'[5]

The infantry, when not crowded on the southern slopes, took turns behind *schanzes* of the firing line. The Boer riflemen and artillery had the range of the firing line, and it was hazardous

1   Olive Schreiner, *The South African question* (Chicago: Sergel, 1899), p.115.
2   Durand, *The life of Field-Marshal Sir George White*, p.176.
3   Atkins, *The Relief of Ladysmith*, p.234.
4   Churchill, *London to Ladysmith via Pretoria*, p.330.
5   Hart, *Letters*, p.314.

to be seen standing up. To relieve the firing line half-companies of about 50 men crawled up the slope to replace their comrades. This meant groups standing up together, which soon brought that section of the line under intense fire. Lieutenant Kearsey noted the Boer pom-pom behind Langkop: 'was especially annoying, being principally aggressive during the time the firing line was relieved, so the plan of one man at a time being relieved was adopted. These tactics later became universal.'[6]

Private O'Mahony, with the West Yorks on Spur 5, recalled:

> ...no one walked on Rangeworthy [Tabanyama], everyone crept on all fours... the crouching attitude... was necessitated by the continuous stream of lead passing overhead... The orderly men trotted down to the cook-house on all fours, resembling short-legged, broad-backed cats. When returning with the camp kettles they crawled forward for some yards, then rested, and on again, looking like so many huge felines playing with gigantic mice.'[7]

On Spur 1, the Connaught Rangers were in a similar position. From sunrise to sunset the rattle of musketry practically never ceased, as their Digest of Service records: '...only at intervals the hum of the passing bullets was drowned by the clang of bursting shrapnel. The Boer guns, posted both directly in front and on the right flank, burst their shells just over the crest, and fired intermittently all day...' When not in the firing line, the men lay behind the slope, each company being protected by a parapet of earth or stone. Immediately below the amphitheatre the ground fell steeply into ravines in which the cooks set up their field kitchens in comparative security. 'It was characteristic of the British soldier that whereas during the greater part of the day he crouched behind his cover, the sight of a fatigue party with the kettles made him forget the shells and bullets, and he dashed off for his food regardless of danger.'[8]

Lieutenant Kearsey of the York & Lancasters was on Spur 4, where he described his men: 'perched on the edge of an almost precipitous hill, their supports massed close behind, where they were exposed to the enemy's shells.'[9] Sergeant O'Hara of the Royal Lancasters noted: 'Shelling still going on – using Lyddite. Bullets whistling around. Sniped 43 rounds.'[10] The West Yorks built a substantial stone fort nicknamed 'Blarney Castle' on Spur 5. This can be seen today at GPS -28.62805, 29.46786. Sheltering in it, Private O'Mahony overheard Colonel Kitchener and Captain Mansel Jones who commanded 'D' Company, West Yorks, discussing the stalemate:

> Kitchener: 'We are doing no good here.'
> Mansel Jones: 'Anyway we're frightening them.'
> Kitchener: '...If I had my way I would rush across that open and get, if not to Ladysmith, to Heaven anyway.'

6   Kearsey, *War Record of the York & Lancasters*, p.19.
7   O'Mahony, *A Peep over the Barleycorn*, p.147.
8   Anon., *Connaught Rangers Regimental Records*, p.51.
9   Kearsey, *War Record of the York & Lancasters*, p.21.
10   T. W. O'Hara, Royal Lancaster Regiment, 'Diary', National Army Museum 1974-11-6, 23 January 1900.

Mansel Jones: 'And I would do my best not to be far behind as your sky-pilot led you aloft.'[11]

The *Manchester Guardian* correspondent wrote of the loss of life which would follow an assault on the Boer trenches, anticipating the mind set which would follow in the First World War: 'If we attack with a sufficient number of men – how many Heaven only knows! – some must get through and be alive at the end of the day. Shall we... disregard losses when we call the issue of the day a victory? We may come to that. But we have not yet.'[12]

The Importance of Taking Spioenkop

Warren hoped to break the stalemate by taking Spioenkop. It is not difficult to understand Warren's plan from what was written at the time, and from studying the battlefield. Once on Spioenkop, the effectiveness of artillery fire would be greatly enhanced, because observers would, for the first time, have a line of sight to the Boer guns and laagers on the plain behind. As 'Defender' wrote in 1902:

> [Spioenkop] was higher by about 160 feet than any portion of the enemy's lines, and could enfilade their trenches at long rifle range, and could see into their works, and also dominate their camps to the north... The occupation of Spion Kop was necessary before an advance could take place, but when it was captured the advance could be made, and would have been made if the hill had not been abandoned... the Boers could not have held their trenches.[13]

Next, infantry on Spioenkop, and especially its northern extension called Conical Hill, would permit a breakthrough by Coke's Right Attack. Conical Hill is 50 metres higher than the Boer trenches on Green Hill, which are only 700 metres away. Private Phipps of the Border Regiment clearly expressed the plan: 'Warren... must first capture the conical hill of Spion Kop on his right flank.'[14] So could the *Manchester Guardian* correspondent: 'If we could get on to the southern crest [of Spioenkop] we could probably push on to the northern end, [Conical Hill] and once there we could open a flanking fire on the Boer lines which ran east and west.'[15] Green Hill was the Boers' weak point; it was the eastern end of the Tabanyama trench line, and only 1,100 metres north of Picquet Hill. Green Hill sticks out like a thumb from the Boer line, and could be isolated from the rest of the line by shrapnel. With Spioenkop secure, Green Hill could be brought under converging small arms fire from Spioenkop, Conical Hill, Picquet Hill and Three Tree Hill. Warren would move 19th Battery from Three Tree Hill to a koppie further south, so shrapnel would converge on Green Hill from two directions. Once the Boers abandoned Green Hill, the rest of the Tabanyama trenches would be open to enfilading fire from the east, and an assault up both sides of Battle Spruit ravine could follow. During General

---

11   O'Mahony, *A Peep over the Barleycorn*, p.147.
12   Atkins, *The Relief of Ladysmith*, p.228.
13   'Defender', *Sir Charles Warren and Spion Kop*, pp.129 & 134.
14   Phipps, *Diary, 1st Border Regiment*.
15   Atkins, *The Relief of Ladysmith*, p.235.

Coke's Right Attack, the East Surreys would be the front line on Picquet Hill, supported by the Connaught Rangers. From behind Three Tree Hill would come the Devons, Somerset Light Infantry, East Surreys and South Lancashires. Hart's Left Attack would join the advance west of Battle Spruit once the time was right. Even if this plan failed, the force on Spioenkop could still advance eastward on the heights, to Aloe Knoll, Twin Peaks and Brakfontein.[16]

In a letter to his brother from Spearman's Camp on 3 February 1900, Thorneycroft wrote: 'The attack on Spion Kop should have been part of a general plan of attack and directly it was known that we had carried the crest at 4 am (and it was known at once) the hill to N.E. of our position [Green Hill] should have been carried at the point of the bayonet. We should then have been able to bring our artillery to bear on the Boer guns.'[17]

Buller Visits Warren

At 5:00 a.m. on 23 January, Warren, Coke and Thorneycroft rode out to reconnoitre the route up Spioenkop, and discussed how to defend it against counter-attack. While they were scouting, Buller had arrived, looked around Tabanyama, and had become clearly annoyed:

> 'I walked round General Warren's firing line... I afterwards pointed out to him that his troops were getting stale, and that his positions were insecure, and told him that unless he could attack he must withdraw. He represented the disadvantages of an attack, but proposed the occupation of Spion Kop. This, he said, he had intended to effect on the previous night without reference to me; but General Coke, to whom be had given the order, had refused to occupy the hill, because he had never reconnoitred the approach. I did not like the proposal, saying that I always dreaded mountains, but after considerable discussion I agreed to his suggestion.'[18]

When Warren told him of the plan to assault Spioenkop, Buller vetoed Coke as commander of the assault. Buller was unaware that Coke had delegated Colonel Hill of the Middlesex Regiment to lead the attack, and considered that Coke, limping from a recently broken leg, would be too slow and cautious. Buller indicated that Warren should remain in the centre of the battlefield, and that the assault should be led by Major-General Sir Edward Woodgate.[19] Although these were only suggestions, they carried the force of direct orders. Buller then returned to Spearman's Hill, leaving Lieutenant Colonel à Court of his staff to assist Woodgate, but otherwise washing his hands of Spioenkop. Buller telegraphed the War Office optimistically: 'Warren holds the position he gained two days ago. In this duel the advantage rests with us...'[20]

16   Amery, *The War in South Africa*, Vol. III p.248.
17   John Stirling, *The Colonials in South Africa, 1899–1902: their record, based on the despatches* (Edinburgh: Blackwood, 1907), p.68.
18   Commission into the War in South Africa, Vol. II, p.178.
19   Commission into the War in South Africa, Vol. II, p.650.
20   Commission into the War in South Africa, Vol. II, p.650.

154   The Spioenkop Campaign

Woodgate Prepares for the Night Attack

Woodgate, commanding in place of Hill and Coke, would require his own troops for his assault. Hart, who had been borrowing the Lancashire Fusiliers since 20 January, was requested to return them to Woodgate. Colonel Blomfield, who commanded them, was relieved: '...the Battalion [Lancashire Fusiliers] returned (with much thankfulness) to its own Brigade... Spion Kop was to be taken that night, and that as he "must have tried troops" for such a hazardous operation, he had determined that the Lancashire Fusiliers should lead the way.'[21] Woodgate's other units – the Royal Lancasters, South Lancashires and TMI – were already on Spur 1 and during the afternoon, they were brought down from their positions. At midday, Bloomfield withdrew the Lancashire Fusiliers from Spur 5. They formed up and marched to Wright's Farm where they spent the afternoon resting. About 3:00 p.m. the Devons noticed their comrades gathering for a night attack: '...but where and what was a mystery.'[22] The field artillery spent the afternoon finding the range of targets they would fire upon in the dark. To prevent the inevitable Boer counter-attack, the path of Boer reinforcements would be illuminated by magnesium star shells.[23] An artillery officer and signallers would accompany the column up Spioenkop and would, when daylight came, direct the fire of the British batteries. They would also report whether it would be feasible to drag artillery onto Spioenkop. 19th Battery was ordered to move the next morning to a koppie with a good view of Green Hill and the saddle to Conical Hill (GPS -28.66260, 29.48881). The Medical Corps made preparations for a dressing station on the summit and another at the foot of the hill. They arranged stretcher-bearers and the supply of water, food and emergency rations.[24] The Natal Volunteer Ambulance Corps and the bearer companies of the brigades received orders to wait at the foot of Spioenkop after dark. No.4 Stationary Hospital, anticipating 600 casualties, erected an additional 100 bell tents.[25]

Woodgate Makes Enquiries

The Connaughts, on Connaught Hill, were closest to Spioenkop, and had long been observing the Boers on the summit. Woodgate went over to them, and Captain Henry Jourdain, commanding D Company, told him that the Boers posted about 10 picquets at night, who withdrew after sunrise, and that he had heard a watch-dog barking.[26]

Lieutenant Charlton of the Lancashire Fusiliers looked out at Spioenkop, which resembled the hump in a camel's back, and worried that, if the enemy were not occupying it, '...the reason could only be that they saw no use in doing so.'[27] The reason was even more obvious: Botha had not entrenched Spioenkop because entrenching on Spioenkop was not possible. There was virtually no soil on the rocky summit.

21 Lewis Childs, *Ladysmith: Colenso/Spion Kop/Hlangwane/Tugela (Battleground South Africa)* (Barnsley, Pen & Sword, 1998), p.80.
22 Linesman, *Words by an Eyewitness*, p.51.
23 Maurice, *History of The War in South Africa, Vol. II*, p.376–377.
24 Amery, *The War in South Africa*, Vol. III, p.241.
25 Treves, *The Tale of a Field Hospital*, p.67.
26 Henry F. N. Jourdain, *Natal memories 1899–1900* (London: Privately printed, 1948), p.13.
27 Charlton, *Charlton*, p.108.

Warren requested 4th Mountain Battery to join the assaulting column, only to learn that the battery was still at Frere, but they would come anyway.

Left Attack Prepares

In preparation for the frontal attack that should follow the capture of Spioenkop, Hildyard ceded control of Spurs 2 to 5 to Hart, the commander of Left Attack. Hart recalled:

> I was told to take command of all troops on the heights of the left attack... I had in the horseshoe (Hart's Hill) the Borders, the Dublin Fusiliers, the Inniskilling Fusiliers (less three companies with [the] artillery), and the York and Lancasters; and, taking up the command of the hill, had also under me at Sugarloaf [Bastion Hill] the Devons, East Surrey, West Yorks, and the Queen's...[28]

Fig 59: Soldiers using volley sights against a distant target. British Lee-Metford and Lee-Enfield rifles had a dial sight (volley sight) on the left of the rifle, allowing a range of up to 2,800 – 2,900 yards.
(National Army Museum)

28   Hart, *Letters*, p.312.

Hart's instructions were to wait until the moment came: '...to use my judgement in opening fire hard to draw off attention, but on no account was I to move...'[29] To be useful, Hart's men used their long range dial sights, calibrated to 2,900 yards (Lee-Metfords) or 2,800 yards (Lee-Enfields), to fire volleys at Boer laagers out of sight beyond Tabanyama:

> One morning, I hope I caught the Boers napping. Knowing their habits of retiring at night and their wagons behind the hills, I began at daylight with a tremendous fire, with side-sights at 2800, [yards] and aim over the crest in front. Those bullets would drop on an area of from about one and a half to three miles from us. I kept it up for over an hour, and I hope it rained bullets upon many an unsuspecting, unprotected bivouac.[30]

The Exhausted Troops

With the exception of Coke's fresh troops, by 23 January Buller's men were exhausted. They had been without shelter in all weathers since the night of 16 January, sleeping little, unable to wash themselves, their socks or their underwear. They had slept under greatcoats or blankets, which offered little protection against the cold drizzle in the hills. Lieutenant Blake Knox noted the khaki drill of their tunics: '...when wet in the presence of a breeze acts as a refrigerator.'[31] Many had lice. Treves said:

> The soldier's tunic, his belt, his pouches, his boots and his face, had all toned down to one uniform tint of dirt colour. He was of the earth earthy. He was unshaven. His clothes had that abject look of want of "fit" that is common to clothes which have been slept in, which have been more than once soaked through, and which have more than once dried upon the body of the owner.[32]

Lieutenant George Crossman of the West Yorks wrote in his diary: 'Tuesday 23 January 1900. This battle has been going now for days. We lost 60 men and 3 officers the day before yesterday... We have now been nine days without our kit or our tents and are awful dirty. Lord knows what we are trying to do.'[33] Not everyone minded, however. Lieutenant Charlton of the Lancashire Fusiliers enjoyed the smell of his men:

> 'A curious, musty, stale odour which emanated from [the British soldier] at all times, the combination of an unwashed body, the thin unabsorbent cloth in which he was clad, and layer on layer of perspiration which had dried between the two. It would have been repellent had it not been bound up with the sentiment of life in camp preparatory

---

29   Hart, *Letters*, pp.311 – 313.
30   Hart, *Letters*, p.315.
31   Blake Knox, *Buller's Campaign*, p.2.
32   Treves, *The Tale of a Field Hospital*, p.6.
33   George Crossman, Lieutenant, 2nd West Yorkshire regiment, 'Diary', Liddell Hart Archives GB0099 KCLMA.

to trial on the battlefield.' Charlton 'liked the men over whom he was in immediate command so much indeed – somewhat, perhaps, in the way a good hospital nurse likes those under her charge, knowing that a few must die while others will recover – that he found their savour at close quarters stimulating to his senses.'[34]

At least the men holding the Maconochie Koppies were near abundant fresh water, and could wash after dark. Captain Talbot of the Rifles found the rocks got red hot; there was no shade; there were 'flies, dust, heat; no luggage except what we stand in; pocket handkerchief & knife is pretty well all my stock in trade; we all look and are filthy; fork, toothbrush, clean socks & shirt badly wanted. Fortunately there is the river to bathe in.' He found the situation tolerable, but he was bored. There was nothing to read or smoke. They had one delivery of mail; no letters, only newspapers, which they devoured.[35]

The Boer Response

To Dr Maxwell, with the Ermelo Commando Ambulance, it seemed by 23 January that the Boers were near collapse:

> Excitement everywhere is intense, and if things continue like this for a few days longer, the Boers will break and run. Things are hanging in the balance, and the officers and burghers are looking more anxious now... I verily believe the English are going to break through at last. The wear and tear and strain of the last two days' fighting is telling very much on the burghers.[36]

Reverend Kestell was also concerned:

> The number of our dead and wounded had already reached nearly a hundred. We began to tremble as to how matters might turn out. How long would it last, we asked when the fourth day [23 January] had passed and our burghers continued to suffer terribly under the bombardment. How long, we asked ourselves, would our burghers be able to hold out? ... The night was dark and rainy, and this did not help to dispel the depression which prevailed; but the burghers were not discouraged; neither the four days' attack, nor the six days of shelling, nor the depression caused by the drizzling rain, could quench the quiet determination and courage of our men.[37]

Deneys Reitz described casualties from the British bombardment that day: 'I saw some men fearfully mutilated, including a father and son of the Frankfort Commando who were torn to pieces by a howitzer shell, their rifles being sent spinning down the incline at the back of us.' It was a day of strain. Not only was there the horror of seeing men killed and maimed, but there was the long-drawn tension and fear of the approaching shells. 'This tremendous volume of

34 Charlton, *Charlton*, pp.98–99.
35 Talbot, *Letter*.
36 'Defender', *Sir Charles Warren and Spion Kop*, pp.122–123.
37 Kestell, *Through Shot and Flame*, pp.61–62.

fire indicated an early attack, and throughout the day we looked to see the storm break at any moment...'[38]

In the afternoon, Louis Botha decided to place a 75mm Krupp on Spioenkop. *Commandant* Hendrik Prinsloo of Carolina, Prinsloo's adjutant J. C. Fourie, and *Commandant* Grobler of Vryheid all went up to select the gun position (likely approx. GPS. -28.64595, 29.51792). The Krupp had been dragged part of the way up when the afternoon drizzle began, so it was taken down again, and parked near General Botha's tent on Groote Hoek Farm, about 1km north of Conical Hill. About 300 Carolina and 100 Lydenburg burghers were camped north of the eastern Twin Peak, under Schalk Burger. Each day, two wagons shuttled between their wagon lager, 3km away, and the camp.[39] The Boers thought the Twin Peaks were too steep to be attacked, so they dug concealed trenches at their foot, facing the Tugela. The guns on Spearman's Hill had shelled this area intermittently since 17 January, wounding Gert Strydom, a Carolina burgher. Then, on 23 January, the British began to bombard the Carolina laager behind Twin Peaks, which was visible from Ladysmith, as a prelude to the Spioenkop assault. *Veldkornet* Steenkamp with 50 Rustenburg men arrived to reinforce this sector, and that evening a group of Heidelberg men joined them.[40] Schalk Burger ordered Colonel Trichardt of the *Staatsartillerie* to bring a field gun and a pom-pom, and Major Wolmarans selected their positions, which would prove crucial the following day.[41]

Fig 60: Colonel Alexander Thorneycroft (1859–1931). A veteran of the Zulu War and Transvaal War of 1881, he raised Thorneycroft's Mounted Infantry in Pietermaritzburg four days after the war broke out, with a strength of 500 men. Thorneycroft carried a C96 Mauser pistol on his left hip. He commanded the Spioenkop summit. (Courtesy Neville Constantine)

38   Reitz, *Commando*, p.73.
39   Grobler, *Die Carolina-kommando in die Tweede Vryheidstoorlog*, p.41–43.
40   Grobler, *Die Carolina-kommando in die Tweede Vryheidstoorlog*, p.42.
41   Grobler, *Die Carolina-kommando in die Tweede Vryheidstoorlog*, p.46.

Final Preparations for Spioenkop

That afternoon, Woodgate shortened the intended route up Spioenkop by selecting the south-western route up the spur, and changed the rendezvous from Wright's farm to the Royal Engineers camp at the head of a small valley (GPS: -28.65337, 29.48460). This shortened the march by about 4km. Warren issued orders for the attack (Appendix V (a)) and Thorneycroft rode out again late in the afternoon to sketch the landmarks on the Spioenkop Spur, and re-examine the route.

The Royal Dragoon patrols confined the Africans to their kraals, to prevent news of the coming attack from reaching the Boers.[42]

That evening, while Woodgate was preparing to set off for Spioenkop, the Dorsets and Middlesex moved up to Picquet Hill, to become the most forward units on Tabanyama. The Imperial Light Infantry, who would support the Spioenkop assault the next day, bivouacked above Wright's Farm. Then, all preparations being completed, the soldiers of the attacking column waited for darkness.

---

42   Maurice, *History of The War in South Africa*, Vol. II, p.376.

12

23–24 January, Night Attack

'It now appears that the English made a great blunder in the manner in which they took up their positions on the top of the hill.' Robert Maxwell, Boer doctor[1]

The Night Climb

The Spioenkop assaulting column comprised 1,700 men, which was fewer than one tenth of Buller's force. The remaining 19 battalions of infantry, the artillery, and the Mounted Brigade, were kept in readiness for the main attack.

The Lancashire Fusiliers reached the assembly area about 8:30 p.m. Lieutenant Charlton 'burnt for the enterprise.'[2] Two hours later they set off, Lieutenant Colonel Alex Thorneycroft leading, in the following order: Thorneycroft's Mounted Infantry (18 officers and 180 men selected from all companies); all eight companies of the 2nd Lancashire Fusiliers; six companies of the 2nd Royal Lancasters; C and D Companies of the 1st South Lancashires, half 17th Company Royal Engineers, and two African guides.

They failed to notice the pile of 2,000 empty sandbags waiting for them alongside the path. The officers, including General Woodgate, all carried rifles. A recent recruit to the TMI was Lieutenant Hugh McCorquodale, correspondent for the *Liverpool Daily Post*, who had joined up at Churchill's suggestion a few hours earlier; he would not survive the next day. The Royal Engineers carried picks, shovels and crowbars; 20 more picks and shovels were carried in stretchers and 5 mules carried more tools.[3] The medical officers carried panniers of splints, bandages, instruments, medicines, stimulants and comforts.[4] Every few minutes Thorneycroft and his scouts, Lieutenants Farquhar and Forbes and Privates Shaw and McAdam, went forward to check the route. Forbes and McAdam would both be wounded the next day. The soldiers were silent and did not smoke; their rifles and magazines were carried unloaded in case of accidental discharge. The night was drizzly, and when the quarter-moon rose just before midnight, it was

---

1   'Defender', *Sir Charles Warren and Spion Kop*, pp.164–165.
2   Charlton, *Charlton*, p.108.
3   Amery, *The War in South Africa*, Vol. III p.250. Maurice, *History of The War in South Africa, Vol. II*, p.376.
4   Blake Knox, *Buller's Campaign*, p.59.

Fig 61: Thorneycroft's Mounted Infantry on the march. This rare box camera photograph shows dismounted TMI, carrying Martini-Enfield Mk I rifles and P1895 spike bayonets; their greatcoats are rolled into a bundle. (National Army Museum)

obscured by clouds. By midnight they had reached the south-western spur and began climbing. Woodgate, who appeared unwell, was helped up the slope.[5][6] Private Cosgrove of the Royal Lancasters wrote: 'There were so many rocks and stones on the hill that we soon got scattered while climbing...'[7] During the pauses, the men snatched a few minutes' sleep; as Lieutenant Charlton recalled: 'Night marches were distinctly bad for the nerves... The halts became more frequent and more nerve-racking...'[8]

After climbing five terraces, Cosgrove asked a comrade beside him, 'I wonder if this is the top?' – which it was.[9] As they neared the summit the officers whispered orders and the men quietly spread out. Thorneycroft recalled: 'As the front broadened I got the Thorneycroft's Mounted Infantry into line, right across the hill, and the remainder followed in successive lines up the last slope, when we were suddenly challenged.'[10]

5   Commission into the War in South Africa, Vol. II, p.442.
6   Burleigh, *The Natal Campaign*, pp.329–330.
7   Cosgrove, *Letter*.
8   Charlton, *Charlton*, pp.108–109.
9   Cosgrove, *Letter*.
10   'Defender', *Sir Charles Warren and Spion Kop*, p.228.

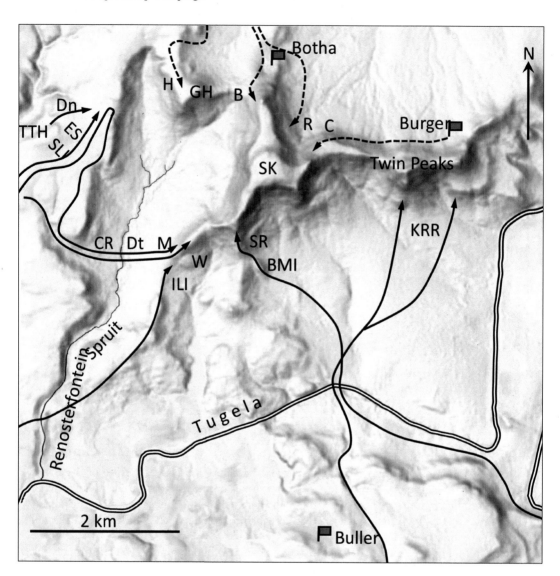

Map 7: Troop Movements on 23–24 January 1900. In the night of 23 January, the Middlesex (M) and Dorsets (Dt) move to Picquet Hill while Woodgate (W) leads the ascent up Spioenkop. Morning of 24 January: East Surreys (ES), Devons (Dn) and Somerset Light Infantry (SLI) move up to face Green Hill (GH), while Middlesex, ILI, Dorsets and part of Connaught Rangers (CR) move to Spioenkop. Lyttelton sends Kings Royal Rifles (KRR) to attack Twin Peaks; Scottish Rifles (SR) and part of Bethune's Mounted Infantry (BMI) move to Spioenkop. Botha sends mixed reinforcements (R) to support Carolina Commando (C); Boksburg Commando (B) occupy Conical Hill and Heidelberg Commando (H) reinforce Green Hill (GH). SK = Spioenkop, TTH = Three Tree Hill.

The Boer Picquet

Commandant Grobler and about 70 men of the Vryheid Commando and the German Corps were asleep at the half-completed Krupp gun emplacement, on flat ground north of the summit. A handful of men were posted about 600 metres south of them, to guard the top of the spur. This is the only way up Spioenkop from the south.[11]

Fig 62: German Corps on Twin Peaks. Taken just after the battle, the eastern Twin Peak is in the background. Often assumed to be the Carolina Commando, there are clues that most of these men are German volunteers, such as their partial uniforms, their style of hats, and Mauser carbines.

About 3:45 a.m. a German picquet heard a sound, and shouted *'Werda?'* ('Who goes there?'). He initially misheard the response, 'Waterloo' as *'Wakkerstroom'*, which was the Boer password that night,[12] but soon realised his mistake and the Boer picquets opened fire. Lieutenant Charlton wrote: 'Immediately came two or three shots in rapid succession. A sound of scampering, which died away in the distance, then all was quiet.'[13] Thorneycroft had ordered the men to lie down

11 Grobler, *Die Carolina-kommando in die Tweede Vryheidstoorlog*, p.47.
12 Kemp, *Vir Vryheid en vir Reg*, p.281.
13 Charlton, *Charlton*, p.109.

when challenged, and they did so. When Thorneycroft thought that the Boers had emptied their magazines, he gave the order to charge; an officer on his left also gave the order to charge. Thorneycroft: '...the whole line advanced at the double and carried the crest line at 4 a.m., when I halted and reformed the line. There were about ten men wounded altogether.'[14]

Lieutenant Vere Awdry of the Lancashire Fusiliers bayoneted one of the Boers, possibly an *agterryer*, who was later buried nearby (GPS -28.65019, 29.51742).[15] Awdry himself was killed later that day; he is buried nearby.

Woodgate and the Engineers Prepare the Summit

Cosgrove recalled that Woodgate: '...requested us to give three cheers, which we heartily did...'[16] and on hearing this, the two howitzers on Three Tree Hill fired magnesium star shells into the sky. Hiley & Hassell described these as: '...brilliant illuminations [which] appeared a most ominous foreboding to the Boers as their trenches were lighted by the various hues.'[17]

All the British batteries now opened fire in the dark, hoping to hit the targets they had identified the evening before.

On Spioenkop summit, Major Hampden Massy, 17th Royal Engineers, laid out tapes to mark the trenches. His sappers found digging was almost impossible – a few centimetres down, they hit stones, and below the stones was rock. Warren had advised Woodgate to entrench on the rear crest of Spioenkop, just as on Tabanyama, thinking that this would give the British shelter from enemy artillery, and Boer riflemen counter-attacking over the flat dome of the summit would be exposed to British rifle fire and shrapnel.[18] However, the summit was found to be a field of boulders, and at the southern crest of Spioenkop was a sheer cliff. There was no suitable place to entrench. Holding the forward crest around the perimeter would not prevent men climbing the steep slope, and would silhouette the defenders against the skyline. Conical Hill, 600 metres to the north, was vitally important, for it was the position from which Green Hill would be enfiladed. But they could not venture towards it, for British shrapnel was bursting in the misty darkness over Conical Hill. Captain Wilson of the Royal Field Artillery wrote:

> At about 4 a.m. on the morning of the 24th the British batteries began to bombard the Boer position in front of Three Tree Hill. The guns had been trained the evening before on the enemy's trenches, and, the positions of the wheels having been marked, they were fired during the night by means of clinometers and lamps. A thick mist prevailed at the time, and the bursting of the shells could only be indistinctly seen.[19]

Shelling in these conditions was haphazard. The target was invisible, the guns shifted after each shot, the shrapnel bursts were indistinct, and the location of British troops was unknown. The risk of casualties from 'friendly fire' was high. It is very likely that these conditions contributed to

14   'Defender', *Sir Charles Warren and Spion Kop*, p.228.
15   Burleigh, *The Natal Campaign*, p.330.
16   Cosgrove, *Letter*.
17   Hiley and Hassell, *The Mobile Boer*, p.118.
18   Amery, *The War in South Africa*, Vol. III p.249.
19   Holmes Wilson, *The Relief of Ladysmith*, p.69.

Woodgate and Massy siting the trench to the south. Dr Maxwell with the Ermelo Commando Ambulance wrote:

> It now appears that the English made a great blunder in the manner in which they took up their positions on the top of the hill… Instead of intrenching along the front ridge, they threw up trenches in the middle of the top; and varying from fifty to 150 yards from the edge. The Boers were thus enabled to climb up their side of the hill without being fired on, and as soon as they reached the ridge the positions of the two forces were equal, or, rather, the Boers had the better of it, as the English artillery could not get at them. If the trenches had been at the front edge, not a Boer could have got up, as the ascent is very, very steep.'[20]

Aloe Knoll to the east, another key feature, was ignored. It was invisible from Three Tree Hill and nobody had made a sketch of the summit, so it was not included in Woodgate's perimeter. The first Boers to counter-attack took possession of Aloe Knoll, after which it could not be occupied. A sapper who was on Spioenkop wrote:

> We then commenced to make some kind of defence works, and the ground being so rocky we had to make them of stones. We only had an hour to make a covering for some thousand men. It was impossible to do it to perfection. A heavy fog was on the hill all the time, and for an hour after daylight, but the Boers kept firing through the fog, and killed and wounded a lot of our men whilst they were working.[21]

It was just becoming light when a mounted Boer, probably an *agterryer*, rode up through the dense mist to the men digging trenches. While the soldiers ran for their rifles, he discovered his mistake and made off, followed by a few harmless shots.[22]

Before Daylight – the First Few Shots

Thorneycroft described the situation at that time:

> Orders were immediately given to form a trench and breastwork. There was a mist on the hill, and in the darkness and mist it was difficult to get the exact crest line for a good field of fire, and the boulders made it difficult to dig, but we made a rough trench and breastwork. At 4.30 a few Boers came up and began firing. The men lined the trench, but the picquets in front replied to the fire, and firing ceased for a time.[23]

20   'Defender', *Sir Charles Warren and Spion Kop*, pp.164–165.
21   Spiers, *Letters from Ladysmith*, p.90.
22   Blake Knox, *Buller's Campaign*, p.64.
23   'Defender', *Sir Charles Warren and Spion Kop*, p.228.

Map 8: Aerial view of Spioenkop at 7 a.m. 24 January 1900. Looking due north, the sheer southern cliff is in the foreground. The sun had been up since 4:30 a.m. but the summit was covered in dense mist. The British have dug a main trench and outlying trenches, and have sent out picquets to the fringe of the plateau. British reserves lie among the rocks south of the main trench. C = Carolina burghers (grey triangles); only 25 Boers of Abraham Smit's corporalship have reached the summit and divided into three small groups. CH = Conical Hill; this is being shelled with shrapnel by 15-pdr guns; note the Fairview-Rosalie road just beyond it. Louis Botha's HQ is at Charles Coventry's abandoned farm, Groote Hoek. Three sheep kraals provide cover for Boers on Aloe Knoll. H = the field hospital or dressing station, which moved down the spur at noon. LF = Lancashire Fusiliers; RL = Royal Lancasters; S = heliograph station, it faces Three Tree Hill but is unable to signal in the mist; SL = South Lancashires; TMI = Thorneycroft's Mounted Infantry.

Sergeant Hartley of the Lancashire Fusiliers wrote: 'The Boers kept firing on us from an adjoining hill [Aloe Knoll] during the time we were making the trenches, and someone fell almost every shot because we were all in groups in the dark. Dawn came and the fun commenced.'[24]

The Trenches

Photographs show the trenches provided only partial shelter from rifle fire, and only from the front. They consisted of low walls of stones and sods, rising 30–45cm in front of wide shallow ditches in which men could lie prone. A Boer officer wrote: 'The English had employed the night in making some wide but low shallow trenches, with corresponding parapets of stones, earth, and sods to shelter behind… more or less in the centre of the plateau, which was a fatal blunder, this being the very spot where… concentrated artillery fire would tell with the deadliest effect.'[25]

Woodgate posted four companies of the Lancashire Fusiliers on the east of the main trench, and in a separate small trench east of the trench: from south-east to north-west were C, F, A and G companies.

The other four companies lay in support behind the main trench; from south-east to north-west were B, D, E and H companies.[26] Thorneycroft's MI were stationed in the centre; west of them were the Royal Lancasters and on the western extremity were C and D companies of the South Lancashires. The main trench accommodated only 400 men lying 1 metre apart; the remainder waited in reserve behind *schanzes* or among the rocks to the south: 'After cheering, we advanced through the thick mist to the crest of the hill, and made trenches, one along the edge of the hill, and one in the centre of the hill. The front trench was lined with troops, and the rest remained in the centre trench ready to reinforce when required to.'[27]

The Boers Awaken

Reitz and his Pretoria tent-mates behind Tabanyama were awakened by an angry sputter of rifle fire coming from Spion Kop: 'As there was nothing we could do in the rain and darkness, and as after a while the firing died down, we fell asleep again.'[28] The Boers who had been on the summit, including Hendrik Kay, wounded in the arm, went immediately to the headquarters of Schalk Burger in the laager behind the eastern Twin Peak and that of Louis Botha just north of Conical Hill.[29] The whole situation was unusual; the British artillery had not previously fired at night, and had awakened the generals. When Botha heard the news, at 5:00 a.m. he telegraphed the Boer headquarters at Colenso: 'Report received that that enemy has taken the Vryheid position. Genl. Burger with all available burghers to proceed there.' Joubert replied: 'Was the Kop still unfortified? Can't you and all the men and officers from all sides re-take the

24   Spiers, *Letters from Ladysmith*, p.92.
25   'Defender', *Sir Charles Warren and Spion Kop*, p.160.
26   Amery, *The War in South Africa*, Vol. III, p.252. Blake Knox, *Buller's Campaign*, p.63.
27   Cosgrove, *Letter*.
28   Reitz, *Commando*, p.74.
29   Hiley and Hassell, *The Mobile Boer*, p.118.

Kop? Everything must be done.'[30] The Carolina Commando laager was closest to the summit, and it fell to them to begin the counter-attack. They were led by *Commandant* Hendrik Prinsloo, a veteran of the 1881 war, who immediately sent Corporal Abraham Smit with 25 men to reconnoitre the summit.

Fig 63: The Carolina Commando before Spioenkop. About a third of the 350-strong Commando are in this photograph. All carry Boer Mauser rifles. Most wear a strip of coloured cloth around their hat. The location is the Carolina laager, just north of the eastern Twin Peak; their A-frame tents were visible from Ladysmith. (Arnold van Dyk collection)

Prinsloo then galloped over to Botha to confer, before he and his adjutant, J. C. Fourie, joined *Veldkornet* Steenkamp and a further 60 Carolina men at the foot of Aloe Knoll. Once it grew light, the Boers heard the bombardment accompanied by rifle volleys along the British firing line, but during daylight this was considered normal. Reitz said he and his comrades behind Tabanyama were: '...not unduly perturbed and sat sipping our morning coffee in the lee of the wagon out of the way of the spent bullets that whined over our heads.'[31]

30   Grobler, *Die Carolina-kommando in die Tweede Vryheidstoorlog*, p.53.
31   Reitz, *Commando*, p.74.

Abraham Smit's Corporalship

When Abraham Smit's men reached the summit, they fired into the dense mist, aiming at the sounds of digging. Corporal Walter Herbert of the Royal Lancasters wrote:

> [We] at once set to work entrenching ourselves before it became too bright, as at present we were amongst the clouds. Before we had done much trench-digging our 'brethren' began sniping… we could hear them snapping over our heads. We laughed at that and continued digging, little dreaming of what was to come.[32]

Smit's small group waited for the mist to clear; as Kestell related: '…everything looked dark. The mountain was enveloped in a dense mist, and for a long time the men lay behind their schanzes waiting for what would happen when the vapours were dispelled.'[33] Each Boer silently piled rocks in front of him; any noise was answered by a blaze of rifle fire from the British line.[34] When daylight came at 4:30 a.m., the mist was dense but brightly-lit, and the British casualties increased as the first few Boer shells began landing. Sergeant E. Dickson, of Thorneycroft's Mounted Infantry wrote:

> There was a very heavy mist on, but at about six they began sending shells up and a stiff rifle fire… They advanced under their heavy artillery fire, and [we] popped them over as they came running from rock to rock. They now brought another gun into position and let drive. Things were getting very hot, and they could not get our wounded away fast enough, so rapidly did they tumble down to it.[35]

Warren – Early Morning

Back at Three Tree Hill, once he had heard the cheers from the summit, Warren sent Colonels Sim and Wood, commanding the engineers, to Spioenkop. Sim visited the summit, a climb of about two hours, then climbed down and the engineers began building gun slides (one can be seen at GPS: -28.6551, 29.51303), a mule track, and a dam across Renosterfontein Spruit. Warren watched the pre-dawn bombardment, and at sunrise he sent Major Kelly to the summit, followed at 6 a.m. by a messenger asking Woodgate to send back the mules for water and supplies. Warren then rode across to Spioenkop Spur, where mules were taking up water in tins, and inspected the engineers working on the gun slides.[36] Warren chatted to the Imperial Light Infantry who were guarding the engineers, and returned to Three Tree Hill around 9:00 a.m.

32 Walter Herbert, 'Letter from Corporal Herbert, B Company 2nd Bn The King's Own Royal Lancaster Regiment', King's Own Royal Regiment Museum KO1383/01.
33 Kestell, *Through Shot and Flame*, p.62.
34 Hiley and Hassell, *The Mobile Boer*, p.119.
35 E. Dickson, Letter: Sergeant E. Dickson: 'How He Was Wounded: Story Told By Himself. The Thorneycrofts Cut Up' in *The Launceston Examiner*, 15 March 1900.
36 Coetzer, *The Road to Infamy*, p.177.

Lieutenant Colonel à Court arrived from the summit with a message from Woodgate. All was well, and 'the summit could be held till doomsday against all comers.' (Appendix V(e)).[37]

Daylight and Mist on the Summit

Around 7:00 a.m. Woodgate realised the main trench was inadequate. Massy's engineers began frantically making outlying *schanzes* in the mist, and Thorneycroft and Colonel Crofton of the Royal Lancasters ordered groups of men forward to occupy them.

Thorneycroft wrote: 'It was found that the trench did not command the [Boer] ascent, and men were pushed forward to line the crest. Defensive works were about to be commenced on the crest, about 180 yards in front of the trench, when the mist lifted – this was between 7.30 and 8.'[38]

Lieutenant Charlton of the Lancashire Fusiliers had fallen asleep and awoke to find that the light had come, bringing with it:

> ...a dense, white cloud that enveloped the mountain-top and blotted out vision beyond a distance of fifty yards... the air was again full of those whip-like cracks and that shrill hissing noise, the full significance of which he had learnt... A few minutes later these disconcerting noises increased to a constant crackling, and he sat up to take notice. There was a certain commotion in the vicinity. The colonel's [Blomfield's] distinctive tone could be heard speaking in a peremptory manner, and the company next door was moving forward at a run... It seemed that affairs were taking a serious turn... the position which had been chosen from the point of view of defence had turned out to be faulty. The enemy was already attacking under cover of the mist and would gain a sure foothold unless new dispositions were taken immediately. The order was for them to leave their present cover and occupy the forward edge of the plateau, trusting purely to luck for natural shelter from the stream of bullets which went sleeting by... Holding themselves in a crouched position and mindless of the weight of their equipment, they plunged forward, and as they did so the air around seethed with the hiss and crack of rifles fired at short range...[39]

Charlton flung himself down behind a boulder fringing the plateau, with men of other units. 'In this spot for hours on end he was pinned by a fierce, short-range fire which plastered his shelter... His own men seemed to have evaporated into space... and [he] found himself in the midst of strange men of other units... There was no other officer to be seen.'[40]

Prinsloo's Counter-Attack

Around 6:30 a.m., Hendrik Prinsloo and Corporal Kritzinger assembled about 60 men to join Abraham Smit's group, making 84 members of the Carolina Commando who would fight on

---

37   'Defender', *Sir Charles Warren and Spion Kop*, p.140.
38   Stirling, *The Colonials in South Africa*, p.70.
39   Charlton, *Charlton*, pp.110—111
40   Charlton, *Charlton*, pp.111—112

Fig 64: *Commandant* Hendrik Prinsloo (1861–1900) led 84 members of his Carolina Commando on Spioenkop summit. (Free State Archives)

Spioenkop summit. Before leaving, Prinsloo asked his artillerymen to reposition their guns.[41] Prinsloo led the men from their laager up a footpath which still exists, and which emerges just north of Aloe Knoll, less than 300 metres from the British trench (GPS: -28.64824, 29.52270). About 7:00 a.m., halfway up the slope, Prinsloo stopped and addressed the group in the mist: 'Burghers, we are going in amongst the enemy, and not all of us will return. Do your duty and trust in the Lord.' Then they spread out and climbed from rock to rock, '…like hunters stalking their prey.'[42]

Prinsloo's men split into three sections. The first made their way up a fold in the ground (approx. GPS -28.64719, 29.51804, behind the present-day Burgher Monument). As this section reached the summit, the British fired on them at close range; Jacob Malan, Theunis Breytenbach, and Hendrik Prinsloo's brother, Willem, were all killed. Another of Hendrik Prinsloo's brothers, Christiaan, was hit in both legs and Hendrik carried him to cover. Burgher J. G. Korf was hit in the arm, but continued firing until his other arm was hit.[43] The second section of Carolina burghers ran into British soldiers 100 metres further south. Tobie van Niekerk, Cornelis Potgieter, Louw van der Merwe and Cornelis Meyer were killed, and *Veldkornets* A. J. Viljoen and A. J. Lange, and burghers Pretorius, Harries, Meyer, McCallum, van Heerden, Breytenbach, Smit and Pincham were wounded. The third section, under *Veldkornet* Steenkamp, were more fortunate. They took cover on Aloe Knoll, although burgher de Koker was killed, and in this position, they were later reinforced by 50 Heidelbergers.[44] Between Aloe Knoll and the eastern outlying British trench were three abandoned stone sheep kraals, each comprising a stout, circular stone wall about 0.5 metre high and about 10 metres in diameter. They provided cover about 200 metres from the outlying Lancashire Fusiliers trench, and the Boers took up positions behind them in the mist. The kraals are still there today: GPS -28.64931, 29.52169; GPS -28.64957, 29.52187; and GPS

41   Grobler, *Die Carolina-kommando in die Tweede Vryheidstoorlog*, pp.42, 51, 52
42   Grobler, *Die Carolina-kommando in die Tweede Vryheidstoorlog*, pp.52–53, 55; Barnard 2 MHJ.
43   Grobler, *Die Carolina-kommando in die Tweede Vryheidstoorlog*, pp.55–56.
44   Grobler, *Die Carolina-kommando in die Tweede Vryheidstoorlog*, p.58.

-28.65007, 29.52191. The British could no longer hope to include Aloe Knoll in their perimeter, which would prove to be crucial.

While Prinsloo was leading his men to the summit, 30 Heidelbergers also began to climb, in the dense mist, up the north-western slope.[45] They ran into outlying British units, and suffered heavily. Willem Kamffer was shot in the shoulder, Willem Marais through the head, and David van Staden high in the forehead. Hendrik Kamffer watched in horror as his friend van Staden writhed about, hitting his face against the stones, spattering it with blood and brains until he died. A. P. van Schalkwyk was hit while lying prone – the bullet entered behind his neck and exited at his buttock. Despite being in severe pain he was unable to withdraw until after dark, when Hendrik Kamffer, the only uninjured member of the group, helped him down the hill.[46]

The Mist Lifts

Prinsloo's signaller was the Carolina schoolteacher, Louis Bothma, who carried his heliograph up the path and set up the instrument on the northern edge of Aloe Knoll (approx. GPS -28.64832, 29.52318). The mist burnt off on Spioenkop about 8:00 a.m., but persisted on Tabanyama for another half hour and prevented signalling.[47][48] When the sun was finally seen, Bothma flashed his first heliogram to Botha: 1,200 British were on Spioenkop. Botha replied that he was sending 400 reinforcements: 'hold the Kop at all costs.'[49]

In the mist, the opposing fighters found themselves among each other's lines, sometimes on either side of the same boulder. Lieutenant Charlton of the Lancashire Fusiliers peered round his cover: 'A few paces away he saw the crown of a slouch hat behind a large boulder, and as he gazed, transfixed, it rose slowly bringing into view a face which was all beard... He fired point-blank into the beard and instantly took cover again...'[50] Burgher Kilian of the Carolina Commando saw his comrade, C. J. Davel, behind a boulder, unaware that a soldier was on the other side of the rock. Kilian shot the soldier, but soon he and Davel were both wounded.[51] Corporal Herbert of the Royal Lancasters wrote: 'As the clouds lifted the sniping, intermittent up to this, became a general rifle fire and presently... we were under the hottest fire, from about 8000 [sic] rifles, that I ever hope to be under.'[52] An engineer wrote: 'When daylight came the bullets came like hail, and hundreds of men were killed and wounded. Out of my Company we lost the Major commanding and three sappers killed, a lieutenant and four sappers wounded. I should have been killed myself... [but] kept under cover as much as possible.'[53]

In clear daylight, the soldiers out in front of the main trench lay pinned down behind rocks. From about 9:00 a.m. they were hit or abandoned their positions, except in the north-west part of the summit.

45   N. M. Lemmer, 'Die Slag van Spioenkop 24 Januarie 1900' in *Military History Journal, The South African Military History Society*, Vol.1 No.1, December 1967.
46   Ian Uys, *Heidelbergers of the Boer War*, (Privately published, Heidelberg, 1981), pp.23–25.
47   Grobler, *Die Carolina-kommando in die Tweede Vryheidstoorlog*, p.54.
48   'Defender', *Sir Charles Warren and Spion Kop*, p.228
49   Grobler, *Die Carolina-kommando in die Tweede Vryheidstoorlog*, p.58.
50   Charlton, *Charlton*, p.112.
51   Grobler, *Die Carolina-kommando in die Tweede Vryheidstoorlog*, pp.56 & 57.
52   Herbert, *Letter*.
53   Spiers, *Letters from Ladysmith*, p.91.

Thorneycroft recorded:

> ...the Boers' rifle fire now became extremely severe, while 3 guns and a Maxim-Nordenfeldt pitched shells on to the plateau with great accuracy from a range of 3,000 yards. It was also now discovered that the trench which had been cut was enfiladed. Most of the advanced parties, being also enfiladed, were completely wiped out, but these were constantly reinforced or replaced.[54]

'They mowed us down like rabbits.' wrote Private Turner of the Royal Lancasters: 'Fancy having dead and wounded men on either side of you, and the moans of the wounded would break the heart of a stone. Hundreds died from loss of blood...'[55]

Lieutenant Charlton was pinned down in front of his trench: 'The sun was most infernally hot... to show a finger even in that inferno of bullets was to have it shot off.' While crawling out to help a comrade, Charlton was hit:

> ...he felt his flesh just above the left knee to be as if threaded in lightning swiftness by a red-hot bodkin, and at the same time he was knocked over on to his side... He scrambled as best he could to his feet and made for the nearest cover at top speed, reckless of the consequences to his wound... he threw himself down behind the rock which his instinct had marked for him, to find that another was there before him. He had unwittingly rejoined his captain [Whyte] who, he gathered, had been unable to move for a long time owing to the intensity of the fire. The captain knew nothing either of what had become of the men. A finger tip had been touched by a bullet. His senior was in a rather shaken condition and most gloomy as to eventualities. He bound his wound, which was stiffening but by no means painful. His captain offered him a brandy flask, which at first he refused... and the next moment accepted. They lay talking, and the day wore on.[56]

Thorneycroft's Mounted Infantry, in the centre of the main trench, were unable to move. Herbert Unwin of the TMI wrote:

> I was laid in one position nearly all day, cramped, and parched with thirst; the trenches piled with dead and dying men. One poor fellow in our trench had his arm blown off close to his shoulder. He picked it up with the other hand, saying "My arm, my arm. Oh God, where's my arm!" Quite mad with pain, he jumped out of the trench, and was instantly shot again, and saved further pain.[57]

Private J. E. Sharples, Royal Lancaster Regiment, lay flat, '...expecting every minute to be blown to pieces ... Bullets and shells were now raining down on the hill, and our artillery could

---

54   Stirling, *The Colonials in South Africa*, p.70.
55   Spiers, *Letters from Ladysmith*, p.90.
56   Charlton, *Charlton*, pp.114–115.
57   Spiers, *Letters from Ladysmith*, p.93.

not touch the Boer guns... All we could do was keep up a rifle fire.'[58] Private McGowan of the Royal Lancasters wrote: '...it was death to stand up. If you wanted to shift, you had to crawl on your stomach. We got no food or drink all day, wounded men asked for water which we had not got.'[59]

Thorneycroft records:

> I sent out more men to the flanks as the Boers were working round, and the replacing of casualties gradually absorbed all the men of the force. The firing became hotter on both sides, the Boers gradually advancing; twice the men charged out from the entrenchments in the centre and kept them back, but at length the entrenchment became the firing line in the centre (the left maintained their advanced position).[60]

58   Spiers, *Letters from Ladysmith*, p.97.
59   James McGowan, Royal Lancaster Regiment, 'Letter dated 28 January 1900', National Army Museum, 1990-12-66.
60   'Defender', *Sir Charles Warren and Spion Kop*, p.229.

13

24 January, Morning on Spioenkop

'...for the next 16 hours our noses were buried in the ground except when we were firing.' Corporal Walter Herbert, The King's Own Royal Lancaster Regiment.[1]

Boer Artillery Intensifies

From about 9:00 a.m. Boer shellfire increased in volume and accuracy. Louis Bothma on Aloe Knoll acted as the forward artillery observer, heliographing to Major Wolmarans where each gun's shells were falling. Wolmarans relayed this information to the five Boer field guns and two pom-poms. Accounts differ as to the precise location of the five Boer field guns and two pom-poms at Spioenkop, but approximate positions are shown on Map 8.

The first to come into action were Prinsloo's Krupp and pom-pom on Twin Peaks. The Krupp was an older OVS black powder gun, and to conceal its smoke it was kept well concealed behind the flank of Twin Peaks. The Carolina pom-pom went out of commission at 10:00 a.m. when it broke a wheel, but it resumed firing from near Botha's tent, propped up by stones. At Botha's request, the two Creusot 75mm guns on the Acton Homes road under von Wichmann were brought within range. A 75mm Krupp under Grothaus, and a pom-pom nearby, which had been in action behind Tabanyama since 20 January, were swung round to face Spioenkop.[2]

From his hospital marquee in Ladysmith, Sergeant Maidment watched an ambulance cart with a Red Cross flag go up to the Aloe Knoll saddle from the Carolina laager. This seemed dangerous: '...especially as a piece of light artillery opened fire beside the cart a moment later. I could see needles of light flashing out like electric sparks, only redder, but could hear no report. Nothing but a 'pom-pom' could have made those quivering flashes...'[3] The pom-poms, nicknamed 'Hell's Bells' by the troops, were lethal against men crowded together without shelter.[4] Atkins thought: 'The hollow rapping of the Vickers-Maxims [pom-poms] was a horrid

---

1   Herbert, *Letter.*
2   Barnard, *General Botha in the Spioenkop Campaign.* Amery, *The War in South Africa*, Vol. III, p.268. Grobler, *Die Carolina-kommando in die Tweede Vryheidstoorlog*, p.60.
3   George C. Maidment, 'Diary of the Siege of Ladysmith', Royal Army Medical Corps Muniments Collection, Wellcome collection RAMC/1011/1.
4   Kestell, *Through Shot and Flame*, p.59.

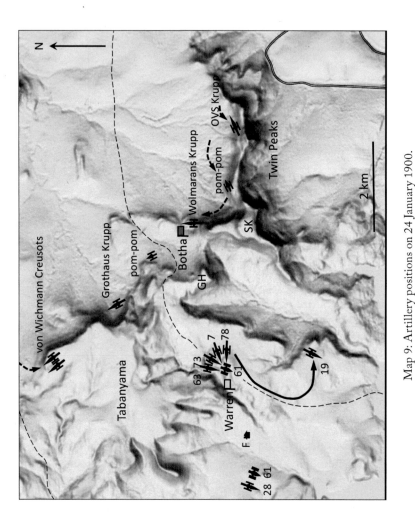

Map 9: Artillery positions on 24 January 1900.

British artillery: At dawn, 19th Battery moves to fire up the Renosterfontein Spruit valley at Green Hill. Two of 61st Battery howitzers fire with 28th Battery from Fairview Farm and two howitzers fire from Three Tree Hill. The 7th, 63rd, 73rd and 78th Batteries fire from Three Tree Hill.

Boer artillery: Botha brought von Wichmann and two Creusots closer to Spioenkop and Grothaus turned his Krupp and pom-pom to face Spioenkop. Wolmarans commanded a Krupp from near Botha's HQ. Prinsloo brought an OVS Krupp closer and moved a pom-pom onto the Aloe Knoll–twin Peaks saddle; when it was damaged it moved to Botha's H.Q.

F = Fairview Farm, GH = Green Hill, SK = Spioenkop.

sound; the little shells from them flapped and clacked along the ground in a long, straight line like a string of geese.'[5]

Reitz recalled how:

> The Transvaal artillerymen got their guns into action on a commanding spur a mile away, and they began to fire over our heads into the troops crowded on the restricted space on the plateau before us. As the guns searched the hill-top the English fire slackened, and from then onward our losses were less.[6]

Corporal Walter Herbert of the Royal Lancasters wrote:

> ... shortly their Nordenfeldt [pom-pom] started barking... And then they started shelling us from both sides, and for the next 16 hours our noses were buried in the ground except when we were firing. Shells are a terrible thing to have whizzing over one, but a confounded sight worse to have bursting close to one's head – as dozens did that day. One man within a few feet behind me was blown in pieces by one, and the trenches were soon filled with dead and wounded.'[7]

Thorneycroft recalled:

> ...the Boers brought a gun and Maxim-Nordenfeldt to bear on us from the east, thus sweeping the plateau from the east, north, and northwest, and enfilading our trenches. The men held on all along the line, notwithstanding the terrific fire which was brought to bear on them as the enemy's guns (which now numbered 5, and 2 Nordenfeldts [pom-poms]) were absolutely unmolested.'[8]

The Boer shells mainly fell on the southern half of the summit and the ascent spur, where there was less risk of hitting their own men, and where British reinforcements were crowded together. From Three Tree Hill, Captain Grant of the Devons watched:

> ...the mob of tiny figures swayed and shook, disintegrated and re-formed into packs... Now a trio of shells would burst at the rear end of the mob, which appeared to surge forward a little... then another placed with diabolical skill in advance of the first; the men in rear edged still farther forward, until a solid mass of humanity stood relieved upon the sky-line. Quick as a flash the whole Boer battery was upon them bang! Bang! Bang! Bang! a storm of projectiles tore into the black lump, which broke up into agitated patches, some edging forwards, some back, some disappearing altogether, as the men composing them fall lifeless below our line of vision. Again the same performance,

5   Atkins, *The Relief of Ladysmith*, p.241.
6   Reitz, *Commando*, p.77.
7   Herbert, *Letter.*
8   Stirling, *The Colonials in South Africa*, p.72.

shells behind, more forward, herding their victims onto the slaughter ground for the coup-de-grâce of that appalling salvo...'[9]

Kestell wrote that:

> ...reinforcements... were subjected to a merciless bombardment, at one point especially, where they were particularly exposed. They were cut to pieces by the shells of the quick-firing guns, and mown down by the tiny projectiles of the Maxim-Nordenfeldt.[10]

Sandberg was with Wolmarans' Krupp just north of Conical Hill:

> Krupp's ammunition turned out to be excellent, and except for the two pom-poms on the flanks, the enemy certainly suffered the most from this gun. It was operated by Major Wolmarans himself, who received heliographic notification of the effect [from Bothma on Aloe Knoll] after each shot.[11]

Colonel Blomfield, commanding the Lancashire Fusiliers, described the effect of being shelled:

> Nearly every [Boer shell] fired took its toll in killed or wounded. I well remember one shell that hit some men lying in a row behind some rocks that afforded protection to their front only. Two [pom-pom] shells passed through the thighs of one man, and on through the legs of the man next to him, leaving only the trunk of the first and carrying away one leg of the second man. A sergeant of the R.E. was lying on the near side of the two men killed and I noticed that his canteen was glittering in the sun, and possibly drawing fire. I told him to turn it round out of sight. The sergeant looked at me, but never spoke or moved, merely turning his eyes towards me, and I learned afterwards that this unfortunate NCO had also been hit by this shell, which had touched his spine and completely paralyzed him.'[12] The paralyzed man, Company Sergeant-Major Plumley, later recovered. His injury was probably spinal cord concussion.[13]

General Woodgate Falls

About 8.30 a.m., Colonel Blomfield of the Lancashire Fusiliers spotted a party of Boers coming up the footpath to Aloe Knoll, reported it to General Woodgate and: 'He came back with me to the spot from which I had been on the look-out, and as we were watching the path the General was shot through the head above the right eye.'[14]

Private John Cosgrove of the Royal Lancasters saw Woodgate fall, around 8:45 a.m.:

9   Linesman, *Words by an Eyewitness*, pp.54–55.
10   Kestell, *Through Shot and Flame*, p.63.
11   Sandberg, *De Zesdaagsche Slag aan de Boven Tugela*, p.96.
12   Childs, *Ladysmith*. p.91.
13   De Villiers, *Healers, Helpers and Hospitals*, Vol.2, p.44.
14   Childs, *Ladysmith*. p.89 .

The firing had not been going on long when the firing line had to be reinforced, and the centre trench was emptied. The General and his staff stood in the centre of the hill directing operations, and as soon as the enemy knew it they directed a most galling fire towards them. The General got shot in the head, his brigade-major Captain Vertue, got killed, and his "runner," Captain Carleton, of my regiment, got shot in the arm. The colonel of my regiment, Colonel Malby Crofton (6 ft. 4 in.) and the colonel of the Lancashire Fusiliers [Colonel Blomfield] were to be seen walking about the hill through a storm of bullets, each with a stick in his hand, directing the troops...'[15]

Those who saw Woodgate's head wound thought he must be dead, though he was still conscious. Treves described the wound, which he thought, probably erroneously, was caused by a shell fragment. It was almost certainly a Mauser bullet wound from close range: 'The piece entered at the outer angle of the right orbit, and ploughed along the skull as far as the pinna. It made a linear ragged gap in the bone. Much brain matter was escaping, and the sight in the right eye was lost.'[16]

Woodgate was carried off by Sergeant Price and other bearers, and as they reached the dressing station the wounded general dictated a heliogram: 'We are between a terrible cross-fire, and can barely hold our own. Water is badly needed. Help us' (Appendix V(f)). The message was taken to the signal station 300 metres away (approx. GPS -28.64938, 29.51497), which faced Three Tree Hill. As Woodgate's message was being sent, the heliograph was smashed by a shell. The signallers ran to the south-east of the spur (approx. GPS -28.65339, 29.51459) and sent the message by semaphore. In their new position, the signallers were safer from shell fire, but Warren could no longer see them, as they now faced Spearman's Hill. The message was read by Signalman Large of HMS *Terrible*. Having seen Woodgate hit, Blomfield recalled: 'I went to Colonel Crofton, commanding the Royal Lancaster Regiment, the senior officer present, and told him what had happened. As he was now in command, I asked him if there were any special orders for the Battalion, and he said, No, but that he should signal down to say that we were "hard pressed and needed reinforcements."'[17] The semaphore message which was sent was: 'Reinforce at once or all is lost. General dead' (Appendix V (b, c)). These messages were relayed from Spearman's Hill by telegraph to Warren at Three Tree Hill, who replied: 'I am sending up two battalions, but they will take some time to get up. Hold on to the last. No surrender!'(Appendix 5(h)) None of Warren's subsequent heliograms to the summit were received, because the heliograph station on the summit no longer existed.[18] Artillery signallers, also using semaphore, were on Spioenkop Spur, but they confined themselves to guessing the locations of Boer guns for the British batteries.[19]

As Woodgate was being carried down, his condition deteriorated; he became agitated, and at the field hospital he struggled to rejoin his men and had to be restrained. He was operated on

15   Cosgrove, *Letter*.
16   Treves, *British Medical Journal*, pp.534–535.
17   Childs, *Ladysmith*. p.89
18   Maurice, *History of The War in South Africa, Vol. II*, p.391.
19   Amery, *The War in South Africa*, Vol. III p.299.

later that day by Treves: 'I opened up the wound, and removed all depressed and loose fragments of bone with a relief to the patient which is, I am afraid, only temporary.'[20]

The British Response

Once the mist cleared, the Royal Field Artillery intensely shelled Conical Hill and the north-western approaches to Spioenkop, preventing the summit from being encircled to the west. 19th Battery had moved at dawn to approx. GPS -28.66260, 29.48881where they had clear views of Green Hill and the saddle to Conical Hill.

The gunners took care to avoid their own men, though they were hard to spot in khaki at a distance. The eastern and northern slopes of Spioenkop were out of sight, and the Boers moved freely on these slopes. The gunners on Three Tree Hill spotted men of the Boksburg Commando under *Veldkornet* Alberts on Conical Hill, and fired at them:

> Our guns on Three-tree Hill tried to find the enemy's attacking infantry, whose right flank was exposed to fire, but they occupied the edge of a cliff, and it was not easy to distinguish them among the rocks. Some of us suggested that they were our own men, but the Artillery officers rightly maintained the opposite... still we never quite realised the life and death struggle that was going on before our eyes.[21]

Shrapnel wounded several Boksburg burghers and Stephanus Olivier was killed, so Botha allowed Alberts to evacuate Conical Hill.[22]

About 10:30 a.m. Colonel Blomfield of the Lancashire Fusiliers was about 30 metres away from C Company's trench when a Mauser bullet went through his right shoulder. Captain Tidswell and Sergeant Lightfoot saw him fall, ran out, and dragged him into their trench. Blomfield lay there for the next nine hours, trying to make himself as small as possible. His water bottle was shot off his chest, and his rescuer, Sergeant Lightfoot, was shot through the head.[23] Blomfield lay listening to the sounds of battle. The Mauser fire slackened a little from time to time, but the guns from the north-west and east pounded 'with horrible effect. The Boers were so close that their voices could be heard from among some rocks near at hand, but they showed no inclination to come to close quarters with our men.'[24]

Lyttelton Sends Help

Warren, on Three Tree Hill, received Crofton's distress signal at 9:50 a.m.: 'Reinforce at once or all lost. General dead.' (compare to: Appendix V(g)) Immediately Warren telegraphed Lyttelton

20 Treves, *British Medical Journal* 3 March 1900, p.535.
21 Anon., *Connaught Rangers Regimental Records*, p.20.
22 Sandberg, *De Zesdaagsche Slag aan de Boven Tugela*, p.94. Grobler, *Die Carolina-kommando in die Tweede Vryheidstoorlog*, p.60.
23 Crowe, *The Commission of H.M.S. "Terrible"*, p.155.
24 Childs, *Ladysmith.* p.104.

requesting assistance.[25] In response, at 10:15 a.m., the naval gunners on Spearman's Hill came into action, concentrating on Aloe Knoll and Twin Peaks:

> We could also see Boers, gathering in clouds, dodging about among the great boulders behind the great nek [Aloe Knoll to Twin Peaks]... Directly the mist drove away, with every rifle and every gun they could get to bear, they opened fire on the summit, now crowded with our troops – most of them unable to get the least cover. Some guns began firing from the northern peak of Spion Kop, from a ridge... others from Tabanyama itself, still others from hills behind it – all impossible to be reached by the naval guns on Mount Alice...[26]

At about 10:15 a.m. Crofton on the summit sent a further signal: 'We occupy all the crest on top of hill, being heavily attacked from your side [the west]. Help us. Spion Kop.' (Appendix V(j)) Lyttelton telegraphed to Warren that he was ready to send men wherever they would be useful and at 10:55 a.m. Warren replied: 'Give every assistance you can on your side; this side [the east] is clear, but the enemy are too strong on your side, and Crofton telegraphs that if assistance is not given at once all is lost. I am sending up two battalions, [ILI and Middlesex] but they will take some time to get up.' (Appendix V(i)) Lyttelton decided to attack over a wider front. He ordered up three battalions: the Scottish Rifles, the Kings Royal Rifles, and Bethune's Mounted Infantry. The Scottish Rifles were on the Maconochie Koppies. They waded south across Potgieter's Drift, collected two squadrons of Bethune's Mounted Infantry, waded north across the Tugela further upstream (GPS -28.67734, 29.53214) and climbed Spioenkop via its south-eastern spur – this was a march of 12km. The 3rd King's Royal Rifles, already south of the Tugela, waded across at the same drift and advanced directly north across the broad Tugela valley towards the Twin Peaks.[27]

At 10.50 a.m. Coke asked Warren's permission to leave Connaught Hill and go up Spioenkop; this was granted, and he set off, Warren's parting words being 'Mind, no surrender.'[28] Warren could not see Aloe Knoll and was concerned that the naval gunners were shelling the wrong area; he signalled: 'We occupy the whole summit and I fear you are shelling us seriously; cannot you turn your guns on the enemy's guns?' (Appendix V(k)) About 11:00 a.m. the naval guns stopped firing, until Lieutenant Colonel à Court clarified to Buller that the British were not on Aloe Knoll, when they resumed firing briefly, until silenced again by Warren.[29] One of the naval shells burst near Bothma and his heliograph, flinging both to the ground. The tripod was broken but the mirrors were undamaged, and Bothma continued to signal from a flat stone on Aloe Knoll.

---

25   Maurice, *History of The War in South Africa, Vol. II*, p.385.
26   Jeans, *Naval Brigades in the South African* War, p.256. Burne, *With the Naval Brigade in Natal*, p.34.
27   Amery, *The War in South Africa*, Vol. III p.261.
28   Commission into the War in South Africa, Vol. II, p.442.
29   Amery, *The War in South Africa*, Vol. III p.262.

Thorneycroft Takes Command

At 10.30 a.m. Thorneycroft, commanding from the centre of the main trench, sent forward Lieutenant Sargeant with 20 men to hold a patch of rocks on the north-east crest. They ran forward and reached them at the same moment that the Boers occupied them from the other side. After a fierce fight, the remnants of the TMI ran back to the trench. A few minutes later, Thorneycroft led 40 men of the TMI and Lancashire Fusiliers in a bayonet charge from the main trench across the open. They made it halfway to the crest before they were forced to take cover, Thorneycroft kneeling behind a rock and firing his Mauser pistol. The survivors ran back to the trench; Thorneycroft fell, twisting his knee, but reached the trench in safety. To the north-east of the trench, the crest line was taken progressively by the Boers. By 11:30 a.m., the eastern crest as far as its northernmost tip was held by Boers, who could now fire on troops coming forward across the summit. Major Massy of the engineers was killed around noon while leading men forward to the main trench.[30] On the north-west crest and plateau the TMI, Royal Lancasters, and South Lancashires maintained their outlying positions. They were protected from being encircled to the west by a sheer cliff, and by shrapnel fired from Three Tree Hill against the western slopes. But with the north-east crest and Aloe Knoll in Boer hands, Boer reinforcements could safely reach the summit from the north-east.

About 11:30 a.m., Buller learned that Major-General Coke was climbing the hill to assume command. Buller was not confident in Coke, and Lieutenant Colonel à Court, who had just arrived from Spioenkop, expressed a high opinion of Thorneycroft. At à Court's suggestion, Buller telegraphed Warren: 'Unless you put some really good, hard fighting man in command on the top, you will lose the hill. I suggest Thorneycroft.' (Appendix V(l)) Although Thorneycroft was junior to Coke and Crofton, Warren could not ignore Buller's recommendation. Warren heliographed to Crofton: 'With the approval of the Commander-in-Chief, I place Lieut.-Colonel Thorneycroft in command of the summit, with the local rank of Brigadier-General.' Crofton, now outranked, sent the message to Thorneycroft. The messenger was shot through the head and fell dead across Thorneycroft's legs, his message undelivered. Shortly afterwards, Lieutenant Rose of the TMI shouted to him: 'Sir Charles Warren has heliographed that you are in command; you are a general!'[31] Coke, limping with reinforcements towards the spur, was never informed that Thorneycroft had been given command. Dundonald summarised the confusion:

> Colonel Thorneycroft was, at Sir Redvers Buller's suggestion, placed in command at Spion Kop by Sir Charles Warren, but the messenger conveying the information was shot dead. Communication with Headquarters was difficult, also flag-signallers were shot down. Major-General Talbot Coke, who had an injured leg, and was halfway up the hill, was partly in command, the officer commanding the actual fighting on Spion Kop was partly in command; all the conditions conduced to muddle and there was muddle, but you can't muddle long under shell fire and with an enemy pouring in well-aimed rifle fire at a 250 yards range, with rocky ground in which you cannot dig, with

---

30   Maurice, *History of The War in South Africa,* Vol. II p.265.
31   Stirling, *The Colonials in South Africa,* p.71.

no sand-bags to construct defences and with men overcome by thirst. It would take pages to describe the different forms of muddling that took place in connection with Spion Kop; one might as well attempt to describe what happens to the various wheels in a clock when the mainspring is out of order.[32]

British Reinforcements

At 9:25 a.m., Warren rode over to Coke on Connaught Hill to request reinforcements. Coke had already ordered up 'F' and 'H' companies of the Imperial Light Infantry under Captains Champney and Smith, who had been waiting below Spioenkop to guard the artillery, and they reached the summit around 10:00 a.m. A further three companies of ILI were sent to the foot of Spioenkop, and about 11:00 a.m. were ordered up by a staff officer who had lost his helmet, and was bleeding from a slight wound in the head. Private Jocelyn Shaw, ILI, wrote in his diary:

> ...we commenced the laborious ascent of the mountain, which took a considerable time, owing to the steepness and the constant necessity for halting to take cover behind a huge bolder from the heavy fire... a most deplorable situation came to light. The men lay in the hastily improvised so called trenches literally packed like sardines in a box. For my part, all I could do was to lie down flat as possible clear behind the firing line, and hope for the best. Personally, I never once fired my rifle, firstly because I could not see anything to fire at, and secondly, because to have done so would have been dangerous to our men in my immediate front.[33]

Shaw was not alone in not having an opportunity to shoot – the Middlesex fired 69,012 rounds that day, whereas the ILI expended only 14,300 rounds.[34]

Private T Hughes, ILI, was hit five times.[35] One ILI trooper advised: 'Don't put your head over the top – I know these buggers – fire round the rock, never over the top!'[36]

At 10:30 a.m., Captain Buckland of the engineers sent 1,000 sandbags to the top of the spur with the Dorsets and African drivers,[37] but by then the men were unable to attend to sandbags. The Lancashire Fusiliers to the east and TMI in front suffered most, as Sergeant Hartley of the Lancashire Fusiliers recalled:

> Well murder was not in it, as from dawn until dark the enemy kept up a fire like hailstones. Our regiment and Thorneycroft's Mounted Infantry were in the front line and we caught the brunt of it. Our fellows fought like lions. Time after time, the Boers

32   Dundonald, *My Army Life*, p.191.
33   Jocelyn Shaw, 'Moving up to Spion Kop', *Military History Journal, The South African Military History Society*, Vol.2 No.2, December 1971.
34   Commission into the War in South Africa, Vol. II, p.445.
35   Stirling, *The Colonials in South Africa*, p.86.
36   Kenneth Griffith, *Thank God We Kept the Flag Flying. The Siege and Relief of Ladysmith 1899–1900* (New York, Viking Press, 1974), p.267.
37   Coetzer, *The Road to Infamy*, p.147.

tried to rush our trenches, and every time we drove them back with heavy losses. Our general was shot down, our staff officers, our own officers – we had no one to command us, our ammunition very nearly gone.'[38]

Private Tom Davis, ILI, described his experience:

When we reached the front line, which we had to do on the right of the hill, we found them behind the rocks peppering it into the enemy as hard as they could... soon the I.L.I. was in the thick of it... The instant you put your head up to take aim properly you had a bullet unpleasantly near, and that is an awful feeling...[39]

Private Beat of G Company, ILI, wrote: 'We got a biscuit the night before, and got nothing until the following morning (36 hours). Water was at a premium on the hill...'[40]
   Private Abbott of the Dorsets remained in reserve on the spur all day:

The firing at daybreak was terrific ... We moved out to reinforce the troops on the kop about 11a.m. & remained about 2 hours half way up the hill there. We had 20 extra rounds of ammunition per man served out to us, and then moved on up to the top of the Hill. It was so steep & rough to get up that we had to go up in single file. As we went up one path, the wounded were being brought down another & it was the most horriblest sight I ever hope to witness... We were just behind the firing line ready to rush when General Coke, at our Colonel's suggestion, would not let us, as the troops in front were suffering very heavy owing to being too thick. 1 shot would knock over 5 or 6 men at a time so we had to lay down under the best cover we could get. It was here the Boers noted Pom-pom guns done so much damage. We were close by the Field Hospital [the dressing station in its 2nd position, approx. GPS -28.65208, 29.51530] & although there was a great Red Cross flag flying the Boers shelled the place unmercifully & the sight of the wounded was horrible. Some walking down with toes & arms off, some being dragged down & others led down. Dead men could be seen in all directions, not a man of us got hit up there though the shells & bullets was flying around in all directions.'[41]

After two hours of slow climbing, General Coke reached the spur and at 11.40 a.m., he ordered the horses of 19th Battery to try, unsuccessfully, to haul up the Dorsets' Maxim machine gun. At 12.50 p.m., he heliographed to Warren that the summit was holding on well (Appendix V(o)). By then, it was so crowded that he had stopped sending up reinforcements. Coke then went to sleep; he can't be entirely blamed for sleeping, as he had slept little the previous two nights and it is likely he was sedated by opiates, which were the only pain relief available. Aspirin, although patented in 1899, had not reached South Africa. Captain Talbot of the Rifles,

38   Spiers, *Letters from Ladysmith*, p.92.
39   Spiers, *Letters from Ladysmith*, p.94.
40   Spiers, *Letters from Ladysmith*, p.97.
41   Abbott, *Diary*.

and presumably the rest of the army, was unimpressed, writing in a letter: 'One general slept, under fire, for 3 hours and could not be found!'[42]

Boer Reinforcements

Boer volunteers came to Spioenkop throughout the morning. Willie Pohl of the Johannesburg Commando reached the summit with Bernardus Rudolph Buys, the joker who had exposed his buttocks on Tabanyama. They were near the British, who were firing volleys on command. Buys waited until a volley had been fired and then stood up and emptied his magazine, before taking cover and reloading. This happened a few times before a soldier held his fire, waited, and Buys was killed. Buys was among 9 Johannesburg men killed and 18 wounded.[43]

Deneys Reitz filled his bandolier and rode through the shells falling behind Tabanyama to the north-east base of Spioenkop, where hundreds of saddled horses stood in long rows in the dongas. As he climbed, he saw comrades, like Jan Malherbe:

> ...with a bullet between his eyes; a few paces farther lay two more dead men of our commando. Farther on I found my tent-mate, poor Robert Reinecke, shot through the head, and not far off [Lambertus] de Villiers of our corporalship lay dead.

Two more of his pals, 'Tottie' Krige and Walter de Vos, had chest wounds.

Reitz found the edge of the summit strewn with Boer dead, and just 20 metres ahead the British were firing from a behind a long *schanz*. Reitz settled down to snap shoot at any soldier he glimpsed.[44]

About 50 Heidelbergers reinforced the Utrecht Commando on Green Hill, where they could aim at the western flank of the summit and the spur, forcing the crowded troops on the spur onto its eastern slopes.[45] The German Corps and the Krugersdorp Commando under Kemp also sent up reinforcements.[46] *Oberst* Constantin von Braun of the German Corps described the death of a volunteer, Henning von Brusewitz: '...he had just risen and walked forward a few steps, when a chance bullet crashed into his forehead, and he fell a corpse.'[47] Reitz knew ex-Lieutenant von Brusewitz's reputation; he had drawn his sabre and run through a stranger in a restaurant in 1896 in Karlsruhe, simply because the man had bumped into his chair. Von Brusewitz seemed to have a death wish; he repeatedly stood up among the rocks to fire and stood smoking a cigarette, careless of the flying bullets until he fell dead within a few feet of Reitz.[48] Reitz vividly described fighting at close range:

---

42 Talbot, *Letter*.
43 Ben Viljoen, *My Reminiscences of the Anglo-Boer War*, p.36.
44 Reitz, *Commando*, p.75.
45 Michael Davitt, *The Boer Fight for Freedom* (New York: Funk & Wagnalls, 1902), p.341. Amery, *The War in South Africa*, Vol. III p.267.
46 Grobler, *Die Carolina-kommando in die Tweede Vryheidstoorlog*, p.60.
47 Pienaar, *With Steyn and De Wet*, p.43.
48 Reitz, *Commando*, p.78.

Fig 65: Deneys Reitz and comrades in the Isaak Malherbe Corporalship of the Pretoria Commando.
Reitz (1882–1944) wrote *Commando*, the most famous account of the war. Photograph taken on
9 December 1899 at Vaalkop near Ladysmith. Some of these men went to the Upper Tugela with Reitz.
Back row, from left: Isaak Malherbe, L. de Villiers**, Jacobus Retief, Jan Malherbe**, Kenne Malherbe,
Hennie Malherbe, Joubert Reitz, Deneys Reitz, Danie de Villiers, Flip Tulleken, Johannes Retief.
Middle, from left: Charles Jeppe**, David Malherbe, Walter de Vos*, P. R. de Villiers, Gert Coetzee, J.
de Villiers (kneeling); Front from left: Solms, B. van Rensburg, Samuel van Zyl, J. Rattray, Jan Luttig.
Key: * = wounded at Spioenkop; ** = killed at Spioenkop. (Arnold van Dyk collection)

About fifty soldiers had run forward to surrender, but otherwise things were going none
too well. We were sustaining heavy casualties from the English schanz immediately
in front of us, and the men grew restive under the galling point-blank fire, a thing not
to be wondered at, for the moral effect of Lee-Metford volleys at twenty yards must
be experienced to be appreciated. The English troops lay so near that one could have
tossed a biscuit among them...[49]

49   Reitz, *Commando*, p.76.

Most of the Boer losses were sustained at close range early in the morning. By 9:00 a.m., the Boers were in well-concealed positions. The estimates of the numbers of Boers on Spioenkop summit vary. Despite the exhortations of their officers, burghers came and went during the battle, some bringing up water and ammunition as others were going down. Eyewitnesses tended to overestimate the numbers of men, and the numbers of dead bodies they saw. Reitz estimated 800 burghers climbed Spioenkop;[50] Kemp said 500,[51] and Botha said no more than 350 burghers fought on Spioenkop.[52] The pro-Boer Irishman, 'Colonel' John Blake, thought the number engaged in the area was about 600 and the actual number on the Kop about 250. [53] Henri Slegtkamp, the hero of Platkop, was on the summit, and wrote: '...only 300 Boers participated in the battle... all were volunteers. No one sent them there to fight. They got the victory. The fame belongs just to them. And this is the true history of Spioenkop.'[54]

Veldkornet Barend Jacobus de Lange Badenhorst of the Vryheid Commando, was hit by either a ricochet or a spent bullet. His death was witnessed:

> Swinging on his heel he sank with a groan in a sitting posture, his back supported by the rock he so lately fired over. Hour after hour he sat with wide open eyes. His death certain, no one moved him... Men with spare ammunition hurrying past would give this well-known man a glance of pity as he sat with open eyes, and angry wound, on the crest of the hill he had given his life to repossess. The noise of the battle and the passing men had no apparent effect on the deadened brain or staring gaze, but sitting erect until noon, suddenly... a stream of blood poured from the hole in his forehead and the bravest man we ever knew sank dead and limp to the earth.[55]

With Badenhorst killed, *Veldkornet* Solomon Grobler, although also shot through the hand, took command of the Vryheid Commando. Badenhorst was buried at Clydesdale, (GPS -28.59362, 29.55637). In 1978, his remains were exhumed for re-burial at Platrand. His skull showed fractures consistent with a spent bullet striking, but not penetrating, his forehead.

The British Surrender

During the campaign on the Upper Tugela 222 soldiers were taken prisoner, and all but 2 of these were captured on Spioenkop on 24 January: 144 Lancashire Fusiliers, 30 ILI, 28 Royal Lancaster, 10 South Lancashire, 6 Middlesex, and 4 TMI.

The most significant incident took place in the Lancashire Fusiliers trench, probably the outlying trench that was exposed to Aloe Knoll and the crest. About noon, when most of their officers were wounded or dead, a white cloth waved above the parapet. Firing continued, but Pretoria burghers under *Veldkornet* Opperman and *Veldkornet* Zeederberg crawled closer.

50   Reitz, *Commando*, p.74.
51   Kemp, Vir Vryheid en vir Reg, p.289.
52   Grobler, *Die Carolina-kommando in die Tweede Vryheidstoorlog*, p.61
53   Blake, *A West Pointer with the Boers*, p.116.
54   Mostert, *Slegtkamp van Spioenkop*, p.44.
55   Hiley and Hassell, *The Mobile Boer*, pp.119–120.

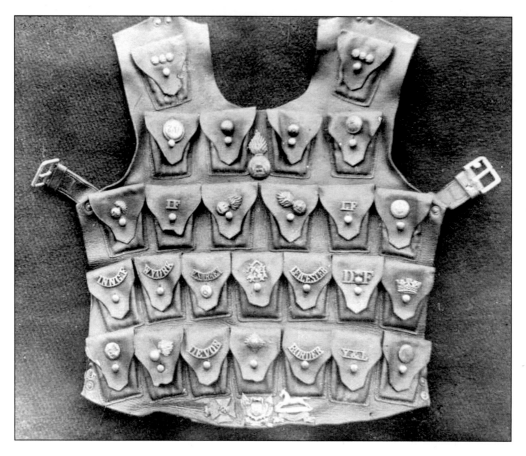

Fig 66: Boer waistcoat bandolier. The owner has affixed souvenirs from units who fought on the Tugela, including: Lancashire Fusiliers, Dublin Fusiliers, Inniskilling Fusiliers, Leicesters, East Surrey, Devons, West Yorks and York & Lancasters, King's Royal Rifles. There are also Boer badges of the ZARPs and OVS.

Raised hands, rifles with the butt uppermost, and white cloths appeared above the parapet.[56] Jan Celliers of Pretoria cried out: 'Hands up! Come out' and the Lancashire Fusiliers in the trench stood up with hands raised. Celliers and about 50 others moved towards the trench, some jumped in among the British, taking their rifles, and the Fusiliers were shepherded down to the footpath north of Aloe Knoll.

Thorneycroft, who was about 100 metres away, noticed what was happening on his right and ran over with a few men, shouting: 'I am the officer in command; back to your positions, men; the fight must go on.'[57] He described the incident:

56   Sandberg, *De Zesdaagsche Slag aan de Boven Tugela*, p.97.
57   Davitt, *The Boer Fight for Freedom*, p.345.

Fig 67: Lancashire Fusiliers outlying trench. After the battle – looking towards Aloe Knoll, the western Twin Peak beyond. The Boer photographer, thought to be Jan van Hoepen, is standing just beyond the main trench, which is now a communal British grave. Beyond him is an outlying trench, which is no longer present, but which was the site of the Lancashire Fusiliers surrender just after noon. The stones of the outlying trench were probably used to build up the communal grave.

The Boers closed in on the right and centre. Some men of mixed regiments at the right end of the trench got up and put up their hands; three or four Boers came out and signalled their comrades to advance. I was the only officer in the trench on the left, and I got up and shouted to the leader of the Boers that I was the commandant and that there was no surrender. In order not to get mixed up in any discussion I called on all men to follow me, and retired to some rocks farther back. The Boers opened a heavy fire on us.[58]

Celliers and his men ducked back to their positions, both sides firing, and several men were hit in the crossfire. Soon the fighting recommenced with, Davitt thought: '...if possible, a deadlier spirit on the part of the burghers... It was resolved that no more attention would be given to British white flags or emblems of surrender...'[59]

58   Stirling, *The Colonials in South Africa*, p.70.
59   Davitt, *The Boer Fight for Freedom*, p.345.

Fig 68: Inside outlying Lancashire Fusiliers trench. This outlying trench formed the eastern flank of the British defence on the summit, and was the site of the Lancashire Fusiliers' surrender just after noon. The three bodies in the trench have been smashed by explosions, and have been stripped of their equipment and boots. Three discarded foreign service helmets lie beyond the parapet. On the slope towards Aloe Knoll, 250 metres away, one of the three stone sheep kraals is visible – it is still present today, though the stones of the trench have disappeared in building up the nearby communal grave.

Lieutenant Charlton, trapped behind his boulder 100 metres front of the trench, saw his comrades surrender: '[They] were all in a very tight corner, so tight indeed, that there seemed no way of escape... There was great commotion ... men were standing up and gesticulating. Surely those others with them could not be some of the enemy. The commotion died down, and firing went on as before.'[60]

Captain George Freeth of the Lancashire Fusiliers, wounded in both arms, refused to surrender. He was dragged from the trench, and once in captivity was provided water and a can of sardines.[61]

Thorneycroft's action prevented the surrender from becoming a general collapse, aided by the fortunate arrival of two companies of the Middlesex.

One company, under Major Savile, had turned east towards Aloe Knoll. When they reached an old sheep kraal (this no longer exists, GPS approx. -28.65012, 29.51928), Savile ordered 'fix bayonets', and led a charge round the shoulder of the summit, reaching the trench where

60   Charlton, *Charlton*, p.112.
61   Sandberg, *De Zesdaagsche Slag aan de Boven Tugela*, p.99.

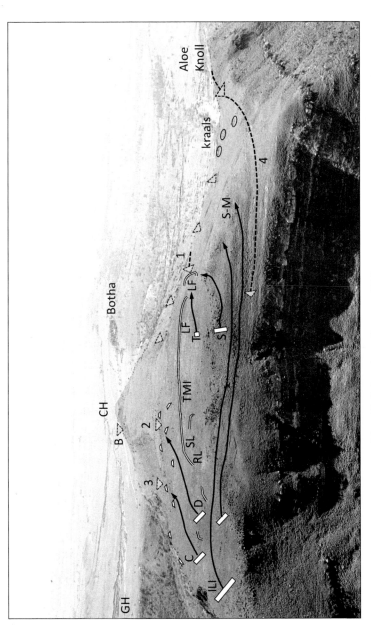

Map 10: Spioenkop afternoon 24 January.

Aerial View of Spioenkop, afternoon of 24 January 1900. Aerial view looking north. 250 Boers are concealed on the north and east fringes of the summit and on Aloe Knoll (grey triangles). British outlying positions in the north-east have been wiped out or captured. The British occupy the main trench and the outlying *schanzes* north-west of it. Reinforcements (Middlesex, ILI and Scottish Rifles) arrive up the spur. A Krupp and a pom-pom fire from near Botha's HQ, four other Boer field guns and a pom-pom fire from further away.

Boer attacks, 1: 12:15 p.m, Jan Cilliers of the Pretoria Commando captured the outlying Lancashire Fusiliers trench, repulsed by Thorneycroft and Major Savile of Middlesex. 2: 2:00 p.m. a limited surrender in outlying positions, repulsed Colonel Crofton (Royal Lancasters) and Captain Dyer (Middlesex). 3: A limited surrender, repulsed by Colonel Cooke (Scottish Rifles). 4: Encircling of the summit to the south resisted by ILI; Major Scott-Moncrieff, Middlesex charges towards Aloe Knoll. The dressing station and signal station have moved down the spur. British shrapnel drove the Boksburg Commando off Conical Hill. B = Boksburg Commando; C = Colonel Cooke; CH = Conical Hill; D = Captain Dyer; ILI = Imperial Light Infantry; LF = Lancashire Fusiliers; RL = Royal Lancasters; S = Major Savile; SL = South Lancashires; SM = Major Scott-Moncrieff; T = Colonel Thorneycroft; TMI = Thorneycroft's Mounted Infantry.

the surrender was taking place. At the same time, a second company of the Middlesex was beckoned directly over the summit by Thorneycroft, who led them in a charge down the slope in front of him. Their momentum carried them past the trench to the fringe of the plateau, but rifle fire soon forced them back.

Thorneycroft recalled:

> On reaching the rocks I saw a company of the Middlesex Regiment advancing. I collected them up to the rocks, and ordered all to advance again. This the men did, and we reoccupied the trench and crestline in front. As the companies of the Middlesex arrived I pushed them on to reinforce, and was able to hold the whole line again.[62]

Around 2:00 p.m. a second group attempted to surrender, this time in the centre of the main trench (see Map 9). Colonel Blomfield, lying wounded, described this as an 'odd incident':

> About 2 pm two companies of the Middlesex Regiment, and a little later two of the Scottish Rifles, came up to reinforce… It was while the Middlesex were fighting that an odd incident occurred. Our men and the Boers apparently advanced simultaneously, both thinking the others were surrendering. After much shouting, and neither showing any signs of giving in, firing was again opened at pistol shot range, and the casualties over this incident must have been extremely heavy.[63]

Blomfield had seen the Boers advancing, causing groups of soldiers to run back to the rocks behind them. Colonel Crofton rushed forward to rally them, and Bugler Russell at his side sounded the advance. The men rallied and ran back to the trench, and once again, the Middlesex checked the surrender, Captain Dyer's Company sweeping forward through the panic-stricken mob.

When the rest of the Middlesex, under Major Blake, and the Imperial Light Infantry reached the summit they were sent towards the east. This was where the fiercest fighting in the afternoon would happen.[64]

Private Herbert of the Middlesex wrote that he was: 'engaged for the rest of the day in one of the most horrible battles… it was the most awful sight that mortal man could possibly witness… If you would know of any one volunteering to come out here to fight just advise them to remain where they are…'[65]

A third surrender attempt, sometime after 2:30 p.m., was relatively insignificant. Soldiers in the western part of the main trench began to wave white handkerchiefs, and the Boers advanced towards them. Sandberg wrote: 'The Utrecht commando [on Green Hill] (on the right, below the summit) continued to fire… without knowing that above, for the third time a surrender was offered and accepted.'[66] Colonel Cooke led the leading company of the Scottish Rifles directly

---

62   Stirling, *The Colonials in South Africa*, p.70.
63   Childs, *Ladysmith*. p.99.
64   Amery, *The War in South Africa*, Vol. III p.270.
65   Herbert, 2nd Bn Middlesex Regiment, 'Letter of 1 February 1900', National Army Museum 2008-02-16.
66   Sandberg, *De Zesdaagsche Slag aan de Boven Tugela*, p.97.

to the front trench, under heavy fire (see Map 9). The Boers fell back, and both sides committed themselves to a battle of attrition.[67]

Coke Reaches the Summit

About 1:15 p.m. Coke had ordered up the remaining four companies of the Middlesex and five companies of the Imperial Light Infantry, and then he slowly climbed the spur. He reached the final terrace, but did not make contact with Thorneycroft or Crofton.

This was the first time in action for Private Evans, of D Company, Middlesex Regiment:

> '...simply walking up the hill to be murdered. The sight I saw what with fellows arms and legs being blown off, some having their brains blown out and their blood splashing all over you. I fainted when I saw a poor fellow's head blown off his shoulders and there he stood till they pushed him down. I was fighting for six hours... I had just fixed my bayonet to make a charge when I got hit... [it] went in at the top of the shoulder and came out of the arm without touching the bone, so I was lucky in fact we were all lucky, wounded or not, to come off that hill alive.'[68]

---

67   Amery, *The War in South Africa*, Vol. III p.273.
68   Frederick Evans, 'Letter, 3025 Pte Evans, D Company, 2nd Bn Middlesex Regiment,' National Army Museum 2008-02-16.

14

24 January, Afternoon on Spioenkop

'Dead, dead; everybody's dead; the British army is all dead.' British prisoner of
war.[1]

At 2:00 p.m. for the first time Thorneycroft found it possible to leave his section of trench in
order to direct the defence of the summit from the outcrop of rocks in the centre, assisted by
Colonel Crofton of the Royal Lancasters. However, they faced north, and were unaware of
events on the rocky slope to their south.[2]

Sergeant E. Dickson of TMI was wounded at 3:00 p.m., shot through the knee. He was still
able to help to carry in some of the wounded until his leg gave in. He tried to scramble away, and
finally a stretcher party picked him up and carried him down to the hospital wagon, a distance
of about three miles; he wrote:

> I saw a shell blow both legs off a man, and another blew a man to pieces. I went with
> another man to get in a poor fellow, and as we carried him my poor mate was shot
> through the head and fell dead, and the wounded man was hit twice. I dragged him
> behind some rocks, but he died, so I made the best of my way back to the others.[3]

During a lull, Lieutenant Charlton, wounded in the leg, and Captain Whyte, wounded in the
finger, managed to crawl back 100 metres to their trench:

> The fire slackened on all sides. It seemed reasonably safe to leave the cover and go in
> search of their men. Slowly and with infinite caution, on hands and knees and stomach,
> they made their way and finally found themselves among their own men again. The
> company had not suffered heavy casualties, but they had been leaderless and were
> rattled. They were thirsty and exhausted by the sun's rays and quite dispirited. A few
> had been killed and lay there unnoticed. A man, severely wounded, and who, according
> to his own broken account, was hit all over his body, kept crawling up and down the

---

1   Stirling, *The Colonials in South Africa*, p.75.
2   Amery, *The War in South Africa*, Vol. III p.270.
3   Dickson, *Letter*.

line, whining pathetically and incessantly... As he approached, those in his path looked over and round him as one does when the cap is passed by an itinerant musician. The captain said, "Poor fellow, poor fellow!"[4]

The Scottish Rifles Reinforce

The Scottish Rifles reached the summit around 2:30 p.m. As Private James Murray climbed the spur, he could see men of the Lancashire brigade coming down:

> some of them horrible to behold... We then got to the zone of fire, and if ever I was glad that I was a short man it was at that moment. Just as I was turning a corner to get into the firing line (and we had to go one at a time, in single file), three [pom-pom] shells flew in rapid succession over my head, and if I had been only a few inches taller I should not have lived to write this letter. At last, however, we got into the trenches … I then had time to look about me, and what did I see – dead, dying, and wounded scattered all over the field … after seven hours hot firing and hard fighting, in as tight a hole as it was ever the lot of any of us to be in...'[5]

The Scottish Rifles arrived by companies, and Thorneycroft sent them to the right and left flanks.[6] Sergeant Raisbeck estimated that he fired 500 to 600 rounds: '...although I must confess I aimed and fired in anything but a deliberate manner … For about six hours we lay packed in that trench – the well, the wounded, and the dead, and the two latter were greatly in the majority by nightfall. Our throats were parched with thirst, and the cries of the wounded for water were piteous...'[7]

Private John Cosgrove of the Royal Lancasters, in the western part of the main trench, was relieved to see the Scottish Rifles arrive:

> After keeping up the firing for several hours we were very hard pressed... the Boers were gaining considerably on the right side of the hill... C Company of the Scottish Rifles came to the left of the hill where I was, and under the command of a cool, calm major did some splendid work. One of them, who was close to me and the major, got ripped open with a shell, and a sergeant of my regiment got a hole through his left arm with the same shell. The worse cases were on the right [east] of the hill where the right half of my company were. And when the fray was at its hottest they were reinforced by a company of the Imperial Light Infantry, who, I believe, did splendid work...'[8]

---

4   Charlton, *Charlton*, p.115.
5   Spiers, *Letters from Ladysmith*, p.94.
6   Stirling, *The Colonials in South Africa*, p.70.
7   Spiers, *Letters from Ladysmith*, p.98
8   Cosgrove, *Letter*.

Fighting on the Southern Slope

The southern slope of Spioenkop summit is steep and narrow, only about 150 metres wide, and bordered to its south by a sheer cliff (see Map 9). It is not possible to dig trenches on the southern slope; large boulders offer cover, but there is very little soil. From about 2:00 p.m. the fiercest fighting took place here, involving mixed units of Middlesex, Imperial Light Infantry and Scottish Rifles.

Colonel Hill of the Middlesex Regiment was in command of the southern slope, out of sight of Thorneycroft, but less than 200 metres away. In the early afternoon, Captain Charles Muriel of the Middlesex led an advance across the boulders towards Aloe Knoll, but fell wounded, and lay exposed for some hours until another bullet killed him. Lance Corporal Putland was among Muriel's men:

> I was lying on the ground firing with the remainder on the extreme right of the firing line, when Capt. Muriel told us to go 60 yards to our right front and about 30 of us went, 2 or 3 was [sic] hit getting there, and directly we got in position. Colour Sergeant Morris was talking and telling me where to fire, he was hit through the nose, he was my right hand man, and directly after this a young fellow was shot on my left, soon after this I was ordered to go to the Main Body on our left with a message, as it was not safe to lift your head up off the ground. I did not like the job, but I had to do it and there was little time for thinking, so I said a prayer to myself and off I went, and the bullets was like rain round me, it was a terrible time for me, and there was any amount of dead here by this time, and the shouts was fearful while I was doing this, Capt. Muriel was shot dead after being fairly riddled with bullets...[9]

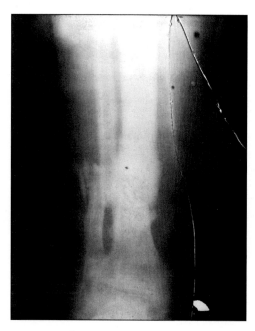

Major Scott-Moncrieff of the Middlesex then led an advance to within 350 metres of Aloe Knoll before he was hit. He fell, rose, and was hit again; he tried to rise again and was hit a third time. Despite bullets passing through his back, abdomen, and three limbs, he survived.[10]

Fig 69: X-Ray of Major William Scott-Moncrieff. Both the British and the Boers used X-ray apparatus in their stationary hospitals. Major Scott-Moncrieff of the 2nd Middlesex was hit in five places while leading a charge towards Aloe Knoll. This radiograph shows his tibia and fibula, shattered by a bullet about 10cm above the ankle joint , are beginning to heal. (Wellcome collection)

9   Putland, *Diary.*
10   Treves, *British Medical Journal,* 1900, p.862.

Some Boers tried to surrender, as Lance Corporal Putland described in his diary:

> ... of course "E" Company of the Middlesex Regmt being in the best position and nearest to were the flag was raised went towards them; as this meant surrender on their part, but this was only their treacherous work, when the Company got within a few yards from them they ordered them to put down their arms which they did, when this was done our fellows were fired on from another party concealed at a few yards distance, and they were mowed down like dogs, here with this party my pal was killed, (shot through the head) Sergt Hudson, we also had some taken prisoner and several got away during the night, we also captured a few...[11]

The British on the southern slope then gradually fell back until the firing line on the southern slope had all but disappeared, and by about 3:30 p.m. the summit was in danger of being encircled. The Boers were able to fire on the spur, choked with British reserves and wounded. At the crucial moment, No.1 Company, Scottish Rifles, reached the summit and turned east, joining the ILI and Middlesex, and holding back the Boer advance. Captain O'Gowan followed,

Fig 70: Scottish Rifles on Spioenkop Spur. From the album of Lieutenant A. C. Northey, it shows a company of Scottish Rifles resting in a line on the Spioenkop ascent spur, 24 January 1900, waiting to advance onto the summit. The standing figure is thought to be Lieutenant Northey himself. On the rear of the photograph is written: 'This is the one where he says the shells were bursting all round and the bullets humming like bees overhead.' (Courtesy Neil Drummond)

11   Putland, *Diary*.

with the 2nd, 3rd and 4th Companies, Scottish Rifles. They fixed bayonets and charged, with groups of ILI and Middlesex joining them, reaching the saddle leading to Aloe Knoll.[12]

Despite the heroism of the British on the southern slope, it was probably the attack on Twin Peaks to their east that was critical in preventing the Boers from encircling the summit.

Fig 71: View east from the southern slopes of Spioenkop. Taken soon after the war, this is the view seen by the ILI, Middlesex, and Scottish Rifles. In the foreground is the sloping southern summit, looking towards Aloe Knoll (left); the western Twin Peak is on the skyline beyond. The KRRC attacked from the right of the picture. (Arnold van Dyk collection)

The Kings Royal Rifles were climbing Twin Peaks, and as the Boer defenders fell back there, the Boers on Aloe Knoll had British on both sides of them. Because of this, from about 4:30 p.m. the fight on the southern slope became stationary, as it had been on the rest of the summit for some time. Putland of the Middlesex recalled: '… this position we held all day and without food or water, and once during the day we were ordered to fix bayonets and charge but had to retire again owing to the fire…'[13]

12   John Stirling, *Our Regiments in South Africa, 1899–1902: Their Record, Based on Dispatches* (Edinburgh; Blackwood 1903), p.72. Amery, *The War in South Africa*, Vol. III p.275.
13   Putland, *Diary*.

The fighting on the southern summit was visible through telescopes from Spearman's Hill, where Atkins wrote: 'I could see men running to and fro on the top, ever hunted to a fresh shelter. Some Boer riflemen crept forward, and for a few minutes fifty Boers and British heaved and swayed hand-to-hand. They drew apart... The shelling did not cease.'[14]

Fig 72: Watching Spioenkop from Spearman's Hill. A crowd of observers looks north across the Tugela valley to watch fighting on the southern slopes of Spioenkop on 24 January. (National Army Museum)

Casualties

The stretcher-bearers, under Captain Tyack and Lieutenant John Stansfeld, found it impossible to get the wounded back from the trenches. The dressing station moved twice under Boer artillery fire. It was at approx. GPS -28.65077, 29.51791 until noon, then moved 250 metres to approx. GPS -28.65208, 29.51530 and at 4 p.m. it moved 300 metres to approx. GPS -28.65437, 29.51384.[15] Regimental stretcher-bearers and the Natal Volunteer Ambulance Corps carried the wounded from the dressing station about 2.5km to Lieutenant Blake Knox at the foot of Spioenkop. From there, stretchers or ambulance carts took casualties to the hospital at Fairview Farm. During the night, pom-pom shells and Mauser bullets overshot the summit and landed around Blake Knox's dressing station, forcing him to move (to approx. GPS -28.66581, 29.49670).[16]

14   Atkins, *The Relief of Ladysmith*, p.240.
15   Amery, *The War in South Africa*, Vol. III, facing p.280.
16   Blake Knox, *Buller's Campaign*, p.75. Amery, *The War in South Africa*, Vol. III p.295.

Fig 73: Wounded being carried from Spioenkop. NVAC bearers carrying wounded from Spioenkop, an ambulance wagon in the background. The men have just left Lieutenant Ernest Blake Knox's dressing station in the Renosterfontein Spruit valley, and are at GPS -28.66274, 29.49010. The skyline is the Spioenkop Spur. (*Black and White Budget*)

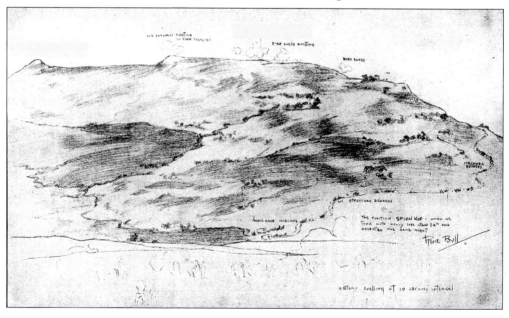

Fig 74: Route of wounded from Spioenkop. Sketched during the battle of Spioenkop by Rene Bull, it shows British shrapnel bursting on the saddle towards Conical Hill, and Boer shells bursting on the southern summit and spur. In the foreground, 19th Battery is firing shells towards Green Hill at 10-second intervals. A line of stretchers winds down Spioenkop Spur, to meet ambulance wagons in the Renosterfontein valley. (Forbes, *Battles of the Nineteenth Century*, Cassell, 1901)

Sheltered behind rocks in a static battle, each side's losses were evident only to their own men, as Reitz wrote: '...we on our side did not know that we were inflicting even greater damage upon them. Our own casualties lay hideously among us, but theirs were screened from view behind the breastwork...'[17]

Those lying wounded and exposed were often hit again. Lieutenant Harry Lockwood of the Scottish Rifles was hit in both ankles, leg and back; he died a month later in hospital in Durban. Henri Slegtkamp of Edwards' *Verkenner Korps* was on the summit of Spioenkop – the other two heroes of Platkop, Jack Hindon and Albert de Roos, were with the Ermelo Commando on Twin Peaks.[18] Slegtkamp saw his friend, Captain Guillaume Wolfaardt of Krugersdorp, lying wounded and in pain. On seeing Slegtkamp, Wolfaardt lifted his head slightly, and Slegtkamp yelled at him: 'Stay flat! Me and Moll would come and fetch him!' A moment later, Moll was shot through the chest. Slegtkamp dragged Moll to cover and helped him down the slope, then filled his water bottle and ate some tinned meat he found near a dead soldier. He went back with another Boer to help Wolfaardt, but had to abandon the rescue attempt when his comrade was shot through the head. The next morning, Slegtkamp found Wolfaardt's body; he had been hit multiple times.[19]

Reinforcements Cease

By 3.50 p.m. the British reinforcements were crowding Spioenkop summit and upper Spur. Coke said:

> Large numbers of men were held in reserve out of fire; many more employed in helping wounded comrades down the hill, others in carrying empty water bottles to be filled, so that generally there were not more men in the trenches than were required to keep back the Boers; but in some cases the trenches, which were badly constructed, were far too crowded. The chief losses were from shrapnel...[20]

About 4,500 troops were by then on the spur and summit of Spioenkop, and 800 more on Twin Peaks: '...the more men, however, that were crowded on the hill the more were killed, the fact is it was a death-trap.'[21] On the summit were the survivors of the original 1,700 men of the assaulting column, plus about 1,900 reinforcements: 800 Scottish Rifles, 800 Middlesex, and 300 Imperial Light Infantry. On the spur were 4th Mountain Gun Battery, General Coke and his staff, a dressing station packed with wounded men and bearers, a signal station, the Dorsets, two squadrons of Bethune's Mounted Infantry and two companies of the Imperial Light Infantry. A little lower down were two companies of the Connaughts, engineers, and two naval guns with their crews. Down the path went a procession of wounded men and stretcher-bearers. Treves thought the temperature was 'that of a hot summer's day in England'[22] but on

17   Reitz, *Commando*, p.76.
18   Preller, *Hindon*, p.88.
19   Mostert, *Slegtkamp van Spioenkop*, p.42.
20   *Commission into the War in South Africa*, Vol. II, p.443.
21   Dundonald, *My Army Life*, p.190.
22   Treves, *The Tale of a Field Hospital*, p.68.

the summit the thirst and heat were intolerable. There was a trickle of water at a spring on the spur (in the summer it is still there, at GPS: -28.65611, 29.51172), but this was 1km from the main trench, and none reached the British firing line. The 1½ pints in their water bottles did not last long.

Deneys Reitz was exhausted by heat, thirst and hunger. Around him lay scores of dead and wounded men and a feeling of discouragement gained ground that was only kept in check by 'Red' Daniel Opperman's forceful personality and vigorous language to any man who seemed to be wavering. Had it not been for him the majority would have gone far sooner than they did, for the belief spread that they were being left in the lurch. They could see large numbers of horsemen collecting at the laagers on the plain behind, but no reinforcements reached them throughout the day. Reitz recalled:

> I repeatedly heard old Red Daniel assure the men that help would be forthcoming, but from the way he kept scanning the country below I could see that he was getting uneasy himself. As the hours dragged on a trickle of men slipped down the hill, and in spite of his watchful eye this gradual wastage so depleted our strength that long before nightfall we were holding the blood-spattered ledge with a mere handful of rifles, I wanted to go too... No further attempt was made to press forward, and for the rest of this terrible day both sides stubbornly held their ground, and, although the battle remained stationary, the heavy close-range rifle-fire continued hour after hour, and the tally of losses mounted while we lay in the blazing heat.[23]

By late afternoon, Reitz was at his limit:

> We were hungry, thirsty and tired; around us were the dead men covered with swarms of flies attracted by the smell of blood. We did not know the cruel losses that the English were suffering, and we believed that they were easily holding their own, so discouragement spread as the shadows lengthened. Batches of men left the line, openly defying Red Daniel... when at last the sun set I do not think there were sixty men left on the ledge.[24]

Corporal Walter Herbert of the Royal Lancasters wrote: 'Just picture to yourself lying for sixteen solid hours under a perfect hail of shell & rifle bullets without a second's intermission, & in saying that I am not exaggerating in the very least.'[25]

Evening Approaches

Late in the afternoon General Coke awoke, climbed up the spur again, and around 5.30 p.m. reached the top of Spioenkop Spur. Coke located Colonel Hill under the cover of some boulders. They both believed that Hill commanded the whole summit, and neither attempted to find Thorneycroft or Crofton. Now seeing the southern slope of the battlefield for the first

23 Reitz, *Commando*, p.78.
24 Reitz, *Commando*, p.79.
25 Herbert, *Letter*.

time, Coke's previous optimism vanished. At 5:50 p.m. he sent a message to Warren, by hand and by signal lamp, reporting that the situation was 'extremely critical.' The men could not stand another day of this, he had troops in hand to cover a withdrawal, 'and should you wish me to withdraw, cover retirement from Connaught's Hill' (Appendix V (q)). Then Coke made his way down to the lower part of the spur again, awaiting orders and leaving Hill in command on the summit. Thorneycroft was unaware that Coke was nearby, or that Hill was commanding 200 metres south of him. He was also unaware that Twin Peaks had been taken. At 6:30 p.m., Thorneycroft sent a message by hand to Warren describing the situation and asking for orders. His message ended: 'The situation is critical.' (see Appendix V (r))

15

24 January, Evening on Spioenkop

'I was not altogether dissatisfied with the results, as a whole, of Spion Kop. My men had gained immensely in knowledge of war and in confidence in themselves and their officers.' General Buller[1]

Twin Peaks

Lyttelton, on Spearman's Hill wrote: '...it was imperative that I should do something to relieve the situation.'[2] Having despatched the Scottish Rifles to Spioenkop, he ordered the 3rd King's Royal Rifles, who were resting south of Potgieter's Drift, to attack Twin Peaks. When Lyttelton reported to Buller what he had done: '...[Buller] was furious, and sent a staff officer two or three times to me with peremptory orders to bring the troops back, especially the KRR which eventually I had to comply with.'

Only later did Lyttelton realise the attack on Twin Peaks probably saved Spioenkop from defeat: 'It was a fine feat of arms, a very steep ascent in the teeth of tolerably heavy fire, and the Rifles did not obey the order to retire till they had carried the top. There is little doubt that it was this pressure which relieved that on Thorneycroft.'[3]

The KRRC waded across the Tugela at a drift (approx. GPS: -28.67728, 29.53233) and left their greatcoats on the north bank. Sergeant Shirley, with the attacking force, recalled that Colonel Robert Buchanan-Riddell formed them up and addressed them: '...two regiments were in great trouble, and that we had to relieve them if possible. The position that we had to attack was across an open plain, a mile and a half wide....'[4]

The Rifles then advanced across the plain. Their route for the first 2km from the drift is followed roughly by the modern R600 road. About halfway across the plain, about 1,500 metres from the peaks, they came under Mauser fire, and they advanced at the double until they reached the shelter of a donga (approx. GPS -28.65679, 29.53584), about 300 metres from the foot of the

1   *Commission into the War in South Africa*, Vol. II, p.178.
2   Lyttelton, *Eighty Years Soldiering*, p.188.
3   Lyttelton, *Eighty Years Soldiering*, p.188.
4   Spiers, *Letters from Ladysmith*, p.95.

slope and about 800 metres from the western peak. Then they rushed forward from the donga, in groups of 12 to 20 men, and climbed the slopes of Twin Peaks, which were:

> '...almost like a precipice, with the best shots of the Boers strongly entrenched on the top. All the time we were crossing the plain we were under a murderous fire from the Boers.'[5]

While on the plain, the Rifles had faced rifle fire from 200 men of the Carolina Commando and Edwards' *Verkenner Korps*, but climbing the steep slope was safer.[6] They used their experience gained in hill fighting in India, firing at the skyline over the heads of the advancing men. Lieutenant Grant of G Company, and Lieutenant French-Brewster of E Company, were killed while crossing exposed ledges on the slope, and Major Kays (B Company), Captain Beaumont (A Company) and Colour Sergeant McLoughlin (E Company) were wounded. Lieutenant Blundell had five bullets through his clothing without a wound.[7] They climbed in open formation, A to D Companies against the eastern Twin Peak, E to H Companies against the western peak: '...crawling, climbing, running, firing from every rock and at every opportunity... making use of the dead ground to pause for breath, but always pushing upwards.'[8] Each half-battalion attacked in 4 lines of men, 12 to 18 paces apart, each line separated by 100 to 200 metres. Sergeant Shirley noted that the firing line for each peak was: '...just a company, to attack a position which seemed almost impregnable.'[9] Jeans recalled that, to keep the Boers' heads down, the naval guns: '...pounded the rocks ahead and above them as hard as our men could work, and they carried the summit in the most gallant manner...'[10]

At 3:30pm Schalk Burger telegraphed to Botha that the Twin Peaks were under attack, followed soon by a message that further resistance was futile. Botha sent a written reply: 'Let us fight and die together, but Brother, let us not yield an inch to the English ... besides, the Enemy is so shaken, that if we just believe and trust and don't fall back, the enemy will give in. I am full of courage and convinced that our God will give us victory if only we stand firm.'[11]

By 4:30 p.m., Burger was withdrawing his wagons out of rifle range, along with the Free State Krupp which was only 600 metres from Twin Peaks.[12] The danger was that this very visible tactical withdrawal could easily turn into a disorganised rout. From Ladysmith, Maidment saw the Boers hurrying down in groups from the crest, their wagons trekking from laagers across the plain, and men rounding up cattle as if for a general retreat: 'To us watching it seemed as if the Boers were beaten and knew it'[13]

When the KRRC were about 150 metres from the summit, the Boers abandoned their trenches. At 5:15 p.m. the right half-battalion of Rifles fixed bayonets, and with a cheer took

5   Spiers, *Letters from Ladysmith*, p.95.
6   Maurice, *History of The War in South Africa, Vol. II*, p.393.
7   Hereward Wake, *Capture of the Twin Peaks at Spion Kop by 3rd Battalion King's Royal Rifles*, The King's Royal Rifle Corps Chronicle for 1908 (Winchester: Warren and Sons, 1909), p.127.
8   Wake, *Capture of the Twin Peaks at Spion Kop*, p.128.
9   Spiers, *Letters from Ladysmith*, p.95.
10   Jeans, *Naval Brigades in the South African War*, p.257.
11   Barnard, *Generaal Louis Botha op die Natalse Front*, p.102.
12   Grobler, *Die Carolina-kommando in die Tweede Vryheidsoorlog*, p.66–67.
13   Maidment, *Diary*.

the eastern Twin Peak (also called the Sugar Loaf). A few minutes later the left half-battalion took the western peak. The Boer trenches had been dug into soft soil, practically on top of the peaks: '...and, in order to fire down the slope, the defenders had to lean right over the parapet of the trench, thus exposing their heads against the skyline, and giving the attackers below an immense advantage.'[14]

Observing from Spearman's Hill, the senior officers had got cold feet almost as soon as the KRRC began to climb Twin Peaks. Lyttelton had misgivings that the Rifles were too far from Thorneycroft, and so far in advance that they might be cut off. Around 2:30 p.m. Major Bayly informed Lyttelton that he did not think the Rifles could take Twin Peaks, and at 3:00 p.m. Lyttelton heliographed Buchanan-Riddell to retire. He sent the order again twice in the next hour, but the messages were ignored. Having taken Twin Peaks, Buchanan-Riddell now replied to Lyttelton's heliographs: he would recall the advanced sections if it could be managed.

The Boer riflemen, having retreated from their trenches, hurried down the relatively gentle gradient of the sandy, northern slopes of Twin Peaks. They took up concealed positions behind rocks and aloes about 200 metres down the slope '...and kept up a constant fire till dark, on the flat hill-tops above them, which afforded no cover whatsoever. Every head that peered over the crest was a target for the Boer rifles close below, and in this manner the Colonel lost his life.'[15] While standing on the skyline, Buchanan-Riddell was shot through the head.

Dr Maxwell of the Ermelo Commando Ambulance wrote:

> At dark the burghers decided that they had had enough of it, and retired and left the troops in possession of the Kop. Wild rumours are flying about, and everything is beginning to point to a general retirement on to Ladysmith, or possibly to the Biggarsberg. It is even said that the Upper Tugela laagers have begun to pack up and prepare to trek... Owing to the confusion it is impossible to get authentic news.[16]

Botha had few reinforcements to offer Twin Peaks. Sandberg wrote:

> We had no more men; all we could spare had been fighting since early in the morning. It was a precarious moment... With [Botha] were only some of his aides, the commander of the [Edwards'] *Verkenner Korps*, who had just delivered a report, and a few dispatch riders, and his assistant secretary (I had myself already been sent with some scouts to the summit of the Kop when assistance was needed): about twelve men altogether. Of these, ten were sent to the threatened point, where already a single 'khaki' was visible against the skyline, while the two others went to get reinforcements.[17]

The Utrecht Commando handed over their positions on Green Hill to a group of Free State burghers and galloped round to counter-attack on Twin Peaks.[18]

14   Wake, *Capture of the Twin Peaks at Spion* Kop, p.129.
15   Wake, *Capture of the Twin Peaks at Spion* Kop, p.129.
16   'Defender', *Sir Charles Warren and Spion Kop*, p.122.
17   Sandberg, *De Zesdaagsche Slag aan de Boven Tugela*, p.98.
18   Amery, *The War in South Africa*, Vol. III p.277.

On Spioenkop, the Rifles' success could be clearly seen by those who faced east, such as General Coke on the spur. But Coke was asleep during much of the afternoon, and heliograph communication between the spur and Twin Peaks was not established. On Spioenkop summit, Colonels Thorneycroft, Crofton and Cooke remained entirely unaware of the British attack and victory on Twin Peaks. The main effect was felt by the Boers on Aloe Knoll, who now risked enemy fire both from in front and from behind. Thereafter, Colonel Hill faced no further attacks from Aloe Knoll.

Major Robert Bewicke-Copley took command of the Rifles when Buchanan-Riddell fell. He had climbed down to the foot of Twin Peaks and was arranging ammunition, water, and entrenching tools to defend the position, when he received a direct order to withdraw. As Dundonald wrote: '...the sorely needed assistance on the right flank of our men on Spion Kop was no sooner given than it was withdrawn.'[19]

An unidentified Rifleman wrote they were '...wild at getting the order to retire after getting right up to the top. We had to come down again in the dark, nearly breaking our necks, falling over rocks and down into deep holes.'[20] They withdrew around 8:00 p.m., darkness concealing their movements. They carried Buchanan-Riddell's body with them. The engineers had built a bridge for them over the Tugela, marked by a bonfire, and at midnight the Rifles recrossed the Tugela.[21]

Darkness and Withdrawal from Spioenkop

At 7:00 p.m. the sun began to set. 'Red' Daniel Opperman's burghers kept up their fire in the dusk, as did a group of Carolina burghers looking for the body of Hendrik Prinsloo's brother, Willie.[22] This may have served to convince Thorneycroft that they would face a night of attacks. Once it was dark, men on the summit could not resist the urge to slip away. Colonel Blomfield had lain wounded all day beside Private Bradley, who had been shot through the chest and thigh. When darkness came, Blomfield crawled out of the trench to find Bradley a stretcher-bearer. Blomfield fainted – his shoulder had been bleeding copiously all day – and when he regained consciousness, he crawled the wrong way, down the slope, and into Boer captivity.[23]

Around 8:00 p.m., Colonels Thorneycroft, Cooke of the Scottish Rifles and Crofton of the Royal Lancasters conferred, and all agreed to abandon the summit.

Thorneycroft later laid out his reasons, any one of which would have been adequate:

> ... I gave the order for the troops to withdraw on to the neck and ridge where the hospital was... [approx. GPS -28.65437, 29.51384]. It was now quite dark, and we went out to warn all to come in. The enemy still kept up a dropping fire... In forming my decision as to retirement I was influenced by the following –

19   Dundonald, *My Army Life*, p.191.
20   Spiers, *Letters from Ladysmith*, p.95.
21   Maurice, *History of The War in South Africa, Vol. II*, p.398.
22   Amery, *The War in South Africa*, p.283
23   Childs, *Ladysmith*. p.104.

1. The superiority of the Boer artillery, inasmuch as their guns were placed in such positions as to prevent our artillery-fire being brought to bear on them from the lower slopes near camp, or indeed from any other place.

2. By my not knowing what steps were being taken to supply me in the morning with guns other than the mountain-battery, which, in my opinion, could not have lived under the long-range fire of the Boer artillery and their close-range rifle-fire.

3. By the total absence of water and provisions.

4. By the difficulty of entrenching on the top of the hill, to make trench in any way cover from infantry fire with the few spades at my disposal, the ground being so full of rocks.

5. Finally, I did not see how the hill could be held unless the Boer artillery was silenced, and this was impossible.[24]

The regiments formed up by companies at the top of the spur and felt their way down the path, the Scottish Rifles forming the rearguard. Because of a shortage of stretcher-bearers, Thorneycroft had to leave a large number of wounded on the summit.[25] Lieutenant Oppenheim of TMI summed up the situation:

Towards sundown the men of the old force were completely exhausted. Since six on the night of the 23rd they had been continuously under arms; they had had absolutely no water and no food. Many of them had been served out with six-pound tins of beef the day before, which they could not carry up the hill, and had... with an improvidence frequently seen, thrown away. Of the lack of water General Woodgate had spoken as early as ten o'clock; a few tins of water had since then been brought up on the backs of mules. Of these more than half had been spilt, for the mules had fallen down the hillside, and the rest was inadequate for the hospital. The intolerable strain of the shell-fire and rifle-fire had told on the stoutest.[26]

An anonymous officer agreed; the men could stand no more:

[The] troops were thoroughly disorganized, and had become practically useless ... the officer in command made up his mind that the position was untenable, and possibly he was right when the morale of the troops was taken into account ... The effect of a terrible fire such as was experienced on Spion Kop on the minds of men is very curious. Soldiers who had gone through the day without a scratch were so overwrought that when, overcome with fatigue, they lay down to sleep, they sprang up again and ran off in the dark without knowing what they were doing or where they were going. At other times they ran round and round in circles, and threw themselves down again, crying out for the companions they had lost.[27]

---

24 Stirling, *The Colonials in South Africa*, pp.72–73.
25 Stirling, *The Colonials in South Africa*, p.73.
26 Stirling, *The Colonials in South Africa*, p.75.
27 Spiers, *Letters from Ladysmith*, p.96.

Deneys Reitz remained at his post, staring into the night, so close that he could hear the cries of the British wounded and the murmur of their voices. He remained there until after 10:00 p.m., listening to the British talking and stumbling about in the darkness, but unaware they were withdrawing.[28] The Boers who came down from the summit ate, drank, and slept nearby, intending to renew the fight at daylight.[29] Sandberg, preparing reports for Joubert and Kruger in Major Wolmarans' tent, wrote: 'The volleys of the English still crackled above us…'[30]

Botha asked *Veldkornet* Kemp with 60 Krugersdorpers to come from Green Hill and take over positions on Spioenkop. Kemp did so, finding only *Commandant* Alberts of Boksburg remained, with 15 men. After 9:00 p.m. Kemp no longer heard the British firing, and at 10:00 p.m. he reported this to Botha.[31] Sandberg and Botha nodded off alternately while they worked: Botha dictated, Sandberg wrote, till after 10:00 p.m. In his report, Botha expressed his opinion that the victory was theirs. Botha knew his men needed rest, water and food, but he was confident that the battle had already been won. Though the British might still be able to fight, he predicted they would take advantage of the darkness to retreat. Their inaction on Tabanyama, their hesitation after capturing Twin Peaks, and the resignation with which they endured their punishment on Spioenkop led him to conclude that the British would withdraw during the night. He explained this in his despatch to President Kruger, adding that he would nevertheless take no risk. He would make the necessary preparations for the battle to be resumed the next morning.[32]

The Climb Down

Lance Corporal Putland of the Middlesex recalled the order to retire: '…being pitch dark and properly done up from the days events we was falling over boulders or rocks, this days fight was done with all Rifle fire our Artillery being out of range… the Boers had Big Guns, Pompoms, and Rifles, and the pompom is an awful weapon…'[33] As he clambered down in the dark, Putland heard someone groaning for help. With a man named Ralton and Sergeant Tilby, Putland crawled among the rocks till they found a man of the ILI, shot through both legs and one of his arms, who had fallen over the cliff and lodged against a rock. They carried him on crossed rifles to the crest, gave him water and left him for the bearer company, but Putland doubted he would survive: '…he was almost gone when we left him, he also told us to take his watch and his belt off with his money in, as he knew where he was going… I also passed another man of ours that was groaning with both feet blew away… in the darkness and everyone mixed up together…'[34] Putland got lost, and after reaching the foot of the hill, he lay down to wait for daylight, but could not sleep. He drank some muddy water and wandered about, coming across men looking for their regiments: '…after a lot of walking about we found the Regt in the afternoon and there was a bit of handshaking here etc the roll was called that evening as we had orders to move and

28   Reitz, *Commando*, p.79.
29   Kestell, *Through Shot and Flame*, p.63.
30   Sandberg, *De Zesdaagsche Slag aan de Boven Tugela*, p.100.
31   Kemp, *Vir Vryheid en vir Reg*, p.291.
32   Sandberg, *De Zesdaagsche Slag aan de Boven Tugela*, p.100.
33   Putland, *Diary*.
34   Putland, *Diary*.

Fig. 75: Dawn after Spioenkop. Taken by Lieutenant Colonel Frederic Harvey, medical officer attached to the 2nd Middlesex Regiment. The Middlesex are awakening below Spioenkop, having come down in the night. The men have piled their rifles and slept under blankets on the veldt. The sun has just risen, wisps of mist are rising on the left. (National Army Museum)

a bad result it was… after having some tea to drink and nothing to eat as we had nothing, we moved off about 4 p.m.'[35]

Lieutenant Charlton of the Fusiliers, wounded in the leg, could not walk unaided. He recalled:

> The firing from either side was now desultory in the extreme, like raindrops after a shower. He heard orders being shouted on the right. Every one inclined an ear to listen. Could they be hearing aright? The order was for each man to leave his position and make a way independently from off the hill.[36]

He limped off, supported by a man on either side. They found the dressing station deserted apart from an orderly, who had only remained in order to destroy the last of the supplies rather

35   Putland, *Diary*.
36   Charlton, *Charlton*, p.116.

than allow them to fall to the enemy. Many dead were lying about, and Charlton regarded them with a curious fascination. A stretcher was found, and Charlton was carried down and deposited at Lieutenant Blake Knox's station at the foot of the hill. Charlton recalled: 'He was hastily bandaged, told he was extremely lucky, and put between blankets. 'He slept as one dead… There followed a rough journey by mule ambulance to another, larger hospital with beds and sheets and nursing sisters.' (this was Treves' hospital at Spearman's Farm).[37]

Private Cosgrove of the Royal Lancasters recalled that, when he left the summit, the dead and wounded were lying about in large numbers:

> The Volunteer bearer company did good work that day, but they could not get half the [wounded] off the hill. Every time they came for a wounded man they had to run through a shower of bullets to say nothing of the shells which the Boers kept firing all day… Joe Bailey, a man of my company (C), was shot in about four places on his legs and when the stretcher bearers came for him he referred them to a man named Miller of my company, saying "Take him, he's worse than me."[38]

The Dorsets on Spioenkop Spur carried the ammunition down the hill, and waited for orders at the foot.[39]

Warren Learns of the Withdrawal

On Three Tree Hill, Warren received Coke's earlier message from the summit at 8:00 p.m. indicating the situation was critical (Appendix V(q)). Churchill, who had reached the top of the spur at 4:00 p.m. but had not ventured onto the summit, arrived back and reported the dire situation to Warren. Warren still hoped he could turn the situation around, and sent Churchill back to Spioenkop to tell Thorneycroft of the support he had arranged, including 4th Mountain Battery. The Battery, under Lieutenant Samuel Normand, had reached Trichardt's Drift from Frere at 3:00 p.m., where they bathed, watered their mules, and fused their ammunition. At 6:30 p.m. they began to ascend Spioenkop Spur. Boer shells were bursting about 400 metres in front of them, so they halted on the spur and awaited orders until 1:00 a.m., when the message came from Thorneycroft to withdraw.[40] The Battery would have made no difference. Though their guns were carried dismantled on mules and could have made it up the path, these were obsolete muzzle-loaders, firing a light 7lb shell only 3,000 metres. The only visible targets, the Boer trenches on Tabanyama, were already under fire from 32 heavier guns. Moreover, mountain guns fired black powder, which produced a large pall of white smoke that would reveal their position

37   Charlton, *Charlton*, pp.117–118.
38   Cosgrove, *Letter*.
39   Abbott, *Diary*.
40   Samuel Richard Normand, *The Boer War Letters of Subaltern Samuel Richard Normand, RA*.<https://www.angloboerwar.com/forum/19-ephemera/30466-the-boer-war-letters-of-subaltern-samuel-richard-normand-ra>, accessed 10 Oct. 2021.

Fig 76: Mountain guns firing. Lieutenant Normand's 4th Battery of Mountain guns were on their way up Spioenkop when the withdrawal took place. They were obsolete guns, firing black powder that produced a huge pall of smoke. (National Army Museum)

On Spioenkop summit, they would have quickly been located and knocked out.[41] Two naval 12-pdrs were also being brought up, under command of Major Hanwell and Lieutenant James. They had reached Spioenkop Spur, but needed a road to be made up the Spur. Colonel Blomfield thought they could not have survived on the summit: 'Had our guns ever been got up they would not have remained in action ten minutes… it was, indeed, fortunate for the gunners that they were unable to get guns to the top of Spion Kop.'[42]

General Coke, on the lower part of the spur, was unaware that the assaulting force was making its way down to him. At 9:00 p.m., Warren requested Coke to report to him at once. Coke replied: 'Night so dark and country so rough that the whole night would be taken up in journey. Is it not possible to give orders without my presence?' The paraffin in the signaller's lamp ran out before the message was sent, so at 9:40 p.m. Coke set off to find Warren. Churchill, on his second journey up, reached the spur after Coke had gone. Churchill met Thorneycroft near the top, handed him Warren's note, and congratulated him on being promoted to brigadier. Thorneycroft replied:

41   Darrell D. Hall, 'Guns in South Africa 1899–1902' in *Military History Journal*, Vol.2 No.1, June 1971
42   Childs, *Ladysmith*. p.109.

Precious lot of brigadier there'll be to-morrow… I ordered a general retirement an hour ago… There is nothing definite in this… Reinforcements indeed! There are too many men here already… I have made up my mind. The retirement is already in progress. We have given a lot of ground. We may be cut off at any moment.[43]

As Churchill and Thorneycroft walked from the summit, they saw figures approaching in the dark. '"Boers" said Thorneycroft in a whisper; "I knew they'd cut us off." They drew their Mauser pistols, only to find they were their own men.[44]

On the southern slope, Colonel Hill had planned to attack Aloe Knoll after dark, but had not told Thorneycroft of his intentions.[45] The ILI were told to retire at 8:15 p.m.; they fell in, and had marched about 200 metres, when Hill, astonished, asked Colonel Nash: 'Where are you going?' Nash replied that he had been ordered to take down the regiment, and Hill retorted: '… not a man or regiment is to leave the hill.'[46] The ILI marched back to their positions, put out picquets, and lay down among the dead and wounded. They could see the other regiments walking down the spur, and Trooper Tom Davies of the ILI wrote: 'Firing ceased by mutual consent about 7 p.m., and the regulars left and went to bed, the I.L.I. being in charge of the position, so there was not much sleep for us.'[47] Then, at 2:00 a.m., an order came from Brigade-Major Bonus: the ILI were to withdraw at once.[48]

The Hours Before Dawn

On Three Tree Hill, Captain Grant of the Devons lay awake:

All through the dark hours grey-faced men stole down from the summit, gaunt, dirty, utterly weary, but undefeated, and perhaps hardly aware how much they owed to the man whose courageous order had saved them from annihilation… the whole British army, as well as the fraction of it which left Spion Kop that night, owes it to Colonel Thorneycroft.[49]

Botha learned that Schalk Burger had withdrawn, and around midnight Botha and Hendrik Prinsloo rode over to the Carolina laager. The wagons were being loaded up in a panic, but as the first wagons moved away and the horsemen were getting ready to follow, Botha shouted to them to halt. He addressed them from the saddle, telling them of the shame that would be theirs if they deserted their posts in this hour of danger. So eloquent was his appeal that in a few minutes the men were filing off into the dark to reoccupy their positions.[50] Botha ordered Willem Pretorius of the Heidelberg Commando to come across from Tabanyama to the foot of

43   Churchill, *My Early Life*, p.308. Churchill, *My Early Life*, p.309.
44   Churchill, *My Early Life*, p.310.
45   Amery, *The War in South Africa*, Vol. III p.279.
46   Stirling, *The Colonials in South Africa*, p.85.
47   Spiers, *Letters from Ladysmith*, p.94.
48   Stirling, *The Colonials in South Africa*, p.85.
49   Linesman, *Words by an Eyewitness*, p.56.
50   Barnard, *Generaal Louis Botha op die Natalse Front*, p.102.

Spioenkop to form a fresh assault force.[51] Pretorius went up in the dark to assess the summit, and found it had been evacuated. When dawn broke, Botha asked him to count the British dead; Pretorius counted 650 bodies, which was an exaggeration; some of these casualties were probably wounded rather than dead.

---

51 Barnard, *General Botha in the Spioenkop Campaign*. Reitz, *Commando*, p.81. Grobler, *Die Carolina-kommando in die Tweede Vryheidstoorlog*, p.68.

16

24 January, Right and Left Attack

'Shelters were built for men resting in rear of the firing line as a protection from dropping bullets, and everything made as snug as possible. If Ladysmith had not to be relieved we could beat the Boers in a game of loafing, as we were much the richer side.' Private Jack O'Mahony, 2nd West Yorkshire Regiment[1]

In his orders at 7:00 p.m. on 23 January, Warren clarified that the attack on Spioenkop would be: '…supported from Three Tree Hill by the troops under the orders of the G.O.C. Right Attack. If firing takes place from Spion Kop during the night, the artillery from Three Tree Hill will fire Star Shell and will open fire at the rear of the enemy's position to prevent reinforcements being brought up. Infantry from Three Tree Hill will fire at daylight with the same object.' Meanwhile '… The G.O.C. Left attack will use his discretion about opening fire against the enemy to his front, if firing breaks out on Spion Kop with a view to creating a diversion' (Appendix V (d)).

Right Attack

When the attack on Spioenkop became a disaster, it consumed all of Coke's, Warren's, Lyttelton's and Buller's attention. It eventually tied up eight battalions – the initial column of two battalions, the Imperial Light Infantry, Middlesex, Scottish Rifles, Kings Royal Rifles, Dorsets and Bethune's Mounted Infantry. Even if Warren and Coke had been able to divert their attention from Spioenkop, their force was severely depleted. Buller stated as much: 'In these circumstances I had not sufficient troops to make a counter-attack, and could do nothing but wait till nightfall.'[2]

Those units that were not on Spioenkop summit were standing by all day for the order to advance. Green Hill would be the weakest point in the Boer line once it was enfiladed from Conical Hill. Botha anticipated this, and during the day of 24 January he sent the Heidelberg Commando to Green Hill to reinforce the Utrecht Commando.[3]

---

1   O'Mahony, *A Peep over the Barleycorn*, p.149.
2   *Commission into the War in South Africa*, Vol. II p.178.
3   Amery, *The War in South Africa*, Vol. III p.254.

The Middlesex, Devons, and East Surreys were ready for Right Attack's advance on Green Hill, (see Map 7) and before Woodgate had reached the summit, at 3:00 a.m. on 24 January, the East Surreys and Devons marched onto Spur 1 from Fairview Farm, with orders '...to be in readiness to support the troops on Spion Kop in any way that might be directed.'

The East Surreys relieved the South Lancashires on Picquet Hill, where Pearse wrote: '...we remained all day lying idle and watching the severe fighting of the Lancashire brigade and other troops, of which we had a clear view.'[4]

The Middlesex also moved to Picquet Hill in the dark, Putland recalling: 'when we reached the top of this it was just breaking day and we opened fire directly at 1,500 yards but the Boers never fired at us here...'[5]

The Devons took up positions in the dark between Three Tree Hill and Picquet Hill, with orders to support the attack on Spioenkop. When the mist burnt off, Captain Grant of the Devons watched Spioenkop:

> ...one could see the crowded figures of the British force like little black marionettes against the light-blue sky, and how thick they appeared! Surely the summit must be very narrow, if but one brigade must huddle together in this manner, a mark such as artillerymen dream of... A boom from the high ground... a puff of woolly smoke in the air, and a shrapnel-shell, timed to a fraction, has swept through the pack upon the hill-top. Then the rifle-fire began, sharp, angry, incessant, from every crevice and every knoll; to us below the whole mountain seemed alive with noise.[6]

During the morning of 24 January, both the Middlesex and Dorsets were sent as reinforcements to Spioenkop, and were replaced by the Somerset Light Infantry. The Somersets moved across from Three Tree Hill to Picquet Hill in clear view of the Boers, which proved costly, as Atkins witnessed:

> ...the Somersets emerged from behind Three Tree Hill in open order, and moved towards the Boer line on the north and towards the west flank of Spion Kop. The Boers sniped into them. A man was down – a shot rabbit in the grass with his legs moving. The infantry went a little way further north and east, halted and watched Spion Kop the rest of the day.[7]

When the mist burnt off, the Connaughts turned their Maxim machine guns onto the nek between Spioenkop and Green Hill. The Connaughts wrote: 'Long range volleys were also used for this purpose, and we knew they were effective, as we could see the few Boers who occupied the trenches at that spot clearing rapidly away.'

General Coke, commanding Right Attack, began the day on Connaught Hill. From this position, he would command the attack up Spur 1, once Boer fire from Green Hill died down under the effect of fire from Spioenkop summit. When Coke departed for the summit, around

4   Pearse, *East Surrey Regiment: Digest of Service*, p.12.
5   Putland, *Diary*.
6   Linesman, *Words by an Eyewitness*, p.54.
7   Atkins, *The Relief of Ladysmith*, p.241.

10:00 a.m., there was no longer a commander to lead Right Attack. No one, that is, apart from Warren, who was fully occupied in dealing with Spioenkop. Without a commander, there was no prospect of Right Attack making offensive action, and the troops on Spur 1 went onto the defensive and waited. The Connaughts were moved across to Three Tree Hill to protect the artillery. From there, they wrote: '…we could see our troops move forward, and then back; we watched the shells falling among them and bursting over their heads. The men were apparently crowding many deep behind a couple of shelter trenches, and when a shell fell among the mass there was a general clearance; then an officer would go back and bring them up again…'[8]

Left Attack

Before dawn on 24 January, Hart's men of Left Attack, on Spurs 2 to 5, began their volleys, audible from Three Tree Hill: 'Over all lay a dense mist, and a quiet which was curiously contrasted with the far-off volleys from the spurs and gorges of our left attack.'[9] Lieutenant George Crossman of the West Yorks on Spur 5 was unaware of the disaster that was unfolding, although he could see Spioenkop in the distance:

Battle very quiet today, lost no one so far. Woodgate's Brigade captured Spion Kop this morning. From here I could watch the attack beautifully with glasses as it is only 2 miles off. This show seems to be going to be a great victory. V. glad!!! The battle has now entered its fifth day. One of the longest on record. Glad I am in it. Have not much time for details as am under fire as I write sitting in my little pile of stones. I have personally fired over 100 rounds today. Wonder if I have hit anyone… have not eaten bread or fresh meat and vegetables for over 9 days now. Continual sound of firing and bullets and shells whistling round gets very tiring to nerves after 24 hours.[10]

The York and Lancasters, on Spur 4, before daybreak:

…opened a heavy fire in order to hold the Boer right during our attack on Spion Kop. At the end of two and a half hours' firing were relieved by the Dublin Fusiliers… as the mist cleared off, the attack on Spion Kop could be seen developing, whilst the Boer shells were dropping all over the hill. Notwithstanding being in reserve, the [York and Lancasters] was not altogether out of range of the enemy's shells, and sustained further casualties that day, one shell alone accounting for five men. Our total losses were one officer [Captain Armstrong] and eight men wounded, five of the latter dying of their wounds.[11]

Hart commanded Left Attack, and was eager to advance, but Warren and Buller were both completely focussed on Spioenkop. Captain Talbot wrote: 'Hart wanted to take his Brigade in

8   Anon., *Connaught Rangers Regimental Records*, p.19.
9   Linesman, *Words by an Eyewitness*, p.51.
10   Crossman, *Diary*.
11   Kearsey, *War Record of the York & Lancasters*, p.20.

support – Buller referred him to Warren. Warren sent him back to Buller. Then it was too late.'[12] Hart could have replaced Coke as commander of Right Attack, but neither Warren nor Buller considered this. Captain Romer of the Dublins on Spur 5 recorded his frustration: 'The 5th Brigade [Hart's Brigade] made no advance. The companies behind the sangars fired hundreds of rounds at the Boer trenches, while their comrades below ate and slept.'[13]

The Border Regiment also waited below Spur 5. Lieutenant Hyde Harrison wrote:

> ...as soon as it was light enough, we were able to see our men moving near the crest. Throughout the day heavy fighting continued all along the front and the summit of Spion Kop was smothered in the smoke and dust of bursting shells... Howitzers arrived to assist us, and came into action near Coventry's Farm... It was a most cheering slight to observe the burst of these heavy Lyddite shells in the Boer trenches opposite, and for a spell the Boer position was smothered in a cloud of bright green and yellow smoke. But the actual result was, I fear, more apparent than real.'[14]

The Royal Field Artillery on 24 January

When, at 3:45 a.m., Woodgate's force called out a loud 'hurrah', the two howitzers at Three Tree Hill fired star shells and the 15-pdrs came into action in the dark. At daybreak, 19th Battery moved from Fairview Farm to a koppie with a direct view of the saddle between Conical Hill and Green Hill (approx. GPS -28.66260, 29.48881 – see Map 8). This battery, the *Digest* recorded: '...fired about 400 rounds but the Boer guns were too well concealed for our fire to have much effect.'[15]

The guns on Three Tree Hill shelled Conical Hill and the western slopes of Spioenkop, where they could see Boers. The 61st Battery (howitzers) fired 239 rounds that day.[16] Their *Digest* records: 'Spion Kop carried at 3:30 a.m. Misty morning. Two star shell and some lyddite fired by night to prevent reinforcements coming up. At 9 a.m. mist lifted. The Battery fired all day but could not keep enemy's fire down as their guns were invisible.'[17]

28th Battery and two howitzers remained on Fairview Farm to shell Platkop. The naval guns fired all day at Brakfontein and Twin Peaks, seen by Sergeant Maidment in Ladysmith:

> I see Buller's batteries shelling the whole range of Intaba Mnyama [Tabanyama] from the peaked "paps" or "sisters" [Twin Peaks] past the Kloof north-west of them and along the more commanding Hog's Back [Spioenkop]... The shelling of the heights with Lyddite and shrapnel went on hour after hour, and towards evening some thought they heard a faint sound as of rifle volleys.'[18]

12   Talbot, *Letter*.
13   Anon., *Connaught Rangers Regimental Records*, pp.20 and 52.
14   Harrison p.110–111.
15   Anon, *19th Battery Digest of Service 1900*, Royal Artillery Institution Archives.
16   Amery, *The War in South Africa*, volume VI part 2, p.493.
17   Anon, *61st Battery Digest of Service 1900*, Royal Artillery Institution Archives.
18   Maidment, *Diary*.

17

25 January, The Inevitable Withdrawal

'So you see, Tommy has to bear the blunt of a lot of battles besides the Boers and the rations were awful.' Drummer Goodwin, West Yorkshire Regiment.[1]

Shortly after midnight, Thorneycroft and Churchill reached the foot of Spioenkop. The engineers there reported that guns and working parties were on their way, but Thorneycroft did not alter his instructions, and he and Churchill walked off to find Warren. Around 2:30 a.m., having limped about in the dark for almost five hours, Coke discovered Warren's tent, which had moved a short distance in the night. Almost simultaneously, a messenger carrying Thorneycroft's message arrived (see Appendix V (s)) and so did Churchill and Thorneycroft. Churchill put his hand on Warren's shoulder and woke him: '"Colonel Thorneycroft is here, sir." He took it all very calmly. He was a charming old gentleman. I was genuinely sorry for him. I was also sorry for the Army.'[2]

There were still 1,600 men of the Dorsets, Connaughts and BMI on the lower spur of Spioenkop. Coke's Brigade-Major, Captain Phillips, had found paraffin for the signal lamp, and signalled for Warren for instructions. Warren conferred with Coke and Thorneycroft, and at 4:00 a.m. he agreed that the retirement should continue. Warren telegraphed this decision to Buller, and asked for naval guns to cover the inevitable withdrawal across the Tugela.[3]

Buller reached Warren's headquarters at 6:00 a.m., and later seemed content, if inaccurate, in his assessments:

I was not altogether dissatisfied with the results, as a whole, of Spion Kop. My men had gained immensely in knowledge of war and in confidence in themselves and their officers. They had fought well, and I was certain that they had inflicted on the enemy not only an immense loss in moral, but actually a greater loss than they had themselves sustained in men… Events proved my opinion to be correct. None of the commandoes

1   Goodwin, *Diary*.
2   Churchill, *My Early Life*, p.310.
3   Amery, *The War in South Africa*, Vol. III, p.294.

with which we were engaged at Spion Kop came again into action against us (so far as I could learn) for at least a year.[4]

Early Morning with the Boers

Around 3:00 a.m., Louis Botha asked *Veldkornet* Kemp to bring his men down from the summit to rest. Kemp suspected the British would take up positions further back, and as it grew light, he went to reconnoitre the summit. His burghers ran into seven soldiers, who they promptly 'hands upped.' The prisoners said they had been ordered to leave their positions at 9:00 p.m. when the shooting stopped, but that they had been so demoralised by the previous day's deprivations that they had stayed behind. Kemp recalled: '...in the early morning of 25th January I was master of Spioenkop. Me, one of the most junior Boer officers with just a handful of men... What a feeling!'[5]

Warren and Buller saw no alternative but to withdraw over Trichardt's Drift.

25 January was a cool, cloudy day.[6] Paths were cut and by nightfall Major Irvine's engineers had put a new bridge across Trichardt's Drift.[7] Those who had fought on Spioenkop summit were withdrawn first. The Middlesex, Lancashire Fusiliers, Scottish Rifles and Royal Lancasters all moved to Trichardt's Drift, where they entrenched on both banks. The Dorsets, Imperial Light Infantry and Thorneycroft's Mounted Infantry were withdrawn onto Wright's Farm. Spurs 2, 3 and 4 were abandoned during daylight hours of 25 January, as this movement could be unseen; Spurs 1 and 5, which were under observation by the Boers, were held in strength for another day. Rifle and artillery fire continued, just as on the five previous days.

Lieutenant George Crossman of the West Yorks wrote from Spur 5:

> Battle here still going on and I am still in the firing line. Awfully sick of it. Boiling hot today... Have been on this hill fighting for over 2 days now and in same place. Food sent up to us and we have had two casualties today. Bullets have been dropping thick all around today. Some unpleasantly close.

They stayed on the alert for a night attack:

> We have to keep half the Coy awake all night here...[8]

For Malcolm Riall of the West Yorks on Spur 5 it was:

> Sniping as usual. Colonel Kitchener very uneasy and afraid our hill will be shelled. Made us build up sangars higher and thicker; no more casualties. Several men going

---

4   *Commission into the War in South Africa*, Vol. II, p.178.
5   Kemp, *Vir Vryheid en vir Reg*, p.291.
6   Treves, *British Medical Journal*, 1900, p.534.
7   Kearsey, *War Record of the York & Lancasters*, p.23. Amery, *The War in South Africa*, Vol. III p.302.
8   Crossman, *Diary*, 25 Jan.

sick owing to sleeping out in open and on nights so cold... Out on hill, sniping when anything seen.[9]

On Three Tree Hill, D Company, the Connaughts, took up positions in front of the artillery in case of a Boer attack, which gave them: '...the benefit of fire from both sides.'[10] Late in the morning they learned that Spioenkop had been evacuated: 'But the renewal of the Boer artillery fire against the crest-line had been a sufficiently eloquent announcement of the fact.'[11]

In Ladysmith, Sergeant Maidment could tell the Spioenkop attack had failed:

The Boer trek [from Twin Peaks] continued for several hours this morning and well on into the afternoon when it slackened. Then we saw some horsemen turn back... The roar of our field-guns has died away instead of drawing nearer, and we look in vain for any sign of British cavalry on the broad plain where they should be by now if Sir R Buller's infantry attack had succeeded.[12]

White feared that the victorious Boers would attack Ladysmith and advised Buller:

I think it would be better if you stick to bombardment and slow progress by something like sap rather than commit yourself to another definite attack. Information, which I believe correct, says Boers are discouraged by superiority of your armament, and say they cannot stand it. Keep them, therefore, in their trenches, and bombard them as heavily as you can. I don't think they will stand it long. I trust to your preventing them from throwing their strength on me... Boers can, however, come here from Potgieter's in 90 minutes. In this lies their great strength. You must not let them leave you and throw their strength on me.[13]

The Dead and Wounded on the Summit

Before daybreak, medical officers, including Lieutenant Blake Knox, set off with stretcher-parties for Spioenkop summit. They gathered the wounded and woke those who had overslept.

Warren sent Lieutenant Hamilton-Russell and four Royal Dragoons to reconnoitre the summit. About 7:00 a.m. they were nearly at the top of the spur, when they met stretcher-bearers who warned them they were about to run into Boers.[14] A long line of wounded men were being carried down, and Grant wrote: '...every now and then a stretcher black with blood, containing something alive but not to be looked on, would be carried past the foot of the hill.'[15]

9   Riall, *The Letters, Diaries and Photographs of Malcolm Riall*, p.44.
10   Jourdain, *Natal Memories*, p.13.
11   Anon., *Connaught Rangers Regimental Records*, pp.52—53
12   Maidment, *Diary*.
13   Commission into the War in South Africa, Vol. II, p.164
14   Amery, *The War in South Africa*, Vol. III p.294
15   Linesman, *Words by an Eyewitness*, p.57.

Fig 77: Doctors on Spioenkop, 25 January 1900. The morning after the battle, British medical teams were allowed onto the summit to care for their wounded, and stretcher-bearers carried them down Spioenkop Spur. A medic walks among dead and seriously wounded soldiers, while Boers comb the battlefield for souvenirs. (Courtesy Neville Constantine)

The Times correspondent noted:

> ...the stretchers pass, each with its burden, each with its blue bandage stained a dark brownish crimson. It is only when the figure on the stretcher lies under a blanket that the tumult and push and sweltering mass comes to a quick pause, while the dead man's comrade stands at attention, and the officer raises his fingers to his helmet.[16]

Almost 600 casualties reached the field hospital at Spearman' Farm, as Treves recalled:

> ...they came in the whole day and until late at night, until the hospital was full... Those who were deposited in the bell tents had to lie on stretchers. All were provided with blankets. In spite of the immense number of the wounded, they were all got under shelter by Thursday night, [25 January] and had had their more serious injuries attended to, and were made as comfortable as circumstances would admit. Some of the staff

16   Davis, *Notes of a War Correspondent*, p.145.

Fig 78: Wounded from Spioenkop. Bearers carry a soldier on a stretcher down to Trichardt's Drift, for the onward journey to No.4 Stationary Hospital at Spearman's Farm; four ambulance wagons follow. (Arnold van Dyk collection)

went round with water and food, and others with morphia, while a third party made it their business to see that every man was bestowed as comfortably as extemporised pillows or change of posture could make him. The pillows were represented by helmets, or by the happy combination of helmet and boot, or by haversacks or rolled-up tunics.[17]

When the Boers saw British doctors arriving on the summit, they arrested Blake Knox and his men. At 10:00 a.m. Colonel Allen, the Principal Medical Officer, and Father Reginald Collins, the British chaplain, met Louis Botha on the summit. They agreed a truce to exchange the wounded, and the British were invited to bury their dead. The Pretoria Commando came to collect their dead around noon. They carried them down in blankets, placed the bodies on board the commando wagon, and escorted them to Ladysmith, whence they were sent by train to Pretoria for burial.[18] Hendrik Kamffer buried his Heidelberg comrades, Marais and Van Staden, on the summit, alongside men from Rustenburg, Middelburg and Pretoria. The British Chaplains Reverend Gedge and Father Collins buried 138 men that day, the next day they buried 20, and on 27 January a further 85. Collins wrote: '...there was a total absence of anything like exultation over what they must consider a military success. Not a word, not a look,

17   Treves, *The Tale of a Field Hospital*, pp.67–69.
18   Reitz, *Commando*, pp.81–82.

not a gesture or sign, that could by the most sensitive of persons be construed as a display of their superiority.'[19]

Hendrik Prinsloo wrote to his wife: 'The Middlesex and Lancashire Fusiliers were plucky fellows, and it seems a pity that we, belonging to two God-fearing nations, should kill one another like that.'[20]

Hundreds of curious Boers turned up, and combed the battlefield for loot.

Fig 79: Spioenkop summit, the morning after the battle. In the foreground are dead and wounded soldiers, while medical corps and Boers walk around the summit. These *schanzes* no longer exist, the stones having been used to cover the mass graves. (Transvaal archives)

They gathered 'a fine lot of rifles' and forty crates of .303 cartridges.[21] This ended in tragedy: a British rifle lay under a corpse, and taking the rifle by the muzzle, Wynand Els of the Pretoria Commando pulled it towards himself. The dead man's finger was on the trigger and the rifle discharged, killing Els.[22]

19   Spiers, *Letters from Ladysmith*, p.100.
20   Hendrik F Prinsloo, 'Forty-Seven Years After "Spion Kop"', *Military History Journal, South African Military History Society*, Vol.1 No.1, 1967.
21   Grobler, *Die Carolina-kommando in die Tweede Vryheidstoorlog*, p.70. Anon., *The Bulletin of Official War News*, (Heidelberg, Transvaal Field Press,
22   Pienaar, *With Steyn and De Wet*, p.46.

Commandant de Villiers saw a Boer youth returning from the summit. He wore a soldier's helmet and his pony:

> ...groaned under the equipment of two or three soldiers. He had three Lee-Metford rifles, several water-flasks were slung from his shoulders, and a number of bayonets hung at his horse's side and rattled whenever the animal moved. Besides this, he had also several of the small spades with which the English soldiers are provided; he had got his head through three or four cartridge belts.[23]

From Three Tree Hill, Captain Grant of the Devons watched the Boers moving about on Spioenkop amongst the dead and heard them trying out the rifles they had picked up:

'A few shots rang out from odd corners of the vast mass, and then there was silence. An armistice had been arranged, to allow of the ghastly heaps left from the threshing of the day before being swept up and hidden. All day the work went on, doctors came and went, men could be seen digging against the clear sky.'[24]

Deneys Reitz revisited the summit: '...men who had fallen like heroes now looked like misshapen flesh that had gone through a meat saw. The brave dead lay in the sun everywhere, swelling up, with mouths and nostrils full of blow flies.'[25]

Sandberg described the horrors of the battlefield:

> There were people whose hand, arm or leg had been torn off, wholly or in part, and had been lying here all night without help. Suffocating from thirst, so completely exhausted that they no longer had the strength to utter a single word; they could only indicate with faint, almost imperceptible, movements of their corpse-white faces that life had not yet been completely extinguished. In addition, the hideously distorted, purple-coloured faces of the dead, covered in blood which stiffly pasted the hair on the head, the clothes on the body. Here two entirely charred bodies, one with a torn off head, the chest of his pal next to him completely gone, the intestines exposed...[26]

Reverend Kestell found it heartrending: 'Many of them were flung into the long trenches that had served as breastworks, and so great was the number that the earth did not sufficiently cover them all. Some even remained unburied. We did not know what the exact number was, but we saw the dead lying in heaps.'[27]

When the Boer telegraphist 'Flip' Pienaar returned to his laager behind Twin Peaks, the wagons were gone and the tents deserted, except one serving as a mortuary, in which half a dozen bodies lay. The entire commando was on the summit, and he joined them: '...gazing at the plentiful harvest reaped by our Nordenfeldts... British ambulance men were busy collecting corpses. ...as if war really meant nothing else than butchering men like sheep, quietly,

23   Kestell, *Through Shot and Flame*, p.61.
24   Linesman, *Words by an Eyewitness*, p.57
25   Martin Meredith, *Afrikaner Odyssey* (Johannesburg, Jonathan Ball, 2017), pp.106–107.
26   Sandberg, *De Zesdaagsche Slag aan de Boven Tugela*, p.100
27   Kestell, *Through Shot and Flame*, p.64.

methodically, and without any pomp or circumstance. "A sad sight!" I remarked to the British chaplain. "They only did their duty," was his unfeeling reply.'

Pienaar wired the news of the victory to Pretoria; routine communication the day before had been interrupted because the Boer telegraphists: '…had taken a hand in the fighting instead of attending to the instrument.'[28]

Jack Hindon and his comrades recognised the faces of dead South Africans who had served in the TMI and ILI.

The Boer Photographers

The Boer photographers Lund and van Hoepen took propaganda pictures, of which they later sold thousands of copies, and these became the most familiar images of the war. Sister Izedinova of the Russian ambulance had encountered Boer photographers and noted they were:

> …making a good living… The agents of these photographers travel around the main Boer positions and their laagers, with the permission of the Government, taking pictures of anything more or less interesting… These photographs adorn the windows of bookshops in their hundreds and sell quickly in spite of their relatively high price – a rouble each.'[29] (A rouble was worth more than a shilling.)

In the Spioenkop photographs, dead men's pockets have been turned out, boots removed, and leather straps, cartridge pouches, rifles and bayonets taken. The tunics have been unbuttoned by looters or possibly by stretcher-bearers seeking identification. In the front flaps of the khaki tunic were two internal pockets. One contained the First Field Dressing – a roller bandage, a pad of gauze, another of wool, a piece of jaconet waterproof, and two safety-pins. The other pocket contained a calico card on which were inscribed the soldier's name, number, regiment, and next-of-kin.[30]

Blake Knox noted: 'men often take off their coats in action, and they are temporarily mislaid, or their coats may be taken off to dress their wounds. Should such men be killed or die, all means of identification may be lost…'[31] The Boers carried a similar calico Red Cross identification card in a pocket. Once the identification cards were removed, the fallen man could often no longer be identified, and consequently many men who were buried on the veldt are unknown. The location of graves was often forgotten once the temporary wooden crosses disappeared. The graves of all the Carolina dead, buried near Spioenkop, have been lost in this way. Many who were buried alone or in small groups on the veldt were exhumed and reinterred in cemeteries in the 1970s. Boers were characteristically found buried under a sheet of corrugated roofing iron, or sometimes between two sheets of iron, to deter animals from digging up the grave. If the burial was near a colony of termites, often the skeleton had completely disappeared.

---

28   Pienaar, *With Steyn and De Wet*, p.41.
29   Izedinova, *A few Months with the Boers*, pp.222–223.
30   Blake Knox, *Buller's Campaign*, p.77.
31   Blake Knox, *Buller's Campaign*, p.91.

A Boer Casualty

'Flip' Pienaar visited his wounded cousin in a farmhouse behind Tabanyama. The wounded cousin, a frail boy of fifteen, looked terribly exhausted lying on the floor, his left arm completely shattered:

> We were two together, myself and another boy. We crept closer and closer to one of the small sangars, firing into it as we crept, until there was only one Englishman left alive in it. He called out 'Water!' and I ran to give him my flask. When I got close to him he pointed his gun at me and fired. I sprang aside, and the bullet ploughed up my arm. My chum then shot him dead. Our doctor was too busy with the English officers to attend to me, so I fear I shall lose my arm.

After his arm was amputated, he went to his uncle's farm to recuperate, then went on commando. Three days later he was brought in again, shot through the lungs.[32]

The Boers Reflect

Dr Maxwell with the Ermelo Commando Ambulance wrote:

> All the morning the excitement has been terrible… The burghers are wild with delight, and are now beginning to claim a great and glorious victory. The English have suffered heavy losses, and then go and throw up a hard-won position – a position which practically meant the relief of Ladysmith… Goodness only knows what will happen now, though they still hold the Thaba Nyama ridges and may be able to break through from there… The English loss must have been very heavy, as our artillery was playing on to them all the time.'[33]

From the Boer laagers rose hymns of praise: '…but there was no hint of triumph in the attitude of the men who stood on top of Spioenkop, at the trenches full of British dead; on the contrary there were few men on the Kop who were not filled with feelings of deep sorrow over the horrific slaughter of so many hundreds of innocent people.'[34]

Kemp wrote that the burials were done:

> …very sloppily… The bodies on the battlefield were horribly mutilated. Now it's over, it's better not to try to describe it… Among us Boers it was not for personal glory. We fought for our people, our land, and our liberty. I reported the situation on Spioenkop to Gen Botha, and later, when he came up he could see that he had finished and won the seven-day battle.[35]

32 Pienaar, *With Steyn and De Wet*, p.42.
33 'Defender', *Sir Charles Warren and Spion Kop*, p.166.
34 Preller, *Hindon*, p.88.
35 Kemp, *Vir Vryheid en vir Reg*, p.292.

A few days later a party of visitors from America visited the battlefield:

> ... the dead which had been dragged in the trenches and sprinkled with loose dirt were protruding in a disgusting manner, many more entirely neglected, lying where they had fallen... The ghastly state and stench precluded the Republicans from putting the hill in a state of defence as the burghers refused to do duty upon it...[36]

Fig 80: Half buried soldiers at Spioenkop, 10 days after the battle. The Boer photographer van Hoepen maximised the horror of this image by combining two views of the same three decomposing British soldiers. The British abandoned a large number of unburied dead on Tabanyama and Spioenkop when they withdrew across the Tugela. (Arnold van Dyk collection)

36   Hiley and Hassell, *The Mobile Boer*, pp.125–127.

General Lyttelton confided his feelings in a letter of the 25 January, marked 'Most Private': 'I have lost all confidence in Buller as a General and am sure he has himself.'[37] A few days later, he added:

> Buller is quite confident that he will win this time, but nobody knows why. I only hope he has good grounds for being so, but I don't see them myself, nor does anybody else. The delay in this campaign is suicidal and criminal... I do not think the relief of Ladysmith is feasible by a force of our strength unless by great good luck or first-class generalship.[38]

37   Lyttelton, *Eighty Years Soldiering*, p.191.
38   Neville Lyttelton, 'Letter to his wife of 1 February 1900,' Liddell Hart Archives GB0099 KCLMA.

18

26 January, Recrossing the Tugela

'...our troops are, I am glad and proud to say, in excellent fettle.' – General
Buller[1]
'We were done; done; exhausted.' Christof 'Sandjie' Sandberg[2]

From Ladysmith, Maidment could see the Boers were back in their laagers. A few shells fell on
Twin Peaks, where he could see white Boer tents once more:

> We need no heliograph signal to tell us the meaning of all this. For us there is to
> be another sickening period of hope deferred; but we try to hide our dejection, and
> persuade the anxious townsfolk that it is only a necessary pause while Genl Buller
> brings up his big guns and transport.[3]

On Tabanyama, Spurs 2, 3 and 4 had been evacuated; from Spurs 1 and 5 the British kept up rifle
and artillery fire as usual, waiting until dark when they could withdraw unobserved.[4] Malcolm
Riall of the West Yorks, on Spur 5, wrote: 'Sniping as usual from sangars. No casualties. The
men looking miserable and hungry, all in need of clean and dry clothes... Very tired.'[5]

The light faded after a cold and rainy afternoon, and to prevent the infantry getting lost in
the dark, from 5:00 p.m. cavalrymen were posted on their horses at intervals of 100 yards along
the tracks to Trichardt's Drift.[6] Hart marked out the routes with piles of stones and empty tins,
recalling: '...the guiding officers on foot found it some-times difficult to see the track and stone
boundaries, but could always see a biscuit tin, even on horseback.'[7]

1   Crowe, *The Commission of H.M.S. "Terrible"*, p.159.
2   Sandberg, *De Zesdaagsche Slag aan de Boven Tugela*, p.102
3   Maidment, *Diary*.
4   Maurice, *History of The War in South Africa, Vol. II*, p.402.
5   Riall, *The Letters, Diaries and Photographs of Malcolm Riall*, p.44.
6   Tremayne, *XIII. Hussars South African War*, p.14.
7   Hart, *Letters*, p.36.

The artillery withdrew, and by 10:00 p.m. the last battery, the 78th, had crossed the river. Their 15-pdrs had been in action 156 hours without moving, which they considered to be a record.[8]

Next, Spur 5 was evacuated; the York and Lancasters formed the rearguard while the Dublins, Connaughts and Borders marched past Fairview Farm to Trichardt's' Drift. The paths were slippery; Colonel John Hinde of the Borders stumbled and broke his femur.[9] Lieutenant Harrison of the Borders thought it was:

> ...a perfectly beastly night, pitch dark, misty, and with a heavy drizzle... a grim night, the sort that does not easily escape one's memory... Looking back, as we stumbled our way down the slippery tracks, we could see the glowing embers of the bivouac fires still struggling, fitfully, in spite of the downpour, and marking, roughly, the line held by our Rear Guard. The sounds of battle had however, subsided and a kind of expectant hush hung over the "Valley."[10]

Abruptly, at 10:50 p.m., a roar of Mauser fire burst out from the trenches on Langkop and Green Hill. Hart ordered: 'fix bayonets' and shouted that: 'not a yard of ground was to be given up...' he would have: '...a proper military retirement in due time, but would have no skedaddle.'

The York and Lancasters stood to, and Hart summoned back the Borders. Hart: 'We fired obliquely at the flashes of the Boer rifles, and in about half an hour all was silent again, cold and wet.'[11] The rifle fire was followed immediately by Boer shelling, and Harrison wrote: 'Star shells, too, soared up into the sky, casting a weird light over all of us.'[12] Lieutenant George Crossman of the West Yorks: '...was sure the enemy had spotted our retirement and was attacking... You can't see to aim, but the bullets fly somewhere near the enemy and that is bad enough at night.'[13]

Only two men of the East Surreys were lightly wounded, but the incident served as a vivid reminder of the hazards of night attacks.

Captain Grant with the Devons recalled being among the last to leave Three Tree Hill:

> Hardly were the orders issued when it began to rain, and what rain! Cold, pitiless, incessant, it drenched the thin khaki drill in five minutes (no one had anything but the summer clothing he stood in), and in five more converted thousands of perspiring men into shivering chattering ranks of misery... The men crouched in a long line on the sodden ground in the downpour in absolute silence, immobility, and wretchedness... The darkness was intense. Every now and then a suspicious noise ahead, distinguished in a second from the subdued bustle of the retreat in progress behind would galvanise the frozen limbs into a momentary alertness... Every moment an attack was expected...[14]

8   Anon, *78th Battery Digest of Service 1900*, Royal Artillery Institution Archives.
9   Harrison, *Unpublished memoir* p.114.
10   Harrison, 'Unpublished Memoir,' p.113.
11   Hart, *Letters*, p.316.
12   Harrison, 'Unpublished Memoir,' p.113.
13   Crossman, *Diary*.
14   Linesman, *Words by an Eyewitness*, pp.59–66.

About 1:00 a.m., the Devons moved off, some needing to be carried on stretchers. The companies closed up and moved off, men's teeth clenched and feet contracted in the soaked chilly boots. They trudged through mud and water and reached the Tugela just before dawn. As they neared the pontoon a single Boer shell went through the planks and exploded in the river, then the rain came down and obscured everything. Grant wrote: 'A sorry sight was that beaten army in its camp between Wagon Drift and Potgieter's when daylight broke: muddy, dripping khaki; rusty rifles, helmets almost melted by the rain...'[15]

Last across was A Squadron, 13th Hussars, at 6:00 a.m., and the pontoon bridge was dismantled as soon as they were over.[16] Crossman recalled: 'The men were awfully done up... not a man had more than five hours sleep in all that time. They were falling asleep as they marched...'[17]

Buller greeted each unit as it crossed,[18] and wrote a detailed, cheerful despatch:

> On the morning of the 25th, finding that Spion Kop had been abandoned in the night, I decided to withdraw General Warren's force; the troops had been continuously engaged for a week, in circumstances entailing considerable hardships; there had been very heavy losses on Spion Kop. I consequently assumed the command, commenced the withdrawal of the ox and heavy mule transports on the 25th; this was completed by midday the 26th... In addition to machine guns, six batteries of Royal Field Artillery, and four howitzers, the following vehicles were passed: ox waggons, 232; 10-span mule waggons, 98; 6-span, 107; 4-span, 52; total, 489 vehicles. In addition to these, the ambulances were working backwards and forwards, evacuating the sick and wounded. By 2 p.m. the 26th, all the ox waggons were over, and by 11.30 p.m. all the mule transports were across and the bridge clear for the troops. By 4 a.m. the 27th, all the troops were over, and by 8 a.m. the pontoons were gone and all was clear... Thus ended an expedition which I think ought to have succeeded. We have suffered very heavy losses, and lost many whom we can ill spare; but, on the other hand, we have inflicted as great or greater losses upon the enemy than they have upon us, and they are, by all accounts, thoroughly disheartened; while our troops are, I am glad and proud to say, in excellent fettle.[19]

The same day, Buller sent a memorandum marked 'not necessarily for publication' to the Secretary of State for War. It struck a different note entirely, and began a cycle of recrimination among the generals: '[Warren] seems to me a man who can do well what he can do himself, but who cannot command, as he can use neither his Staff nor subordinates. I can never employ him again on an independent command.'[20] Buller later changed his mind, and Warren successfully commanded the 5th Division until Ladysmith was relieved.

15   Linesman, *Words by an Eyewitness*, p.69.
16   Tremayne, *XIII. Hussars South African War*, p.14.
17   Crossman, *Diary*.
18   Harrison, 'Unpublished Memoir,' p.115.
19   Crowe, *The Commission of H.M.S. "Terrible"*, p.159.
20   'Defender', *Sir Charles Warren and Spion Kop*, p.217.

The darkness and misty weather had made it impossible for the Boers to attack the retreating army. Trichardt's Drift was invisible until dawn broke; when the Boer artillery opened fire, it was too late; the withdrawal was complete and soon the rain again obscured the Tugela.

Botha's small force was spent. Sandberg, Botha's secretary, reflected:

> We were done; done; exhausted. The battle had lasted six days; every day from early morning until late at night, without rest... And at night they could only sleep intermittently, while half the men present kept watch. Those nights on the hills, between rocks and on rocks, the snake-human body twisted in all sorts of bends to avoid the stones to some extent; just a boulder as a pillow underneath bare sky, with few or no blankets; day and night in the same clothes; at the beginning very little food, a bit more in the last couple of days, but food never too good; exhausted by hurrying from one position to the next, sometimes far away and always inaccessible in these steep hills, and the journey sometimes only undertaken for a day because that same evening they had to ride back to their original positions. And these were always the same men who had fought on the first day, because there were no reserves. No, it was trouble and again trouble. At night, after fighting all day, and as soon as darkness allowed, we often had to dig or repair trenches, usually without tools other than our own arms and hands.'[21]

The Border Regiment marched to their tents through what, until recently, had been Buller's headquarters on Spearman's Farm. The ox-wagons were packed and inspanned, ready to move off. In an open space in the centre stood a wooden table, and on it someone had placed an empty champagne bottle. The men saluted it as they marched past.[22]

---

21   Sandberg, *De Zesdaagsche Slag aan de Boven Tugela*, p.102.
22   Harrison, 'Unpublished Memoir,' p.116.

19

27–29 January, Recuperating

'Such a man [Buller] could do anything with soldiers, if he could but invent
anything to do…' Captain Grant, Devonshire Regiment.[1]

By 27 January, Buller's army was back in camp. To discourage the Boers from approaching
the Tugela, the artillery bombarded the north bank. The 15-pdrs had fired 6,766 shells since
17 January, and on 27 January they fired a record 1,530 shells, of which 7th Battery fired 764.[2]

The Dorsets formed a burial party of 100 men who went to bury the dead on Spioenkop.
Private Abbott wrote: '…it was a horrible sight. The Boers were very polite to our men on the
hill but by the look of our dead they had not been polite to some of them.'[3]

Hart's Irish Brigade looked back, as the Connaughts wrote: '…towards Tabanyama, where
the discarded biscuit tins were gleaming in the morning light, [to] say good-bye to that long line
of sangars and trenches… all were finally rewarded by the arrival of the transport with tents and
baggage, and everyone spent the night in comparative luxury.'[4]

Even Hart himself was exhausted:

I arrived [at Spearman's] on the 27th January with my brigade, after a night march and
retirement over the Tugela, having been for seven days and seven nights continually
under fire, no tents, and the men without overcoats or blankets; so I need not tell you
we got inside our tents again with gratefulness, and not a word was heard that night,
nor a sentry's challenge, for we all slept like dead men.[5]

The Times correspondent described the troops relaxing in the days that followed:

The Tommies stretch themselves in the sun to dry the wet khaki in which they have
lain out in the cold night for weeks, and yawn at battles. Or, if you climb to the hill
where the officers are seated, you will find men steeped even deeper in boredom…

1   Linesman, *Words by an Eyewitness*, p.71.
2   Amery, *The War in South Africa*, Vol. VI part 2 p.491.
3   Abbott, *Diary*.
4   Anon., *Connaught Rangers Regimental Records*, p.54.
5   Hart, *Letters*, p.311.

Fig 81: Spioenkop trench grave in the 1960s. The remains of soldiers in the shallow trench were only covered by a few centimetres of soil, so the rains sometimes exposed bones and ammunition. The graves were subsequently protected by layers of rocks and stones, which removed the traces of the outlying *schanzes*. (Photograph by 'Midge' Carter, courtesy of Trish Woodman)

they are unbearably bored now. Below them the men of their regiment lie crouched amid the boulders, hardly distinguishable from the brown and yellow rock. They are sleeping, or dozing, or yawning… They are tired in body and in mind, with cramped limbs and aching eyes.'[6]

After kit inspection, Drummer Goodwin of the West Yorks grumbled about how the men were treated, but had praise for Colonel Kitchener:

[It] was very funny to see mens straps – some had pouches with bullet holes through and water bottles and was emergency Rations as well; and the men had to pay for water bottles damaged and lost in action; and the men got punished for losing the Emergencies [rations] and were made prisoners for not building trenches for the officers while under fire and Tommy was anything but treated fair by the officers as they put us down to the lowest of the low so this was the day of reckoning so a good many were

6   Davis, *Notes of a War Correspondent*, p.147.

doing defaulters so you see what Tommy suffered the people at home was not aware of this... so you see Tommy has to bear the blunt of a lot of battles besides the Boers and the rations were awful.[7]

Captain Jourdain of the Connaughts recalled: 'We had been under sniping rifle-fire and shell fire... from 16th to the 27th January... and during the whole of that time we had no covering of any kind, and our rations were very meagre and nearly always cold.'[8] Captain Fred Talbot of the Rifle Brigade had spent the days among the Maconochie Koppies: 'It is a great relief to get some shade again after 18 days sitting on rocks under a blazing sun... It was a great thing however to have the river to bathe in, & the sunsets are very fine.'[9]

Private Sprague of the Borders reflected:

> The engagement lasted from 20th to 26th January inclusive (7 days) ... We suffered heaviest in the brigade. We are now resting. We drove the enemy from two or three positions and then shelled and fired at them daily. We suffered not only from the firing but from lying there on the hill with naught to shade us from the sun by day (107 in the shade) and wind and rain by night... We are now again under welcome tents, enjoying a deserved rest.[10]

Private McGowan, with the Royal Lancasters, expressed doubts about the war:

> I do not think, in spite of all the troops, that we are making any progress towards the termination of this war – they will have to alter their tactics or they will be outwitted by the Boers – they get in rifle pits and you cannot distinguish with the naked eye where they are, so clever are they at concealment... Tell Willie... to put it out of his head altogether about being a soldier – if he heard the noise of shells and shot flying and other things he would alter his tune.[11]

Sunday 28 January

On Sunday 28 January, Church services were held. The men rested and bathed in the *spruits* (springs), drying themselves and their kit in the sun, and enjoying letters from home.

Cleanliness was at a premium, and when the kit of the late Captain Charles Ryall was auctioned off, his bar of soap fetched 10 shillings.

Private Cosgrove of the Royal Lancasters wrote: 'The men are in fairly good spirits for all our non-success. They have great faith in Buller... I fancy now they are going back to the original

7   Goodwin, *Diary.*
8   Jourdain, *Natal memories,* p.14.
9   Talbot, *Letter.*
10   Sprague, *The Smethwick Telegraph.*
11   McGowan, *Letter.*

Fig 82: A wash at Spearman's after the retirement from Spioenkop. A group of men, unit unknown, wash their feet in a watering hole at Spearman's Camp. (Arnold van Dyk collection)

campaign and possibly we may have very little more fighting up this side. Personally, I have had quite enough already.'[12]

Buller

On the evening of 29 January, Buller addressed his army at Spearman's Camp, and told them that they had found for him the key to Ladysmith – this would be Vaalkrans, the next battle

12   Cosgrove, *Letter*.

to be fought, and lost (Appendix II (b)).[13] Private Abbott of the Dorsets wrote: '…if Buller had found the key to Ladysmith, it must have been rusty, as it took him another month before he unlocked the way. But never mind, Buller is a good man, we all got faith in him & every man would go anywhere with him.'[14]

Hart was touched by Buller's comments: 'Thus he has given me in the course of a few weeks a full measure of blame and a full measure of praise.'[15]

Coke was unsure where he stood: 'Sir R. Buller's conduct was certainly most extraordinary. He neither saw me nor said one word to me regarding the action, though I met him daily.'[16]

Captain Grant of the Devons found Buller enigmatic:

> Most difficult of men to describe: impassive, yet notoriously tender, with heart bleeding for his falling soldiers; determined as fate, yet faltering before the blows of what seemed to be fate; bravest of the brave, yet a very woman in the face of certain losses… Such a man could do anything with soldiers, if he could but invent anything to do… it must be admitted that a man who could by a short, unintelligible address send his defeated and diminished army merry and confident back to camp, as he did on that Monday afternoon, is an anomaly of no small military value.[17]

The Boers Go Over the Battlefield

North of the Tugela, *Commandant* Krause visited Tabanyama, avoiding numerous corpses which were in various stages of decomposition, of which he wrote:

> …poisoned the air with pestilential odours… In some places where the soldiers had taken shelter behind long, low stone walls, from behind which they had fired, the ground was covered for hundreds of yards with empty cartridge cases, several inches deep and two or three yards broad, which crunched like gravel when one walked over it. All around the long rich grassy slopes were dotted with bright red, crimson, purple and brown patches, where the lyddite shells had ploughed up the earth, and had scorched the grass with their yellow fumes…' The surrounding farms were abandoned and ransacked.[18]

Dr Raymond Maxwell of the Ermelo Commando ambulance visited Spioenkop summit:

> … the stench was too dreadful. In some places the English trenches were just behind one another, and quite parallel, and in the flurry and excitement of the fight it would be surprising if some of the men in the front trenches were not shot from behind.[19]

13   Blake Knox, *Buller's Campaign*, p.95.
14   Abbott, Diary.
15   Hart, *Letters*, p.317.
16   Commission into the War in South Africa, Vol. II, p.443.
17   Linesman, *Words by an Eyewitness*, p.70–71.
18   Krause, *War Memoirs*, p.58.
19   'Defender', *Sir Charles Warren and Spion Kop*, pp.167—168.

The Transvaal *Official War News Bulletin* reported: 'On one of the koppies 17 unburied bodies of soldiers were found by Genl. Cronjé. The enemy apparently does not intend to bury their dead, as lots of bodies are still lying on Spioenkop.'[20]

The Injured

Treves, treating the Spioenkop casualties noted the wounds from shell and shrapnel were much more severe. Shell wounds inevitably became infected, unlike Mauser wounds.[21] He noted the psychological strain as well:

> The men, however, were much exhausted by the hardships they had undergone. In many instances they had not had their clothes off for a week or ten days. They had slept in the open without great-coats, and had been reduced to the minimum in the matter of rations. The nights were cold, and there was on nearly every night a heavy dew... The want of sleep and the long waiting upon the hill had told upon them severely. There is no doubt also that the incessant shell fire must have proved a terrible strain... Many were absolutely exhausted and worn out independently of their wounds.[22]

Anthony Bowlby, a surgeon at Cape Town and Bloemfontein, began to encounter soldiers with physical symptoms for which there was no apparent explanation. These men suffered from what would later be called 'Shell Shock' or Post-Traumatic Stress Disorder. They had, Bowlby found, headaches, pains in the neck, back and limbs, and: '...general feebleness of the muscular system amounting to paralysis more or less pronounced.'[23] Some men broke down psychologically: 'It was really terrible to see the condition of fine, strapping men which led them to shrink from the slightest touch and shed tears like children...'[24] A surgeon in Aldershot, Mr Morgan Finucane, reported numbers of soldiers invalided home with a new condition which he termed 'General Nervous Shock'. His cases included four men from Spioenkop whose wounds had healed, but whose health had not recovered. Finucane reported one young man was: '...very unsteady and shaky, with noises in the head and giddiness. His memory is bad and failing. The surface of the body is cold. The patient suffered from nerve shock and panic at Spion Kop before being wounded...' Another suffered 'vertigo, headaches, flushing, and periods of stupidness and unconsciousness. His memory is bad and is getting worse. The patient describes his nerve break-down as due to shock and panic at Spion Kop, even before receiving his wound, as the result of heavy shellfire and rifle fire from the Boers, who were invisible and well under cover while the English troops were freely exposed.' Another had 'tremors in the muscles of the back and both lower limbs. His gait is unsteady and he is incapable of sustained or arduous exertion... He is in a dull, lethargic mental state.' The fourth veteran of Spioenkop was 'scarcely able to walk. There are twitchings and tremors about the face, which has an anxious and pinched appearance. He

---

20   Anon., *The Bulletin of Official War News*, (Heidelberg, Transvaal Field Press, 29 January 1900).
21   Treves, *British Medical Journal*, 1900, p.726.
22   Treves, *The Tale of a Field Hospital*, pp.67–69.
23   Edgar Jones and Simon Wessely 'The Origins of British Military Psychiatry Before the First World War' in *War & Society*, Volume 19, Number 2, October 2001, p.98.
24   Jones and Wessely, 'The Origins of British Military Psychiatry', p.104.

sleeps little, owing to night pain.' Having seen numbers of these cases, Finucane laid the blame with the Generals and their 'badly conceived projects causing panic and disaster.'[25]

As one wounded soldier was being anesthetised, Treves noted: '…in his dream he was back again in the trenches, and was once more among his dead and mangled comrades. The vision of one wounded man especially haunted him and fascinated him, and at last he screamed out: "There goes that bloke again whose leg was shot away; blimy, if he ain't crawling now!"' Another yelled: 'There they are on the hill! For God's sake, shoot! Why don't we shoot?'[26]

Among the prisoners reaching Pretoria from Spioenkop was an officer. His fellow-captives asked for news of their friends and relatives: 'His answer was "Dead, dead; everybody's dead; the British army is all dead." For a month, this was all the man could say.'[27]

Corporal Walter Herbert of the Royal Lancasters wondered how: '…any of us escaped, and what was it all for? All our nerves are shook, so that the sudden crack of a… whip makes us jump… Half our officers are dead, wounded or missing, & the same with our N.C.O.s… I don't believe any of us are funking it.'[28]

Bugler Dennison, of the same unit, wrote: 'I don't think there is one who would go through the same again for £1,000.'[29] Sergeant Riding, of the South Lancashires, wrote home a week after Spioenkop: 'This will affect the whole of Lancashire, and I say, "God help the wives and families, more especially the children, who have been bereaved."'[30]

25   Morgan I. Finucane, 'General Nervous Shock, Immediate and Remote, After Gunshot and Shell Injuries in the South African Campaign', in *The Lancet*, 15 September 1900, pp.807–809.
26   Treves, *The Tale of a Field Hospital*, pp.78–79.
27   Stirling, *The Colonials in South Africa*, p.75.
28   Herbert, *Letter*.
29   Bugler Dennison, King's Own Royal Lancasters, 'Letter' in *Mid-Cumberland and North Westmorland Herald, Saturday 19th May 1900*
30   W. Riding, Sergeant, 1st South Lancashire Regiment, 'Letter' in *Waterloo & Crosby Herald, 3rd March 1900*.

20

Epilogue

Spioenkop became famous throughout the world, while the battles on Tabanyama were forgotten.

Boer casualties on the Upper Tugela on 24 January were 59 killed and 134 wounded, of whom 9 died of wounds. Of these, 25 Boers were killed and 95 wounded on Spioenkop summit. Among Prinsloo's 84 Carolina burghers, 52 were killed or wounded.[1]

The Spioenkop campaign from 17 to 27 January cost the British roughly 464 killed, 1,107 wounded and 240 missing or captured, although the number of British dead on Spioenkop remains disputed. *Commandant* Willem Pretorius of Heidelberg counted 650 British bodies on the summit, but probably included some of the 350 'seriously wounded' men in this count.

The Times History records 322 soldiers killed or died of wounds, and 563 wounded at Spioenkop. Casualties among Thorneycroft's Mounted Infantry were 35 percent of their strength (including 55 percent of their officers); the Lancashire Fusiliers lost 30 percent (including 63 percent of their officers); the Royal Lancasters lost 25 percent.[2] Lyttelton concluded the high proportion of officer casualties was due to recklessly standing up in battle: '...if they do get hit disproportionately, it is because they stand up so much more than the men. However that may be I have ordered them all to carry rifles and shall do so myself.'[3]

The siege of Ladysmith was relieved on 27 February 1900, by a sustained attack on a wide front over several days. During the siege, 541 soldiers died of typhoid.[4] Of the 556,653 men who served Queen Victoria in the South African War, 8,225 died of typhoid, including Prince Christian Victor, the Queen's grandson. He had not been immunised, though he was aware of the illness: his grandfather, Prince Albert, had died of typhoid in 1861, before the vaccine was invented.[5]

Harry Coventry returned to Fairview Farm once Ladysmith was relieved. He found bodies decomposing on Tabanyama, unrecognisable apart from one man with a distinctive tattoo on the back of his hand. Coventry took the piece of tattooed skin into Ladysmith for identification,

---

1 Anon., *The Bulletin of Official War News*, Heidelberg, Transvaal Field Press, 27 January 1900. Barnard, *General Botha in the Spioenkop Campaign*.
2 Amery, *The War in South Africa*, Vol. III p.295
3 Lyttelton, *Letter* to his wife of 1 February 1900.
4 De Villiers, *Healers, Helpers and Hospitals*, Vol. 2 p.129.
5 De Villiers, *Healers, Helpers and Hospitals*, Vol. 2 p.15.

but nobody knew the man. The skin can be seen in the Ladysmith Siege Museum to this day. Coventry buried the bodies in a British trench on the crest of Tabanyama, where the communal grave is marked by a cross of railway iron (GPS: -28.63487, 29.47724).

Major-General Sir Edward Woodgate did not recover. Treves kept the public informed about his condition: 'I am sorry to say that General Woodgate is not progressing favourably, and is indeed losing strength. I had to remove the damaged eye. The General is free from pain, but is seldom really conscious, although he recognises his friends and answers a few questions.'[6] Woodgate was more at ease by the time, on 9 February, No.4 Stationary Hospital followed the army to Chieveley. Gandhi recalled: 'During these days we had to march from twenty to twenty-five miles a day, bearing the wounded on stretchers. Amongst the wounded we had the honour of carrying soldiers like General Woodgate.'[7] Woodgate was accompanied by his brother, who had nursed him with the utmost devotion since the day he was wounded.[8] He died at Mooi River on 23 March 1900, and was buried at St John's Anglican Church.

General Sir Redvers Buller continued to command in Natal and led a successful advance into the Transvaal. He returned to England and retired in October 1901. In his evidence before the Royal Commission, he had a selective recall of events, and a biography of Buller written in 1923 makes no mention of Spioenkop.[9]

General Sir Charles Warren was very publicly blamed by Buller, but led his 5th Division to victory in the relief of Ladysmith. Warren returned to Britain in August 1900, was promoted to Lieutenant-General in 1904, and retired a year later. A 1902 book vindicating him for Spioenkop was probably written by Warren himself.[10]

General Sir George White suffered recurrent fever, and two days after the relief, he broke down. He was invalided home in March 1900, and in 1903 became the Governor of Gibraltar.

General Arthur Fitzroy Hart continued to lead his brigade, and his men continued to have high losses. He retired in 1904.

Lord Dundonald (Douglas Cochrane) was mentioned in despatches six times, and in 1906 was promoted to Lieutenant-General. His autobiography appeared in 1926.[11]

General Louis Botha became *Commandant*-General of the Transvaal forces, fought to the bitter end, and signed the peace treaty with Lord Kitchener on 31 May 1902. He became the first Prime Minister of the Union of South Africa in 1910, and sent South African troops to the assistance of Britain in 1914, once he had suppressed a rebellion of his former Boer comrades.

Hendrik Slegtkamp and Oliver 'Jack' Hindon fought to the bitter end, and biographies were published in Afrikaans of Slegtkamp in 1935,[12] and Hindon in 1942.[13]

Commandant Hendrik Prinsloo of the Carolina Commando was killed by machine gun fire at Witkloof on 7 November 1900. His 12-year old son, also named Hendrik, fought until he was

6   Treves, *British Medical Journal*, 1900, p.600.
7   Gandhi, *An Autobiography or the Story of My Experiments With Truth*, p.244.
8   Treves, *British Medical Journal*, 1900, p.726.
9   Charles H. Melville, *Life of General the Right Hon. Sir Redvers Buller* (London: Edward Arnold, 1923).
10   'Defender', *Sir Charles Warren and Spion Kop: A Vindication* (London: Smith, Elder & Co., 1902).
11   Douglas M. B. H. C. Dundonald, 12th Earl of, *My Army Life* (London: E. Arnold, 1926).
12   Dirk Mostert, *Slegtkamp van Spioenkop: Oorlogsherinneringe van Kapt Slegtkamp* (Cape Town: Nasionale Pers, 1935).
13   Gustav S Preller, *Kaptein Hindon – Oorlogsavontuur van ń Baasverkenner* (Cape Town: Nasionale Pers, 1942).

captured, and later said '...my little heart was full of bitterness and revenge. I was sorry we could not kill you all, and, looking back, I often wonder what would have happened to me if we had not had men like Generals Louis Botha and Smuts to lead us.'[14]

14   Prinsloo, 'Forty-Seven Years After "Spion Kop"', *Military History Journal, South African Military History Society.*

The Battlefield Today

These are among the waste places of the earth – barren, deserted, fit meeting grounds only for men whose object in life for the moment is to kill men. Were you shown over one of these places, and told, "A battle was fought here," you would answer, "Why, of course!" – Richard Harding Davis[1]

Soon after the South African War, a hotel was built for those visiting the Upper Tugela. It was on the site of Warren's headquarters, the ideal spot from which the battles could be understood. The hotel burnt down about 1920. By then, bereaved families in Britain were visiting Great War cemeteries, and Spioenkop became a distant memory. Gradually the veldt grew back over most of the traces of battle, with the exception of Spioenkop summit, where the graves and monuments were maintained and an access road was built for cars.

Planning a Visit

The battlefields on the Upper Tugela have changed little since 1900. All the battlefields are safe to visit. The rainy season is October to April with daytime temperatures around 30° C, rainstorms or light rain in the evenings, and overnight temperatures around 15° C. In April to October, it is dry, cooler and the grass shorter.

Reverend 'Danie' Kestell's description is still accurate:

I used to sit of an evening beneath the camel thorn-tree, under which Commandant de Villiers had pitched his tent, and gaze into the far west. There lay Spion Kop, tinted pink by the last rays of the setting sun. Far beyond rose the Drakensberg Mountains with their rugged, dizzy crags, scored and scarred, already veiled in the shadows of night... I forgot in such moments that we were at war.[2]

Farming is mainly large cattle ranches and the land is strikingly empty. Two main changes are the white-thorn Acacia, which has encroached widely, and Spioenkop Dam and Nature Reserve. The Nature Reserve is surrounded by a game fence that must *not* be climbed. If walking on the battlefield, carry plenty of water, a GPS device or a compass, and a detailed map, or arrange a guide. You will need walking boots, a hat, sunscreen, water, mobile phone for emergencies, and

---

1   Davis, *Notes of a War Correspondent*, p.64.
2   Kestell, *Through Shot and Flame*, p.36

a walking stick. Expect loose boulders underfoot; snakes are occasionally seen. Stream water is safe to drink. There is no malaria or bilharzia here, and in the summer, pools in Battle Spruit can provide a refreshing dip.

Spioenkop Summit

Allow a full day, especially if wishing to walk to Aloe Knoll and Twin Peaks. The summit can be reached by car. The entry gate is at the foot of Conical Hill; the staff will issue a map for a self-guided tour on request. When visiting Spioenkop summit, it is important to realise that only a small part of the trenches still exists, namely the eastern third of the main trench. The visitor will see three long mass graves of British soldiers. Their remains are at ground level; the summit was too rocky for proper graves. All available loose stones have been consumed to build up these graves, as well as the obelisks and the access road. This is why none of the numerous parapets and *schanzes* exist today. Two mass graves are both parts of the Lancashire Fusiliers main trench. The mass grave on the north-west part of summit is not located on any prior trench line, but is built from the *schanzes* on the north-west of the summit. Boer graves were dug in convenient places near where the men fell, and where there was some depth to the soil. The western part of the main trench can be spotted when the grass is short, parallel to the walking trail; thereafter it is lost. The three sheep kraals on Aloe Knoll are still there. A walk to Twin Peaks will bring the visitor to the memorial to Buchanan-Riddell.

Spioenkop – GPS Coordinates of Boer Sites

Botha's HQ -28.63123, 29.51973
Burger's HQ / Carolina laager -28.64528, 29.54211
Krupp position being dug on 23 January -28.64595, 29.51792
Bayoneted Boer grave -28.65019, 29.51742
Prinsloo path to Aloe Knoll -28.64824, 29.52270
Carolina Commando fold in the ground -28.64719, 29.51804
Louis Bothma heliograph -28.64832, 29.52318
Badenhorst buried at Clydesdale -28.59362, 29.55637
Sheep kraals on Aloe Knoll -28.64931, 29.52169; -28.64957, 29.52187; -28.65007, 29.52191.

Spioenkop – GPS Coordinates of British Sites

19th Battery on 24 January -28.66260, 29.48881
Rendezvous / Royal Engineers camp -28.65337, 29.48460
1st position British signal station -28.64938, 29.51497
2nd position British signal station -28.65339, 29.51459
Drift where KRRC and Scottish Rifles crossed Tugela -28.67734, 29.53214
Lancashire Fusiliers mass graves at -28.64899, 29.51886 and at -28.64914, 29.51937
Mass grave not on trench line -28.64834, 29.51737
Western section of trench -28.64974, 29.51674 to -28.64927, 29.51713
Outlying grave -28.65146, 29.51625

Summit dressing station till noon -28.65077, 29.51791; till 4p.m. -28.65208, 29.51530; from 4:00 p.m. -28.65437, 29.51384
Blake Knox's dressing station -28.66581, 29.49670

Spearman's Hill (Mount Alice)

The site is the property of Spion Kop Lodge, who will advise how to visit and where to park. From the summit, the panorama Buller, the Bishop of Natal and the naval gunners enjoyed is almost unchanged. Spearman's Military Cemetery is near Buller's headquarters, on the site of Treves' No.4 Stationary Hospital.

GPS Coordinates

Pretorius' Farm -28.82968, 29.66291
Spearman's Hill site of 4.7-inch guns -28.70768, 29.56191
Naval 12-pdr guns -28.68901, 29.54179
Spearman's Military Cemetery, Buller's HQ and Treves' Hospital -28.72226, 29.54326
Potgieter's Drift -28.68960, 29.56119;
Potgieter's Drift Ferry -28.68650, 29.56547
Maconochie koppies -28.67872, 29.57495
Vaalkrans Farm, -28.67365, 29.59408

Acton Homes Ambush

Drive along the R616 from the N3 towards Bergville. At 16km, you'll pass the narrow nek where the ambush is erroneously considered to have occurred. This is von Wichmann's field gun position. At 17.5km, you'll pass the turning on your left towards Three Tree Hill lodge and Rangeworthy Military Cemetery. At 18.8km, turn right onto an unmarked road; keep left, and after 1km cross Venter's Spruit over an iron bridge. 250 metres after the bridge, turn sharp left up a track. This is all that remains of the old Ladysmith – OVS road. After 650 m, you'll see Mentz's knoll to your left. Looking up the road you will see two low koppies, straddling the road: the south-eastern one held by the Carbineers and the north—western one by the ILH. Between the koppies, the road peters out at a farm gate; the telegraph poles beyond indicate the direction it once followed.

GPS Coordinates

Von Wichmann's gun position -28.60630, 29.45417
Carbineers koppie -28.63118, 29.39087
ILH koppie -28.62834, 29.39054.
Mentz knoll -28.62703, 29.40079
Mentz buried -28.50961, 29.73061
SALH donga -28.63248, 29.40731

Tabanyama

Tabanyama is remarkably unchanged, and there are no new houses, monuments, or car access. The Boer trench line can be seen by climbing Green Hill (park at the Spioenkop gate), or from Three Tree Hill lodge (walk up the Fairview-Rosalie road) or from Easby guest house (walk up the wagon road to Platkop). Platkop is the site of the heroism of Slegtkamp, Hindon and de Roos. From Platkop, a short walk takes you to the donga where the Queens sheltered, and the large British *schanzes* of Spur 5. When walking on Green Hill, Langkop and Platkop, the massive stone parapets of the Boer trenches are evident. Boer shelters can be seen on some reverse slopes. On the southern crest, less impressive than the Boer positions, are the British infantry *schanzes*. Vast quantities of brass cartridges were recycled as scrap after the war, and removing the remaining artefacts is not allowed. The 15-pdr gun sites and Royal Lancaster *schanzes* are a 2km stroll from Three Tree Hill lodge.

If staying in a car, you will see Bastion Hill, Fairview [Rangeworthy] Farm, Rangeworthy Military Cemetery, and Battle Spruit on the way to Three Tree Hill lodge. Rangeworthy Farm looks much as it did in 1900; Harry Coventry's farmhouse on the koppie was the hospital; John Coventry's farm is south of the road. About 80 soldiers including Major Childe rest in Rangeworthy Military Cemetery, on the site of Major Moir's hospital tents. From the cemetery or the road, you can see Spurs 1–5 on the skyline. On the open veldt are several isolated graves; most of the occupants were reinterred in the 1970s.

General – GPS Coordinates

Trichardt's Drift -28.68661, 29.46859
Wright's Farm -28.68132, 29.47896
Fairview Farm -28.651440, 29.46927
Venter's Spruit drift -28.67786, 29.45562
Bivouac 17 and 18 January -28.66179, 29.48708, -28.66930, 29.50030
Rangeworthy Military Cemetery -28.65018, 29.46847
Outlying grave of 4 British soldiers -28.66073, 29.47211
Warren's wagon park from19 January -28.67433, 29.45816
Picquet Hill -28.64353, 29.49473
Connaught Hill -28.65427, 29.49074

Three Tree Hill

No. 1 gun of 73rd Battery -28.64603, 29.48380
Royal Lancasters *schanzes* -28.64627, 29.48302 to -28.64663, 29.48390
78th Battery -28.64709, 29.48677
Battle Spruit Y-shaped ravine -28.63308, 29.48838
Outlying grave with cross of railway iron -28.63487, 29.47724
Warren's HQ -28.64774, 29.47977

Bastion Hill

Mounted Brigade Maxim -28.63934, 29.44839
Childe buried at Mounted Brigade HQ -28.6592, 29.4364

Slegtkamp, Hindon and de Roos

Platkop -28.61912, 29.46172
Ravine -28.62296, 29.46802

Attack on Platkop

Kitchener's starting lines -28.62831, 29.46709
Donga -28.62104, 29.47182 to -28.62285, 29.46824
15-pdrs and howitzers near Bastion Hill -28.64245, 29.45025

Appendix I

British Order of Battle, Upper Tugela

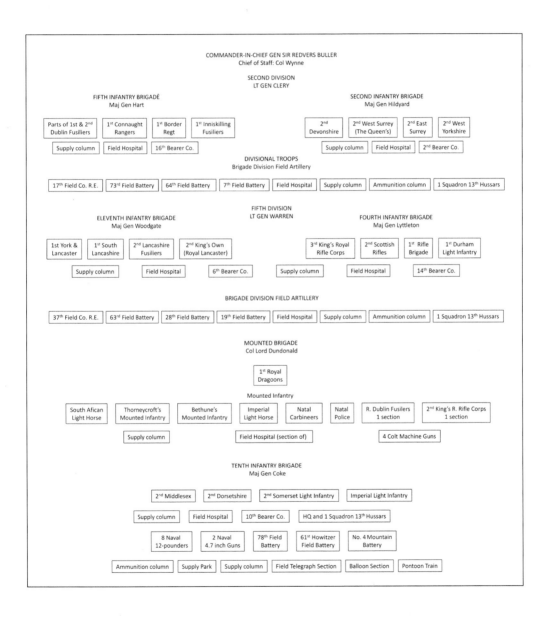

COMMANDER-IN-CHIEF GEN SIR REDVERS BULLER
Chief of Staff: Col Wynne

SECOND DIVISION
LT GEN CLERY

FIFTH INFANTRY BRIGADE
Maj Gen Hart

SECOND INFANTRY BRIGADE
Maj Gen Hildyard

| Parts of 1st & 2nd Dublin Fusiliers | 1st Connaught Rangers | 1st Border Regt | 1st Inniskilling Fusiliers | | 2nd Devonshire | 2nd West Surrey (The Queen's) | 2nd East Surrey | 2nd West Yorkshire |

| Supply column | Field Hospital | 16th Bearer Co. | | Supply column | Field Hospital | 2nd Bearer Co. |

DIVISIONAL TROOPS
Brigade Division Field Artillery

| 17th Field Co. R.E. | 73rd Field Battery | 64th Field Battery | 7th Field Battery | Field Hospital | Supply column | Ammunition column | 1 Squadron 13th Hussars |

FIFTH DIVISION
LT GEN WARREN

ELEVENTH INFANTRY BRIGADE
Maj Gen Woodgate

FOURTH INFANTRY BRIGADE
Maj Gen Lyttleton

| 1st York & Lancaster | 1st South Lancashire | 2nd Lancashire Fusiliers | 2nd King's Own (Royal Lancaster) | 3rd King's Royal Rifle Corps | 2nd Scottish Rifles | 1st Rifle Brigade | 1st Durham Light Infantry |

| Supply column | Field Hospital | 6th Bearer Co. | Supply column | Field Hospital | 14th Bearer Co. |

BRIGADE DIVISION FIELD ARTILLERY

| 37th Field Co. R.E. | 63rd Field Battery | 28th Field Battery | 19th Field Battery | Field Hospital | Supply column | Ammunition column | 1 Squadron 13th Hussars |

MOUNTED BRIGADE
Col Lord Dundonald

| 1st Royal Dragoons |

Mounted Infantry

| South Afican Light Horse | Thorneycroft's Mounted Infantry | Bethune's Mounted Infantry | Imperial Light Horse | Natal Carbineers | Natal Police | R. Dublin Fusilers 1 section | 2nd King's R. Rifle Corps 1 section |

| Supply column | Field Hospital (section of) | 4 Colt Machine Guns |

TENTH INFANTRY BRIGADE
Maj Gen Coke

| 2nd Middlesex | 2nd Dorsetshire | 2nd Somerset Light Infantry | Imperial Light Infantry |

| Supply column | Field Hospital | 10th Bearer Co. | HQ and 1 Squadron 13th Hussars |

| 8 Naval 12-pounders | 2 Naval 4.7 inch Guns | 78th Field Battery | 61st Howitzer Field Battery | No. 4 Mountain Battery |

| Ammunition column | Supply Park | Supply column | Field Telegraph Section | Balloon Section | Pontoon Train |

Appendix II

General Buller's Addresses to the Troops, Springfield

(a) 12 January 1900.

The Field Force is now advancing to the relief of Ladysmith where, surrounded by superior forces, our comrades have gallantly defended themselves for the last ten weeks. The General commanding knows that everyone in the force will feel as he does; we must be successful. We shall be stoutly opposed by a clever unscrupulous enemy; let no man allow himself to be deceived by them. If a white flag is displayed it means nothing, unless the force who display it halt, throw down their arms, and throw up their hands. If they get a chance the enemy will try and mislead us by false words of command and false bugle calls; everyone must guard against being deceived by such conduct. Above all, if any are even surprised by a sudden volley at close quarters, let there be no hesitation; do not turn from it but rush at it. That is the road to victory and safety. A retreat is fatal. The one thing the enemy cannot stand is our being at close quarters with them.

(b) 29 January 1900.

General Coke, Officers and Men of the 10th Brigade, I might thank you for your behaviour during the past 10 days, and that I might express to you how much I have admired your conduct. Nothing could have been better than your behaviour in the firing line and in other ways in the difficulties and trials you have undergone. I don't want you to think that because we have left that position that your trials and labours have been thrown away. I believe that is not the case. We have found the key to the Ladysmith road and I hope shortly will be able to relieve the beleaguered garrison, and if we do so it will be by your gallantry and hard work. I have received a telegram from the Queen this morning and I propose to read it to this Brigade, and then to the other Brigade and then to ask the two Brigades to give three cheers for Her Most Gracious Majesty. The Queen says I must express my admiration of the conduct of the troops during the past week especially those regiments you specify, and of your hard and trying march. The Queen mentions the regiments I have specified; and you have done your best, and a very good best too. I could not mention all the regiments in my telegram that I should like to have done, but you have all done well. As soon as I have spoken to the other Brigade, I will ask you to give three cheers for the Queen.

Appendix III

Orders and Messages, 17 to 19 January 1900

(a) From Sir R. Buller, 17 January 1900. Received 18 January

My dear Warren, I am carrying coals to Newcastle, probably, but on the chance, I write to say I wish you would, if you have not already done so, point out to Woodgate that his advance from Smith's Farm to-day was all wrong. The one thing if we mean to succeed is to keep our left clear. He was at Smith's Farm; the Yorkshires had occupied a kopje to the east, and he had advanced northeast; this was wrong. I give a small diagram. If your direct road is blocked, we must go forward by moving off to the left, and this will have the further advantage that it will keep you near the water at Venter's Spruit—consequently the left flank must always be thrown outward. If you can make a direct advance, it will be in line, but if you are checked, the next advance must be by moving half left; I mean that to get on, your left will creep outward and forward, and your right follow. I don't know if I have made myself clear. Wynne will explain, but until you have so far encircled the enemy that you can wheel to the east, pray always try to overlap their right with your left.

Redvers Buller.

(b) From Sir C. Warren to Lord Dundonald, 18 January 1900:

The G.O.C., as far as he can see, finds that there are no cavalry stationed near the camp, and nothing to prevent the oxen being swept away; you are to send 500 mounted men at once to be stationed round the camp.

(c) From Sir C. Warren to Lord Dundonald, 18 January 1900, 11.45 a.m.:

In case I may not have been explicit this morning in my instructions, I send the following: 500 mounted men to be employed on our rear and flanks to protect the oxen, cover our infantry, and feel for the enemy. The remainder to be employed in scouting to the front, with instructions to cut off any Boers. Parties to patrol about 10 miles to the west and north-west.

(d) From Lord Dundonald to Sir C. Warren, 18 January 1900, 2 p.m.:

I had already arranged to protect your advance by piqueting kopjes. The Royal Dragoons will do this and look after your rear and flanks. I am having sketches made of the Rangeworthy Hills, which will be sent you; the Boers occupy them. To advance with your infantry to attack Rangeworthy (Venter's Spruit) in flank, you will have to cross to the left over the Venter's Spruit, about a mile above its junction with the Tugela, coming along the back of the kopjes which line the south-west bank of the Venter's Spruit; you can then re-cross the Venter's Spruit farther on to make your flank attack; there is plenty of water here and all along the Venter's Spruit, and also camping ground. If you wish to keep on the north—east side of the Venter's Spruit, you will have to advance on the Rangeworthy Hills, without making your detour flank attack, as there is broken ground close under the hills, and it would also be within rifle fire. 1 should recommend your crossing yourself to where I address this letter from, and you will see enough. An officer who knows the road will take this note, and will inform you. I find that the Royals are weaker than I thought they were, being only some 412 instead of 500. As it is a unit, I have detailed them alone, and if you wish more I can send you more men to make up the 500; without the Royals I have about 1,100 men only. I have sent patrols to west and northwest.

(e) From Lord Dundonald to Sir C. Warren, 18 January 1900 (evening):
   My advanced squadrons are engaged with the enemy. I am supporting them. Can you let me have the Royals?

(f) From Sir C. Warren to Lord Dundonald, 18 January 1900, 7.30 p.m.:
   I did not intend you should force on an action until I had arranged to proceed from here and take the initiative; unless you are sure of success you should retire upon the camp. I am sending you 3 squadrons of the Royals to support you.

(g) From Lord Dundonald to Sir C. Warren, 18 January 1900 (despatched at 6.50 p.m., received 9 p.m.):
   The position about two miles west of Acton Homes occupied after a fight; about 20 Boers killed and wounded, 15 prisoners; am holding position and kopjes commanding the west of your line; details further.

(h) From Lord Dundonald to Sir C. Warren, 18 January 1900 (later):
   I remain here for the night with 880 men; the two squadrons 13th Hussars have to connect with occupying a kopje en route.

(i) From Sir C. Warren to Lord Dundonald, 18 January 1900 (in reply to the above):
   The position you have occupied seems to be too far to the north—west, but of this I cannot be certain. I am marching towards Venter's Spruit to-morrow morning, and expect advanced guard to arrive there about 7 a.m. What number of mounted men can you send me, as I have practically none?

(j) Sir C. Warren to Lord Dundonald, 7 a.m.:
   Yours of 4 a.m. Our objective is not Ladysmith. Our objective is to effect a junction with Sir Redvers Buller's force and then to receive orders from him. By detaching your cavalry from me you are hampering all my movements, and forcing me to alter my plans. I am moving up towards you and desire you will not move forward unless you are actually forced to do so. I require your mounted men to act as part of my force. I am shelling a hill close to this in order to draw attention off you.

(k) Lord Dundonald to Sir C. Warren, 9 a.m.:
   Please understand that I have taken up my position here to protect your left flank and assist your plans. I am in close touch with you. If I am to operate on your left flank, the road across which I came is the only one available for my wheeled first-line transport. I quite understand

your general plan, and that it is to unite with Sir R. Buller. I am quite able to protect myself where I am, and shall there await your instructions.

(l). Sir C. Warren to Sir C. F. Clery, 19 January 1900, 6 a.m.:

You command the whole of the troops in rear of General Hildyard, including the rearguard. The object is to push all the baggage and supply wagons to the front as quickly as possible, as until they are away from the vicinity of the camp (Trickhardt's Drift) General Woodgate's Brigade cannot be moved. My objective is to render assistance to Lord Dundonald, who has been in action. I am now shelling the Boer position in order to distract attention from him, but until the whole of our wagons are well to the front I cannot render him assistance.

(m). From Sir C. Warren to Lord Dundonald, 20 January 1900, 5.20 a.m.:

General White states that a force of 1,500 to 2,000 Boers marched from Clydesdale to Acton Homes yesterday at 5 p.m., 19th January. You must take care that you are not cut off, and must keep touch with the main force.

(n). From Sir C. Warren to Sir R. Buller, 19 January 1900 (sent 7.45 p.m., received 8.15 p.m.):

To Chief of Staff. Left Flank, 19th January.

I find there are only two roads by which we could possibly get from Trickhardt's Drift to Potgieters on the north of the Tugela, one by Acton Homes, the other by Fairview and Rosalie. The first I reject as too long: the second is a very difficult road for a large number of wagons, unless the enemy is thoroughly cleared out. I am, therefore, going to adopt some special arrangements which will involve my stay at Venter's Laager for two or three days. I will send in for further supplies and report progress.

C. Warren.

Appendix IV

Orders and Messages – Battle of Tabanyama

(a) Orders Issued By Sir C. Warren To Sir C. F. Clery, 19 January 1900 (Evening).

General Officer Commanding 2nd Division: I shall be glad if you will arrange to clear the Boers out of the ground above that at present occupied by the 11th brigade, by a series of outflanking movements. In the early morning an advance should be made as far as the Hussars reconnoitred to-day, and a shelter trench there made across the slope of the hill. A portion of the slopes of the adjoining hill to the west can then be occupied, the artillery assisting, if necessary, in clearing the western side and upper slopes. When this is done I think that a battery can be placed on the slopes of the western hill in such a position that it could shell the schanzes of the Boers on Spion Kop and the upper portion of the eastern hill. When this is done a further advance can be made on the eastern hill, and artillery can be brought to bear upon the upper slopes of the western hill. It appears to me that this might be done with comparatively little loss of life, as the Boers can in each turn be outflanked. The following cavalry are at your disposal: two squadrons Royal Dragoons and Vth divisional squadron.

C. Warren, Lieut.-General.

(b). From Sir C. Warren to Sir C. F. Clery, 20 January 1900 (evening):

I quite concur that a frontal attack is undesirable, and that a flank attack is more suitable. I intended to convey that we should hold what we get by means of entrenchments when necessary, and not retire, continuing the advance to-morrow if it cannot be done to-night; frontal attack, with heavy losses, is simply playing the Boer game.

(c). From Sir C. Warren to Chief of Staff, 21 January 1900, 6.30 p.m.:

I am under the impression, from various indications, that the Free State Boers are preparing a great trek to the west, and that the present fighting is to secure their line of retreat. If you can push on three battalions to reinforce me as quickly as possible I think I can manage to close the road to the west and secure some of the wagons.

(d). From Sir C. Warren to Sir J. R. Buller, 21 January 1900 (evening):

I find that there is a position now being fortified behind the one we are now engaged on, so that it is impossible to say when decisive attack will take place, but I am under the impression that with continuous fighting we shall clear the range of hills we are now attacking up to the Acton Homes–Ladysmith road in two or three days. I fancy the Boers are fighting as much to retain possession over their communications as to prevent our getting to Ladysmith, and I have great hopes that the Howitzers will add greatly to our progress to- morrow. I find that there are some guns placed concealed in a donga, together with a large number of Boers, overlooking the road between here and Acton Homes, and as soon as the extra battalions arrive I shall endeavour to surround both.

(e). From Sir R. Buller to Sir C. Warren, 22 January 1900, 5:06 a.m.:

I think it possible the enemy may try a counter-attack. They are concentrated. Your troops are widely extended and do not support each other. I should be cautious how I attempted any enterprise further to the left at present. I thought Woodgate's troops very badly placed on your right yesterday, the bulk of them were much too far back to have been of any use in the event of a sudden attack upon the guns. I think before you do anything else, at least one battalion should be strongly entrenched close to the guns. I am riding over this morning and should like to see you. Will you leave an orderly on the hill where I met you out yesterday to tell me where to find you?

(F). Force Orders by Sir C. Warren, 22 January 1900.

Venter's Laager, 22.1.00, 1.20 p.m. 1. As a temporary measure the following arrangements for staff duties are being made: A.A.G.-Major Capper, Provost Marshal-Major Williams. Signalling Officer-Capt. McHardy. 2. The following tactical distribution of troops is made: Right Attack and Right Flank. Troops east of a line dividing Three Tree Hill from Fair View Farm Spur and the 10th Brigade. These are under General Talbot Coke. Left Attack and Left Flank. Troops to the west of above line. These are under General Sir F. Clery. 3. General Talbot Coke will arrange for immediate security of camp and baggage. 4. The Lancashire Fusiliers will rejoin 11th Brigade. 5. The G.O.C. the force will be stationed near the artillery on Three Tree Hill. 6. Two mounted orderlies from each division and one from each brigade division R.A. will be permanently stationed with the Headquarters of the force. To report as soon as possible.

T. Capper, Maj. for A.A.G

Appendix V

Orders and Messages – Battle of Spioenkop

(a) Orders by Sir C. Warren for the Occupation of Spion Kop, 23 January 1900.

To G.O.C. Right attack. 1. The G.O.C. the force has decided to seize Spion Kop to-night. 2. You will detail from the troops under your orders 2 battalions and Thorneycroft's Mounted Infantry and ½ company R.E. to carry out this operation. 3. Major-General Woodgate is to command this force. 4. The Column will parade at the place appointed by you, and you will issue all necessary orders. The Column should move off not later than 12 midnight. 5. Extra ammunition must be carried on ammunition mules drawn from the Regiments of your own force. 6. One day's complete rations are to be carried on the man, and wagons with supplies and greatcoats brought up as far as possible at present without exposure. 7. All natives in the vicinity of the commencement of your line of advance should be confined to their kraals by cavalry piquets, which should act after dark to-night. Wright's Farm should also be piqueted and inhabitants confined to the building. 8. The Imperial Light Infantry now at the Pontoon Bridge will be ordered to occupy the heights E. and W. of the gully above Wright's Farm after dark to-night, ready to support you and keep open your communications. 9. A mountain battery has been ordered to come up, and will be sent up the Spion Kop as soon as they arrive, after you have made your lodgment on the hill. 10. The artillery and infantry of your right attack must be prepared to support the Column occupying Spion Kop by their fire as soon as it is light. 11. Entrenchments must be made on the top of Spion Kop as soon as it is taken; the half company R.E. will bring their extra tools for this purpose. 12. The G.O.C. desires that the regiments you may detail for the Spion Kop Column should be relieved from further duty to-day. 13. Endeavour will be made to collect any pack mules (provided with the Indian equipment for carrying water in skins) there may be in camp to carry water. Failing this, water can be carried on mules in waterproof sheets. 14. Signalling communication must be established as soon as secrecy is no longer possible. 15. A special party from the R.A. to observe and report by signal the effect of Howitzer fire must also accompany the Column.

By order, T. Capper, for A.A.G.

(b). Attack Orders Issued by Major-General Coke, Commanding Right Attack, 23 January 1900.

1. The General Officer Commanding has decided to seize Spion Kop. 2. The operations will be conducted by Major-General Woodgate, who will detail two battalions of his own brigade, to which will be attached about 100 men of Thorneycroft's Mounted Infantry and half company Royal Engineers. 3. Rendezvous just east of the encampment Royal Engineers, at 7 p.m. Men must be kept concealed from the front. 4. One hundred and fifty rounds of ammunition will be carried by the men. The General Officer Commanding 11th brigade will attach three mules to each battalion, and the Officer Commanding 10th brigade three mules, this afternoon. Ammunition for these mules will be furnished by the battalions concerned. One day's

complete ration to be carried by the men. All horses to be left at the Royal Engineer bivouac. The mules will follow in rear of the Column. Men will carry entrenching tools in stretchers. 5. The Officer Commanding the Royal Dragoons will arrange to piquet all native kraals on the line of advance, and also Wright's Farm. All inhabitants should be confined to the buildings. 6. Men will of course carry filled water bottles, and should be cautioned that a re-fill may be difficult. Battalions will endeavour to make some arrangement, by fastening biscuit boxes on to mules, or in some other manner, to carry extra water. 7. The General Officer Commanding 11th brigade will arrange that the Volunteer ambulance and the bearer company of the brigade send detachments. No ambulance to be nearer than the Royal Engineer bivouac till daylight.

J. Talbot Coke, Major-General.

(c). Brigade Orders by Major-General Woodgate, 23 January 1900.

1. The General Officer Commanding has decided to seize Spion Kop this night. 2. The following troops will compose the force: Royal Lancaster regiment (6 companies). 2nd Lancashire Fusiliers. Thorneycroft's Mounted Infantry (180 men). Half company 17th Company Royal Engineers. 3. The above troops will rendezvous at White's Farm about half mile north-west of Pontoon Bridge at 7 p.m. 4. Extra ammunition will be carried on the mules supplied by the 10th brigade. 5. One day's complete rations will be carried. Wagons with supplies and great-coats will be brought up as soon as possible without exposure; also water carts and machine guns. 6. The South Lancashire regiment will hand over six mules, three to each battalion, for water-carrying purposes. 7. Pack mules will be utilized for carrying water in waterproof sheets. 8. Twenty picks and twenty shovels to be carried in regulation stretchers. 9. Password, "Waterloo."

(d). Force Orders by Sir Charles Warren, Relative to the Occupation of Spion Kop.

Three Tree Hill, 23rd January 1900. 7 p.m.

I. An attack on Spion Kop will be made to-night by a force of about 3½ battns. under General Woodgate, the march commencing about midnight.

II. This attack will be supported from Three Tree Hill by the troops under the orders of the G.O.C. Right attack. If firing takes place from Spion Kop during the night, the artillery from Three Tree Hill will fire Star Shell and will open fire at the rear of the enemy's position to prevent reinforcements being brought up. Infantry from Three Tree Hill will fire at daylight with the same object.

III. The G.O.C. Left attack will use his discretion about opening fire against the enemy to his front, if firing breaks out on Spion Kop with a view to creating a diversion.

IV. A Staff Officer from Right and Left attacks will report to the G.O.C. the force at midnight at Three Tree Hill.

V. All troops are to be warned of the operations which will be carried out. No firing must take place without the orders of Battalion Commanders.

VI. Countersign is Waterloo.

VII. If firing commences frequent reports are to be sent to the G.O.C. the force at Three Tree Hill by signal or messenger.

VIII. The division of the Force into Right and Left attack is to be considered purely tactical. For administrative purposes, the troops will be organised as before into IInd and Vth divisions and Corps Troops. This arrangement will apply to casualty returns.

IX. General Talbot Coke will temporarily command the Vth division and will nominate his own Staff.

X. The Imperial Light Infantry joined the force to-day and comes under the orders of the G.O.C. Right attack.

By Order, T. Capper, A.A.G.

(e) Letter from Major-General Woodgate, written about 7 a.m. and handed to General Warren by Lieutenant Colonel à Court at 9 a.m.:

Spion Kop: 24 January 1900.

Dear Sir Charles, we got up about four o'clock, and rushed the position with three men wounded. There were some few Boers, who seemed surprised, and bolted after firing a round or so, having one man killed. I believe there is another somewhere, but have not found him in the mist. The latter did us well, and I pushed on a bit quicker than I perhaps should otherwise have done, lest it should lift before we got here. We have intrenched a position, and are, I hope, secure; but fog is too thick to see, so I retain Thorneycroft's men and Royal Engineers for a bit longer. Thorneycroft's men attacked in fine style. I had a noise made later to let you know that we had got in.

Yours etc., E. Woodgate.

(f) Message sent by General Woodgate after his head wound at 8:50 a.m.:

We are between a terrible cross-fire, and can barely hold our own. Water is badly needed. Help us.

(g) Colonel Crofton subsequently stated that the message delivered verbally by him to the signalling officer of his battalion, and by the latter to the signaller, also verbally, ran thus:

General Woodgate dead. Reinforcements urgently required.

The signalling officer on the other hand stated that the message he handed in was as follows:

General Woodgate is killed, send reinforcements at once.

(h) From General Warren to Colonel Crofton on Spioenkop, exact text unknown but likely to have been approx. 9:45 a.m.,:

I am sending up two battalions, but they will take some time to get up. Hold on to the last. No surrender!

(i) From General Warren to General Lyttelton. Sent from Left Flank Attack Office, 9.53 a.m., received 9.55 a.m., 24.1.00:

Give every assistance you can on your side; this side is clear, but the enemy are too strong on your side, and Crofton telegraphs that if assistance is not given at once all is lost. I am sending up two battalions, but they will take some time to get up."

(j) Heliogram from someone unknown on Spion Kop to General Lyttelton. Received 10.15 a.m., 24.1.00:

We occupy all the crest on top of hill, being heavily attacked from your side. Help us. Spion Kop.

(k) From General Warren to General Lyttelton and General Buller approx. 10:55 a.m., 21.1.00:

We occupy the whole summit and I fear you are shelling us seriously; cannot you turn your guns on the enemy's guns?

(l) From General Buller to General Warren 11.45 a.m.:

Now Woodgate is dead I think you must put a strong commander on top; I recommend you put Thorneycroft in command.

This was followed immediately by heliograph from Warren to Crofton that Thorneycroft was, with the Commander-in-Chief's approval, placed in command of the summit, with the rank of brigadier-general.

(m) From General Coke to General Warren 12:60 p.m.:

I am now on the plateau of Spion Kop slopes. The top of the hill is reported crowded with men, and as these are exposed to shell fire and suffering, but holding out well, I have stopped further reinforcements beyond this point, but the troops engaged know that help is close at hand. Ammunition is being pushed up.

(n) From Colonel Thorneycroft to General Warren 2.30 p.m. (sent with Colonel Sandbach):

Hung on till last extremity with old force, some of the Middlesex here now, and I hear Dorsets coming up, but force really inadequate to hold such large perimeter. The enemy's guns on N.W. sweep the whole of the top of the hill. They also have guns E.; cannot you bring heavy artillery fire to bear on N.W. guns? What reinforcement can you send to hold the hill to-night? We are badly in need of water. There are many killed and wounded. If you wish to make a certainty of hill for night you must send more infantry and attack enemy's guns.

(o) From General Coke to General Warren 3:00 p.m.:

I have ordered the Scottish Rifles and the King's Royal Rifles up to reinforce. The Middlesex Regiment, Dorset Regiment, and Imperial Light Infantry have also gone up. Bethune's Mounted Infantry (120 strong) also reinforced. We appear to be holding our own at present.

(p) From General Coke to General Warren 3:50 p.m. (after Coke had reached the summit):

We are suffering much from shrapnel fire from our left front, bearing magnetic north apparently from Three Tree Hill. The hill is being cleared of Boers. The necessary reinforcements have been ordered up. Scottish Rifles have just reached top of hill. Casualties heavy. More doctors, food, and especially water wanted.

(q) From General Coke to General Warren 5:50 p.m.

Top of Spion Kop,' 5.50 p.m., 24-1-1900. The situation is as follows: The original troops are still in position, have suffered severely, and many dead and wounded are still in the trenches. The shell fire is and has been very severe. If I hold on to the position all night is there any guarantee that our artillery can silence the enemy's guns, otherwise to-day's experience will be repeated, and the men will not stand another complete day's shelling. I have in hand Bethune's Mounted Infantry and the Dorset Regiment intact to cover a withdrawal. If I remain I will endeavour to utilise these units to carry food and water up to the firing line. The situation is extremely critical. If I charge and take the koppie in front [Aloe Knoll], the advance is several hundred yards in the face of the entrenched enemy in strength, and my position as regards the quick-firing guns is much worse. Please give orders, and should you wish me to withdraw, cover retirement from Connaught's Hill.

(r) From Colonel Thorneycroft to General Warren, by hand, 6.30 p.m. 24.1.00:

The troops which marched up here last night are quite done up, Lancashire Fusiliers, Royal Lancaster regiment, and Thorneycroft's Mounted Infantry. They have had no water, and ammunition is running short. I consider that, even with reinforcements which have arrived, it is impossible to permanently hold this place, so long as the enemy's guns can play on this hill. They have one long range gun, three of shorter range, and one Maxim-Nordenfeldt, which have swept the whole of the plateau since 8 a.m. I have not been able to ascertain the casualties, but they have been very heavy, especially in the regiments which came up last night. I request instructions as to what course I am to adopt. The enemy at 6.30 p.m. are firing heavily from both flanks, with rifles, shell, and Nordenfeldt, while a heavy rifle fire is kept up in front. It is all I can do to hold my own. If casualties go on occurring at present rate, I shall barely hold out the night. A large number of stretcher-bearers should be sent up, and also all water possible. The situation is critical.

Alex. Thorneycroft, Lt.-Colonel.

(s) From Colonel Thorneycroft to Sir C. Warren. Sent from Spion Kop, by Lieut. Winston Churchill, 24.1.1900. Delivered 2 a.m., 25.1.1900.

Spion Kop, 24th January 1900. Regret to report that I have been obliged to abandon Spion Kop, as the position became untenable. I have withdrawn the troops in regular order, and will come to report as soon as possible.

Alex. Thorneycroft, Lt.-Colonel.

(t) General Warren to General Lyttelton. Sent from Left Flank 6.45 p.m., received 6.48 p.m. 24.1.00:

The assistance you are giving most valuable. We shall try to remain in statu quo during tomorrow; balloon would be of incalculable value to me.

(u) General Lyttelton to General Warren. Received 8.35 p.m., 24 January 1900:

My position to-night is this: The Scottish Rifles and 2 squadrons Bethune's have joined your extreme right and remain there. The K.R.R. scaled Sugar Loaf Hill, and reached the top, but as they were 2 miles in advance of your extreme right, and as I had no troops to support them, I have ordered them to withdraw again to the foot of my position here. Let me know how you stand, and what you propose to do in the morning.

(v) Force Orders, Issued by General Warren on the Evening of 24 January 1900.

1. The action of to-day commenced with the surprise of Spion Kop by General Woodgate's force, which consisted of: The Lancashire Fusiliers. The Royal Lancaster regiment. Thorneycroft's Mounted Infantry. \ Co. R.E., and detachment R.A. About 8.30 a.m. the enemy made a determined attempt to retake the hill, which was gallantly held by our men all day. in spite of a damaging shellfire. At the close of the day the following regiments were occupying Spion Kop, in addition to the original force: The Dorsetshire regiment. The Middlesex regiment. Part of

the Connaught Rangers. 2 companies Bethune's MI The Scottish Rifles. The two last operating from Potgieters. The remainder of General Lyttelton's brigade also operated on our right. The G.O.C. is confident that the spirit of gallantry and endurance which has marked the conduct of the troops will be continued to-morrow.

2. An issue of rum is sanctioned for all troops.

3. Captain C. B. Levita, R.A., is appointed D.A.A.G. (a), to the force as a temporary measure, from 23: .00. 4. The East Surrey and Devonshire regiments have been temporarily transferred to the right attack.

By Order, T. Capper, for A.A.G.

The countersign to-night is "Victoria."

(w). Letter from General Warren to Colonel Thorneycroft. Sent at 8.20 p.m. by Lieut. Winston Churchill, and delivered at 10.30 p.m., 24 January 1900:

The General Officer Commanding Force would be glad to have your views of the situation and measures to be adopted, by Lieut. Winston Churchill, who takes this note.

By Order, T. Capper, A.A.G.

Bibliography

Manuscrript Sources

Abbott, Walter, Private, Dorsetshire Regiment, *Diary*, National Army Museum 1992-08-335

Anon, *19th Battery Digest of Service 1900*, Royal Artillery Institution Archives.

Anon, *28th Battery Digest of Service 1900*, Royal Artillery Institution Archives.

Anon, *61st Battery Digest of Service 1900*, Royal Artillery Institution Archives.

Anon, *63rd Battery Digest of Service 1900*, Royal Artillery Institution Archives.

Anon, *78th Battery Digest of Service 1900*, Royal Artillery Institution Archives.

Anon., *Battle of Venter's Spruit 21 Jan 1900* in: Digest of Service, 2nd Bttn Queen's, (1900). Surrey Infantry Museum. QEWS 3/5/1

Cosgrove, John, *Letter*, King's Own Royal Regiment Museum KO2926/0

Crossman, George, Lieutenant, 2nd West Yorkshire regiment, *Diary*, Liddell Hart Archives GB0099 KCLMA Crossman

Evans, Frederick, *Letter*, 3025 Pte Evans, D Company, 2nd Bn Middlesex Regiment, National Army Museum 2008-02-16

Goodwin, H., *Diary of 4412 Drummer Goodwin, 2nd Bn West Yorkshire Regiment*, National Army Museum 1976-07-47.

Herbert, Walter, *Letter from Corporal Herbert, B Company 2nd Bn The King's Own Royal Lancaster Regiment*, King's Own Royal Regiment Museum KO1383/01

Herbert, 2nd Bn Middlesex Regiment, *Letter of 1 February 1900*, National Army Museum 2008-02-16

Harrison, George Hyde, Border Regiment, *Unpublished Memoir*, Cumbria's Museum of Military Life: Ch. 5, pp.91—118.

Kearsey, Alec H. C., *Letter dated 29 January 1900*, National Army Museum 1999-12-15

Lyttelton, Neville, 'Letter to his wife of 1 February 1900', Liddell Hart Archives GB0099 KCLMA Lyttelton

McGowan, James, Royal Lancaster Regiment, 'Letter dated 28 January 1900', National Army Museum, 1990-12-66

Maidment, George C., *Diary of the Siege of Ladysmith*, Royal Army Medical Corps Muniments collection, Wellcome collection RAMC/1011/1

O'Hara, T.W., *Diary While Serving in the Royal Lancaster Regiment*, National Army Museum 1974-11-6

Phipps, Harry, *Diary, 1st Battalion Border Regiment,* National Army Museum 1983-02-15

Putland, Walter John, *Personal Diary of Lance Corporal Walter Putland 2785 2nd Middlesex Regiment*, The National Army Museum, London. Archives Reference Number 8107-18

Talbot, Frederick G., Captain, Rifle Brigade, *Letter of 4 February 1900*, Liddell Hart archive, GB0099 KCLMA Lyttelton

Wedd, Laurie D., 2nd Queen's Royal West Surrey Regiment, *Letter*, National Army Museum 1999-06-94

Unpublished Thesis

Grobler, Francois Jacobus, *Die Carolina-kommando in die Tweede Vryheidstoorlog, 1899–1902*, Unpublished thesis, North-West University Repository, South Africa, 1960.

Published Sources, Books

Amery, Leopold S. (ed.), *The War in South Africa 1899–1902* Vol. III. (London: Sampson Low, Marston & Co, 1905)

Anon., *Connaught Rangers Regimental Records* (Ireland: Connaught Rangers, 1901)

Atkins, John Black, *The Relief of Ladysmith*, 2nd Edition (London: Methuen, 1900)

Barnard, Christiaan J., *Generaal Louis Botha op die Natalse Front 1899–1900* (Cape Town: Balkema, 1970)

Baynes, Arthur H., *My Diocese During the War* (London: Bell, 1900)

Belloc, Hillaire, *The Modern Traveller* (London: Edward Arnold, 1898)

Blake, John Y. F., *A West Pointer with the Boers* (Boston: Angel Guardian Press, 1903)

Blake Knox, Ernest, *Buller's Campaign with the Natal Field Force of 1900* (London: R. B. Johnson, 1902)

Breytenbach, Johan H., *Die Geskiedenis van Die Tweede Vryheidsoorlog in Suid-Afrika, 1899–1902* (Pretoria: Staatsdrukker, 1971) Part 3, Ch 5, Sec 7.

Burleigh, Bennet, *The Natal Campaign* (London: Chapman & Hall, 1900)

Burne, Charles R. N., *With the Naval Brigade in Natal, 1899–1900* (London: Arnold, 1902)

Charlton, Lionel E. O., *Charlton* (London: Faber & Faber, 1931)

Childs, Lewis, *Ladysmith: Colenso/Spion Kop/Hlangwane/Tugela (Battleground South Africa)* (Barnsley, Pen & Sword, 1998)

Churchill, Winston S., *London to Ladysmith Via Pretoria* (London: Longmans, 1900)

Churchill, Winston S., *My Early Life*, (London: Thornton Butterworth, 1930)

Churchill, Winston S., *The River War. An Historical Account of the Reconquest of the Soudan* (London: Longmans, 1902)

Coetzer, Owen, *The Road to Infamy* (London: Arms & Armour, 1996)

Commission into the War in South Africa; *Report of His Majesty's Commissioners Appointed to Inquire into the Military Preparations and Other Matters Connected with the War in South Africa*, (London: H.M.S.O 1903), Vol.2.

Creswicke, Louis, *South Africa and the Transvaal War* (Edinburgh: TC & EC Jack, 1900), Vol. III.

Crowe, George, *The Commission of H.M.S. "Terrible" 1898–1902* (London: George Newnes, 1903)

Davis, Richard Harding, *Notes of a War Correspondent* (New York: C. Scribner's Sons, 1911)

Davitt, Michael, *The Boer Fight for Freedom* (New York: Funk & Wagnalls, 1902)

'Defender', *Sir Charles Warren and Spion Kop: A Vindication* (London: Smith, Elder & Co., 1902)

De Villiers, J. C., *Healers, Helpers and Hospitals* (Pretoria: Protea Book House, 2008)

Du Cane, Hubert, *The War in South Africa*, London: John Murray, 1906.

Dundonald, Douglas M. B. H. C., (12th Earl of), *My Army Life* (London: E. Arnold, 1926)

Durand, Henry M., *The Life of Field-Marshal Sir George White, V.C.*, (London: Blackwood & Sons, 1915), Vol. II

Gandhi, Mohandas K., *The Story of My Experiments with Truth*, Vol. 1, (Ahmedabad: Navajivan Press, 1927)

Gibson, George F., *The Story of the Imperial Light Horse in the South African War 1899–1902* (London: G.D & Co, 1937)

Griffith, Kenneth, *Thank God We Kept the Flag Flying. The Siege and Relief of Ladysmith 1899–1900* (New York, Viking Press, 1974)

Hall, Darrell D., *Halt! Action Front!* (South Africa, Covos-Day, 1999)

Hall, Darrell D., *The Hall Handbook of the Anglo-Boer War 1899–1902*, (Pietermaritzburg: University of Natal Press, 1999)

Hart-Synnot, B. M. (ed.), *Letters of Major-General FitzRoy Hart-Synnot* (London: Edward Arnold 1912)

Hiley, Alan R. I., and Hassell, John A., *The Mobile Boer; being the record of the observations of two burgher officers* (New York: Grafton press, 1902)

Hofmeyr, Nico J., *Zes Maanden bij de Commandos*, ('s-Gravenhage: van Stockum & Zoon, 1903)

H.M. Govt., *The Spion Kop Despatches* (London: H.M.S.O., 1902)

H.M.S.O., *Infantry Drill Manual 1896* (London; Harrison and Sons, 1896)

Hillegas, Howard C., *The Boers in War; The Story of the British-Boer War of 1899–1900* (New York, Appleton, 1900)

Inniskilling Fusiliers Regimental Historical Records Committee, *The Royal Inniskilling Fusiliers* (London: Constable, 1928)

Izedinova, Sophia, *A Few Months with the Boers* (Johannesburg: Perskor, 1977)

Jeans, Thomas T., *Naval Brigades in the South African War 1899–1900* (London: Sampson Low, Marston & Co 1901)

Jourdain, Henry F. N, *Ranging Memories* (Oxford: John Johnson, University Press, 1934)

Jourdain, Henry F. N., *Natal Memories 1899–1900* (London: Privately published, 1948)

Kearsey, Alec H. C., *War Record of the York & Lancaster Regiment 1900–1902* (London: George Bell & Sons, 1903)

Kemp, Jan C. G., *Vir Vryheid en vir Reg*, (Pretoria: Nasionale Pers, 1941)

Kestell, John D., *Through Shot and Flame. The Adventures and Experiences of J. D. Kestell, Chaplain to President Steyn and General Christian De Wet* (London: Methuen, 1903)

Krause, Ludwig, *The War Memoirs of Commandant Ludwig Krause 1899–1900* (Cape Town: Van Riebeeck Society, 1995)

Kruger, Paul, *The Memoirs of Paul Kruger* (New York: Century, 1902)

Lasham, F., *Some Notes on the Queen's Royal West Surrey Regiment, together with an Account of the 2nd and 3rd Battalions in the late South African Campaign* (Guildford: Privately published, 1904)

Linesman (Captain Maurice H. Grant), *Words by an Eyewitness – The Struggle in Natal* (London: Blackwood, 1901)

Lynch, George, *Impressions of a War Correspondent* (London: George Newnes, 1903)

Lyttelton, Neville, *Eighty Years Soldiering, Politics, Games* (Hodder and Stoughton., London, 1927)

McKenzie, A.G., *Delayed Action* (Pietermaritzburg: Privately published, 1963)

Makins, George H., *Surgical Experiences in South Africa, 1899–1900, Being Mainly a Clinical Study of the Nature and Effects of Injuries Produced by Bullets of Small Calibre* (London: Smith, Elder, & Co., 1901)

Maurice, John F., *History of the War in South Africa, 1899–1902* (London: Hurst and Blackett, 1907), Vol. II

Melville, Charles H., *Life of General the Right Hon. Sir Redvers Buller* (London: Edward Arnold, 1923)

Meredith, Martin, *Afrikaner Odyssey* (Johannesburg, Jonathan Ball, 2017)

Mostert, Dirk, *Slegtkamp van Spioenkop: Oorlogsherinneringe van Kapt Slegtkamp* (Cape Town: Nasionale Pers, 1935)

Neligan, T., *From Preston to Ladysmith with The 1st Bn South Lancashire Regt.* (Preston: J. & H. Platt, 1900).

O'Mahony, Charles J., *A Peep over the Barleycorn. In the firing line with the P.W.O., 2nd West Yorkshire Regiment, Through the Relief of Ladysmith* (Dublin: J.T. Drought, 1911)

Pearse, H. W., *2nd Battalion East Surrey Regiment: Digest of Services in South Africa 1899–1902* (London: Medici, 1903)

Penning, L., *De Oorlog in Zuid-Afrika* (Rotterdam: Daamen, 2nd edition 1901)

Pienaar, Philip, *With Steyn and De Wet* (London: Methuen, 1902)

Pohl, Victor, *Adventures of a Boer Family* (London, Faber & Faber, 1944)

Preller, Gustav S., *Kaptein Hindon – Oorlogsavontuur van ń Baasverkenner* (Nasionale Pers, Cape Town. 1942)

Pretorius, Fransjohan, *Life on Commando During the Anglo-Boer war 1899–1902*, (Cape Town: Human & Rousseau, 1999)

Reitz, Deneys, *Commando* (London, Faber and Faber, 1929)

Riall, Nicholas, *Boer War: The Letters, Diaries and Photographs of Malcolm Riall from the War in South Africa 1899—1902* (London, Brassey's, 2000) pp.41–45

Romer, Cecil F. and Mainwaring, Arthur E., *The Second Battalion Royal Dublin Fusiliers in the South African War* (London: A L Humphreys, 1908)

Rompel, Frederik, *Heroes of the Boer War* (London, Review Of Reviews, 1903)

Sandberg, Christof G. S., *De Zesdaagsche Slag aan de Boven Tugela, 19 tot 24 Januari 1900* (Amsterdam: De Gids, 1901)

Sandberg, Christof G. S., *Instantanés uit den Zuid-Afrikaanschen Oorlog* (Amsterdam: De Gids, 1901)

Schikkerling, Roland W., *Commando Courageous* (Johannesburg: Keartland, 1964)

Schreiner, Olive, *The South African Question* (Chicago: Sergel, 1899)

Spiers, Edward M., *Letters from Ladysmith.* (Barnsley: Pen & Sword 2010).

Steevens, George W., *From Capetown to Ladysmith; an Unfinished Record of the South African War* (New York: Dodd, Mead & Co., 1900)

Stevenson, William F., Surgeon-General (ed.), *Report on the Surgical Cases Noted in the South African War, 1899–1902* (London, Printed for H. M. Stationery Office by Harrison and Sons, 1905)

Stirling, John, *The Colonials in South Africa, 1899–1902: Their Record, Based on the Dispatches* (Edinburgh: Blackwood, 1907).

Stirling, John, *Our Regiments in South Africa, 1899–1902: Their Record, Based on Dispatches* (Edinburgh; Blackwood 1903)

Tremayne, J. H., *XIII. Hussars South African War October 1899 – October 1902* (Aldershot: May & Co., 1905)

Treves, Frederick, *The Tale of a Field Hospital* (London: Cassell, 1900)

Uys, Ian, *Heidelbergers of the Boer War*, (Heidelberg: Privately published, 1981)

Van Warmelo, Dietlof, *On Commando* (London: Methuen, 1902)

Viljoen, Ben, *My Reminiscences of the Anglo-Boer War* (London: Hood, Douglas, & Howard, 1902)

West Yorkshire Regiment, *Extract from Digest of Service of the 2nd Battalion in South Africa, 1899–1902* (York: Yorkshire Herald, 1902)

Wilson, Charles Holmes, *The Relief of Ladysmith. The Artillery in Natal* (London: William Clowes & Sons, 1901)

Published Sources, Journals, Newspapers

Anon., *The Bulletin of Official War News, Heidelberg*, Transvaal Field Press, 19–29 January 1900

Anon, Letter, *Glasgow Herald*, Wednesday 10th January 1900

Barnard, Christiaan J., 'General Botha in the Spioenkop Campaign January 1900' in *Military History Journal, South African Military History Society*, Vol. 2 No. 1 – June 1971

Dennison, King's Own Royal Lancasters, Letter in *Mid-Cumberland and North Westmorland Herald, Saturday 19th May 1900*

Dickson, Sergeant E., Letter 'How He Was Wounded: Story Told by Himself. The Thorneycrofts Cut Up' in *The Launceston Examiner*, 15 March 1900.

Finucane, Morgan I., 'General Nervous Shock, Immediate and Remote, After Gunshot and Shell Injuries in the South African Campaign' in *The Lancet*, 15 September 1900.

Hall, Darrell D., 'Guns in South Africa 1899–1902,' in *Military History Journal, Vol. 2 No. 1,* June 1971

Hall, Darrell D., 'Ammunition' in *South African Military History Society: Military History Journal. Vol. 3 No. 4*, Dec 1975

Hensley, Charles A., 'Letters of Capt. C.A. Hensley to his Father' in *Military History Journal, The South African Military History Society, Vol.6 No.6*, December 1985

Jones, Edgar and Wessely, Simon, 'The Origins of British Military Psychiatry Before the First World War' in *War & Society, Volume 19, Number 2*, October 2001

Jooste, L., 'Foreigners in the defence of South Africa' in *South African Journal of Military Studies, Vol. 16, Number 2* (1986)

Lemmer, N. M., 'Die Slag van Spioenkop 24 Januarie 1900' in *Military History Journal, The South African Military History Society*, Vol.1 No.1, December 1967

Prinsloo, Hendrik F., 'Forty-Seven Years After "Spion Kop"' in *Military History Journal, South African Military History Society*, 1967, Vol.1 No.1

Treves, Frederick, 'The War in South Africa' in *British Medical Journal* 1900

Riding, W., Sergeant, 1st South Lancashire Regiment, 'Letter' in *Waterloo & Crosby Herald*, 3rd March 1900

Shaw, Jocelyn, 'Moving up to Spion Kop' in *Military History Journal, The South African Military History Society*, Vol.2 No.2, December 1971

Sprague, Aubrey, 'Letter to his father of 27 January 1900' in *The Smethwick Telegraph*, 31 March 1900.

Stakhovich, Pavel A., 'The Despatches of Colonel Stakhovich, of the General Staff Despatched to the Theatre of Military Operations in South Africa' in *Scientia Militaria, South African Journal of Military Studies,* Vol.5, No.3, 1975

Stevenson, R. E., 'A Carbineer Remembers' in *Military History Journal, The South African Military History Society,* Vol.2 No.2, December 1971

Wake, Hereward, 'Capture of the Twin Peaks at Spion Kop by 3rd Battalion King's Royal Rifles' in *The King's Royal Rifle Corps Chronicle for 1908* (Winchester: Warren and Sons, 1909)

West Yorkshire Regiment, *Extract from Digest of Service of the 2nd Battalion in South Africa, 1899–1902* (York: Yorkshire Herald, 1902)

Electronic Sources

Normand, Samuel Richard, *The Boer War Letters of Subaltern Samuel Richard Normand, RA*.<https://www.angloboerwar.com/forum/19-ephemera/30466-the-boer-war-letters-of-subaltern-samuel-richard-normand-ra>, accessed 10 Oct. 2021.

Index

The period 1815-1914 is sometimes called the long century of peace. It was in reality very far from that. It was a century of civil wars, popular uprisings, and struggles for Independence. An era of colonial expansion, wars of Empire, and colonial campaigning, much of which was unconventional in nature. It was also an age of major conventional wars, in Europe that would see the Crimea campaign and the wars of German unification. Such conflicts, along with the American Civil War, foreshadowed the total war of the 20th century.

It was also a period of great technological advancement, which in time impacted the military and warfare in general. Steam power, electricity, the telegraph, the radio, the railway, all became tools of war. The century was one of dramatic change. Tactics altered, sometimes slowly, to meet the challenges of the new technology. The dramatic change in the technology of war in this period is reflected in the new title of this series: From Musket to Maxim.

The new title better reflects the fact that the series covers all nations and all conflict of the period between 1815-1914. Already the series has commissioned books that deal with matters outside the British experience. This is something that the series will endeavour to do more of in the future. At the same time there still remains an important place for the study of the British military during this period. It is one of fascination, with campaigns that capture the imagination, in which Britain although the world's predominant power, continues to field a relatively small army.

The aim of the series is to throw the spotlight on the conflicts of that century, which can often get overlooked, sandwiched as they are between two major conflicts, the French/Revolutionary/Napoleonic Wars and the First World War. The series will produced a variety of books and styles. Some will look simply at campaigns or battles. Others will concentrate on particular aspects of a war or campaign. There will also be books that look at wider concepts of warfare during this era. It is the intention that this series will present a platform for historians to present their work on an important but often overlooked century of warfare.

Submissions

The publishers would be pleased to receive submissions for this series. Please contact series editor Dr Christopher Brice via email (christopherbrice@helion.co.uk), or in writing to Helion & Company Limited, Unit 8, Amherst Business Centre, Budbrooke Road, Warwick, Warwickshire, CV34 5WE.

Books in this series: